CW01024185

ORIGAMI MASTER CLASS
FLOWERS

ORIGAMI MASTER CLASS
FLOWERS

With flower models by:

JOHN BLACKMAN

TOSHIKAZU KAWASAKI

ROBERT J. LANG

JOOST LANGEVELD

ALDO MARCELL

DELROSA MARSHALL

DEREK MCGANN

ALEXANDER OLIVEROS AVILA

DANIEL ROBINSON

DAVID SHALL

Illustrations by
Marcio Noguchi

Additional material written by
Sherry Gerstein

Race Point
PUBLISHING

Race Point
PUBLISHING

A division of Book Sales, Inc.
276 Fifth Avenue, Suite 206
New York, New York 10001

RACE POINT PUBLISHING and the distinctive Race Point Publishing logo
are trademarks of the Quayside Publishing Group, Inc.

© 2014 by The Book Shop, Ltd.
7 Peter Cooper Road
New York, NY 10010

This 2014 edition published by Race Point Publishing
by arrangement with The Book Shop, Ltd.

EDITOR Sherry Gerstein
DESIGNER Tim Palin Creative
FLOWER MODEL PHOTOGRAPHER Andrew Werner Photography

Photo credits:
Andrew Werner—covers, title page, table of contents, 28, 31, 35, 36, 41, 51, 52, 59, 63, 64, 71, 72, 83,
90, 102, 111, 112, 139, 140, 147, 148, 161, 162, 181, 182, 190; Thinkstock—12, 13, 14 (top), 15,
16, 17, 18, 19, 20, 22, 25, 34, 48, 54, 68, 87, 108, 137, 144, 157, 178; Getty Images—14
(middle, bottom); Corbis—21; Tim Palin—26, 27, 183; courtesy of John Blackman—29; courtesy
of Delrosa Marshall—37; courtesy of Joost Langeveld—53; courtesy of David Shall—65; courtesy of
Derek McGann—73; courtesy of Toshikazu Kawasaki—91; courtesy of Alexander Oliveros Avila—113;
Isa Klein—141; courtesy of Daniel Robinson—149; Steven A. Heller—163; Sherry Gerstein—191

ISBN-13: 978-1-937994-40-2

Printed in China

2 4 6 8 10 9 7 5 3 1

www.racepointpub.com

"A flower blossoms for its own joy."

—Oscar Wilde

TABLE OF CONTENTS

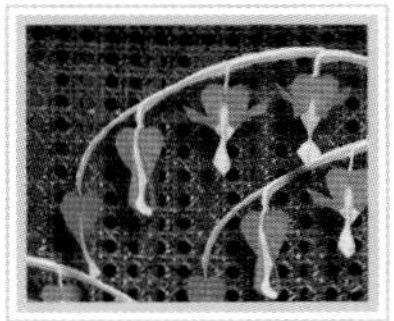

TERMS AND SYMBOLS

Edge

Existing crease

Valley fold

Mountain fold

Fold in front

Fold behind

Fold and unfold

Hidden lines

Rotate

Sink/squash/push

View from here

Turn over

Open

6–10

Repeat

Magnify

View of detail next

Pleat

Crimp

★

Important reference point established earlier

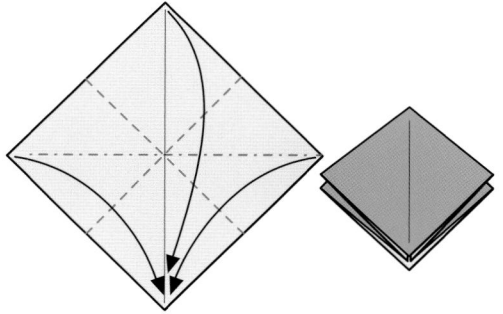 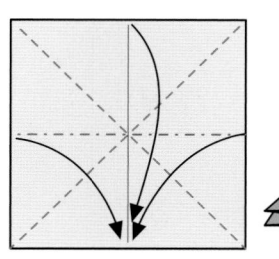 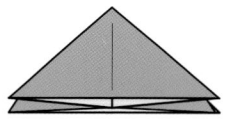

Preliminary base

Waterbomb base

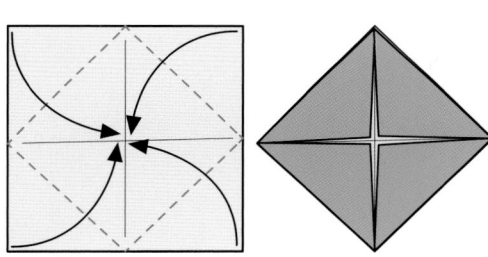 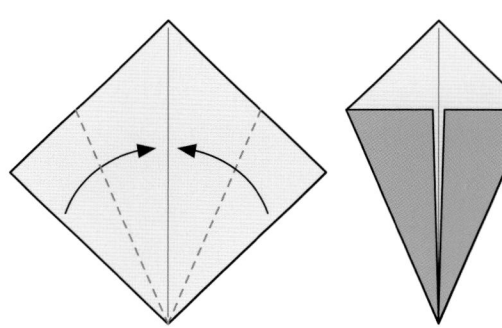

Blintz base

Kite base/fold

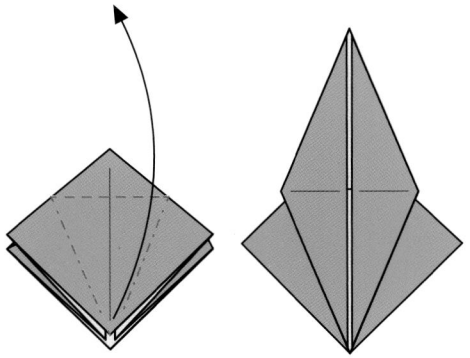 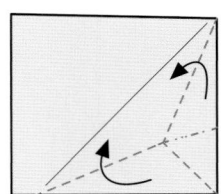 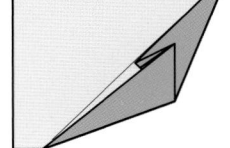

Petal fold

Rabbit-ear fold

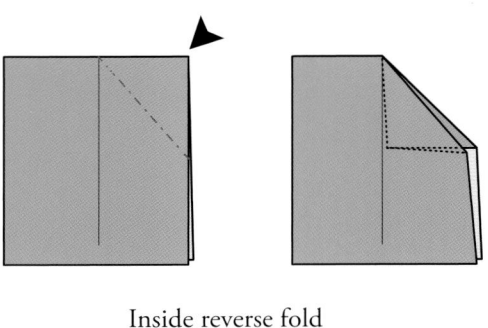

Inside reverse fold

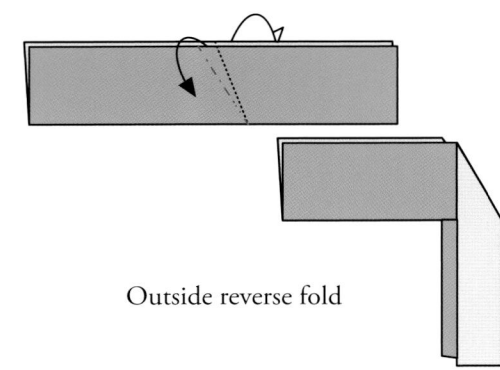

Outside reverse fold

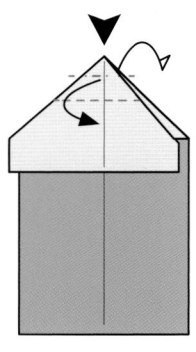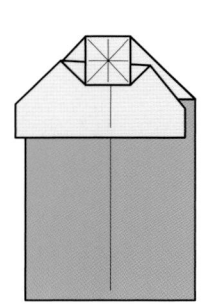

Spread squash

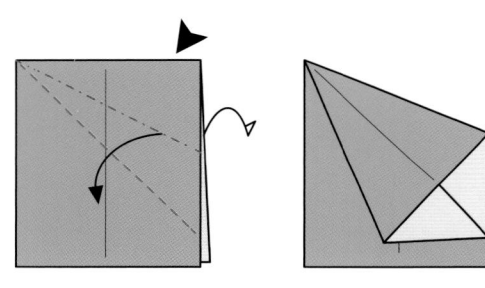

Squash fold

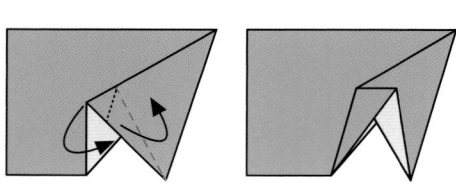

Swivel fold

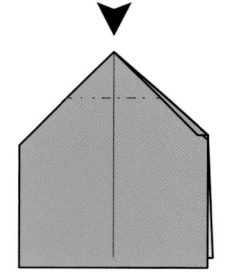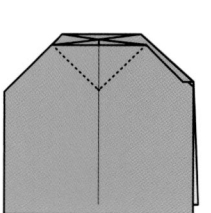

Open sink

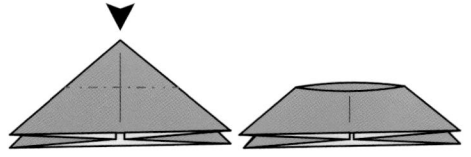

Closed sink

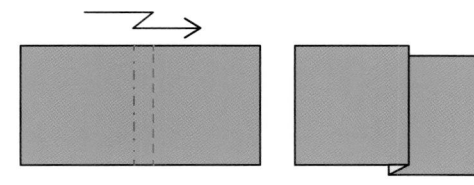

Pleat

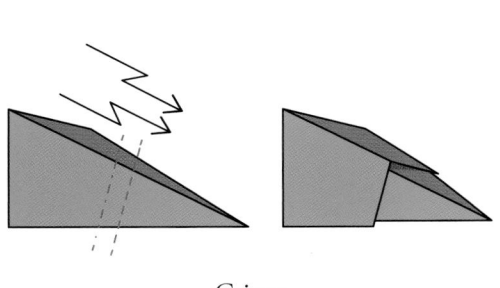

Crimp

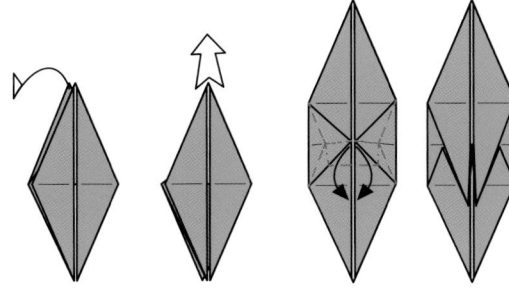

Stretch

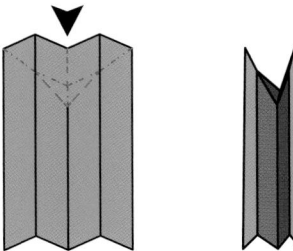

Elias stretch

A FEW WORDS ABOUT PAPER

As long as there has been paper, there has been paper folding. The varieties of paper are endless: it can be made from many different materials, such as tree bark, cloth rags, bamboo, even vegetables! As long as the material can be formed into a pulp that sticks together while being spread into a thin sheet, paper can be made. What kind works best for origami? As you will see, preferences vary from artist to artist. To help you decide what kind of paper works best for your purposes, it may help you to learn more about the history and properties of paper itself.

THE HISTORY OF PAPER

Just about every school child knows that our word "paper" comes from the Greek word *papyrus*, the common name for a marsh grass found in the Mediterranean region. Egyptians learned to soak the stems, separating them into long fibers and pounding them flat. The flattened fibers would be laid out side by side, with other layers laid out on top, perpendicular to the first. These crisscrossing layers would then be treated with a paste and pounded together to make a mat of fibers that could be written on. The mats were light and portable—especially compared to stone tablets. It was the primary material used for writing in that area of the world for 4,000 years.

There were other kinds of writing materials as well. The ancient Hebrews, for instance, set down the text for the Five Books of Moses (the first part of the Old Testament) on scrolls made of parchment—the scraped, stretched, and dried skins of animals.

People have always been inventive. They have always made the most of the materials they had close to hand. In ancient China, people used silk scrolls for writing on, or they used flattened strips of bamboo, but they also experimented with other plant fibers they had available to them. By 105 AD, a courtier of the Han emperor had refined a way of processing the bark of several plants into a pulp that could be spread out and dried. The resulting sheets were the first real papers.

Papryus plant

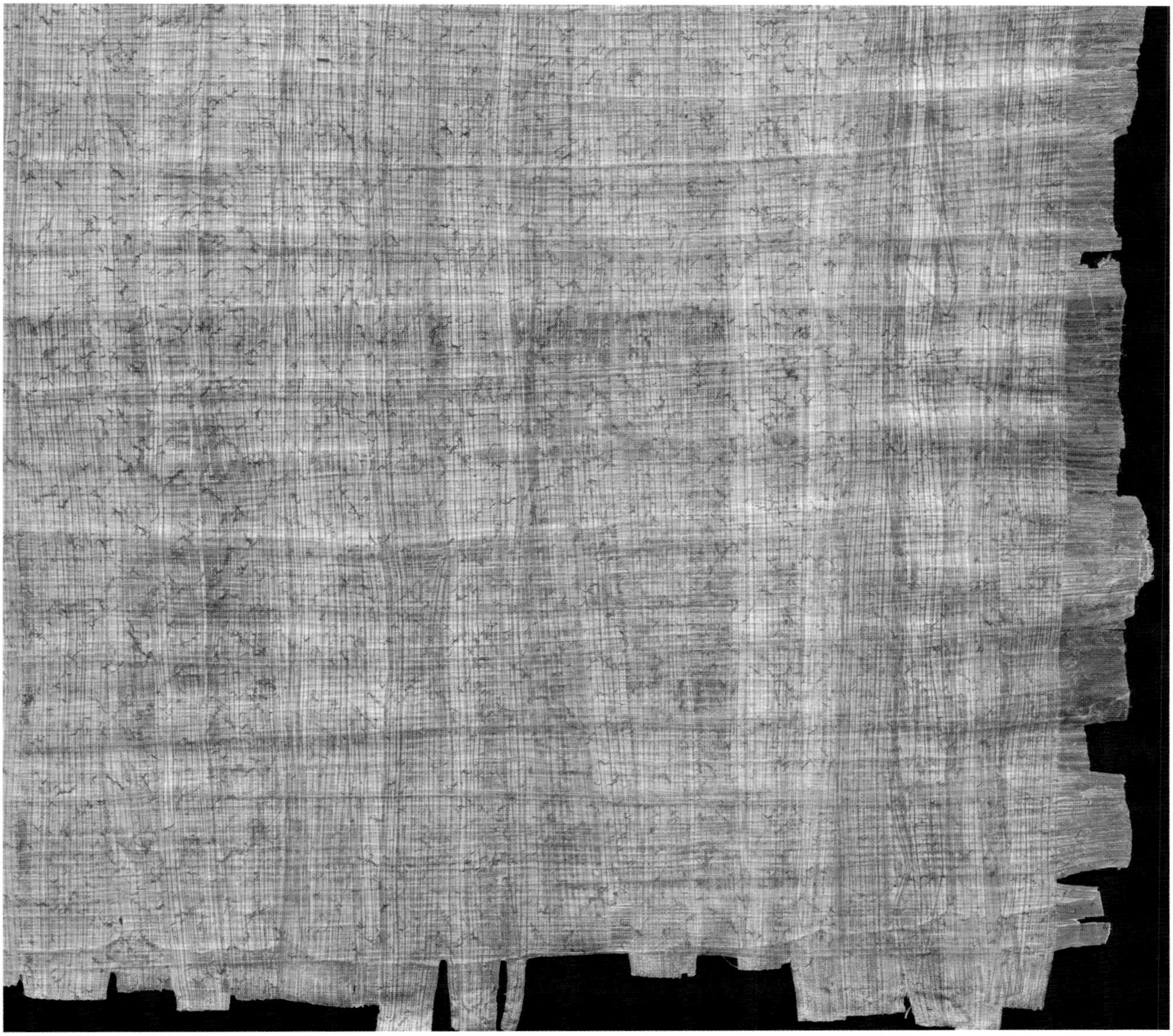

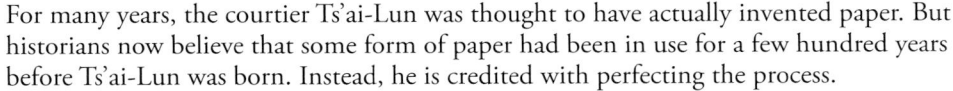

Papryus mat

For many years, the courtier Ts'ai-Lun was thought to have actually invented paper. But historians now believe that some form of paper had been in use for a few hundred years before Ts'ai-Lun was born. Instead, he is credited with perfecting the process.

Paper was a precious invention. It was a closely guarded secret that stayed within Chinese borders for many years. But as Buddhism began to spread to other areas of the far east, so too did the process of papermaking—Buddhist monks brought the process with them as they traveled, using it for their sacred texts.

Papermaking reached Japan in the 7th century. People there refined the process, and it became a staple handicraft for many farmers. Called "washi" (*wa* means "Japanese"; *shi* means "paper"), the paper was made from the bark of one of three main plant fibers: first was *kozo* (paper mulberry); later, *mitsumata* (paperbush) or *gampi* (genus *Wikstroemia*) were used. It was an efficient arrangement of time and resources. Farmers would grow the plants as one of their annual crops. After the rice was harvested and the weather was too cold to work outside, the papermaking would begin. Cold running water from local streams was an important element, too—it retarded bacterial growth and kept the paper pure. Entire families devoted their winter months to the making of fine paper for centuries.

Papermaking was also spreading westward. Islamic warriors in

Paper mulberry

Paperbush

Gampi

Although it is impossible to say for certain when origami was invented, it is assumed that paper folding developed first in China, since paper was invented there. Origami developed in Japan once paper arrived there, but it was originally a craft for the elite only, since paper was so expensive and precious.

Vellum (above) is a type of parchment made from calfskin. Note that it comes from the same root as "veal."

750 AD were known to have captured a caravan of Chinese papermakers. So the process was brought to Samarkand, which became a capital of papermaking in the region, and from there it spread across the Islamic world. Moorish invaders from northern Africa eventually brought papermaking to Spain and Portugal in the 13th century. But as the process spread, the traditions changed, based on the plant materials that were easily available and the work it took to make them usable in paper.

What really helped the spread of paper as the preferred writing material was the development of the printing press. About ⅓ of the original print run of Gutenberg's Bible was printed on vellum, a parchment product that was the other major writing material of the time. But processing vellum through the printing press turned out to be difficult. Paper and the craft of printing became permanently intertwined.

Making paper, however, remained a laborious process for centuries after. It was still largely made from bark and other plant fibers, such as linen and bamboo. The usable plant parts had to be separated from the waste, then soaked or boiled and beaten to tease apart the long fibers. The resulting sludge was washed in cold water, impurities removed by hand, spread out on large screens (of bamboo or other material) and dried, then bleached in the sun. Some paper—depending on the material it was made from—needed sizing agents added to keep the surface from being too absorbent. It was simply too difficult to make large amounts quickly.

Bamboo stalks

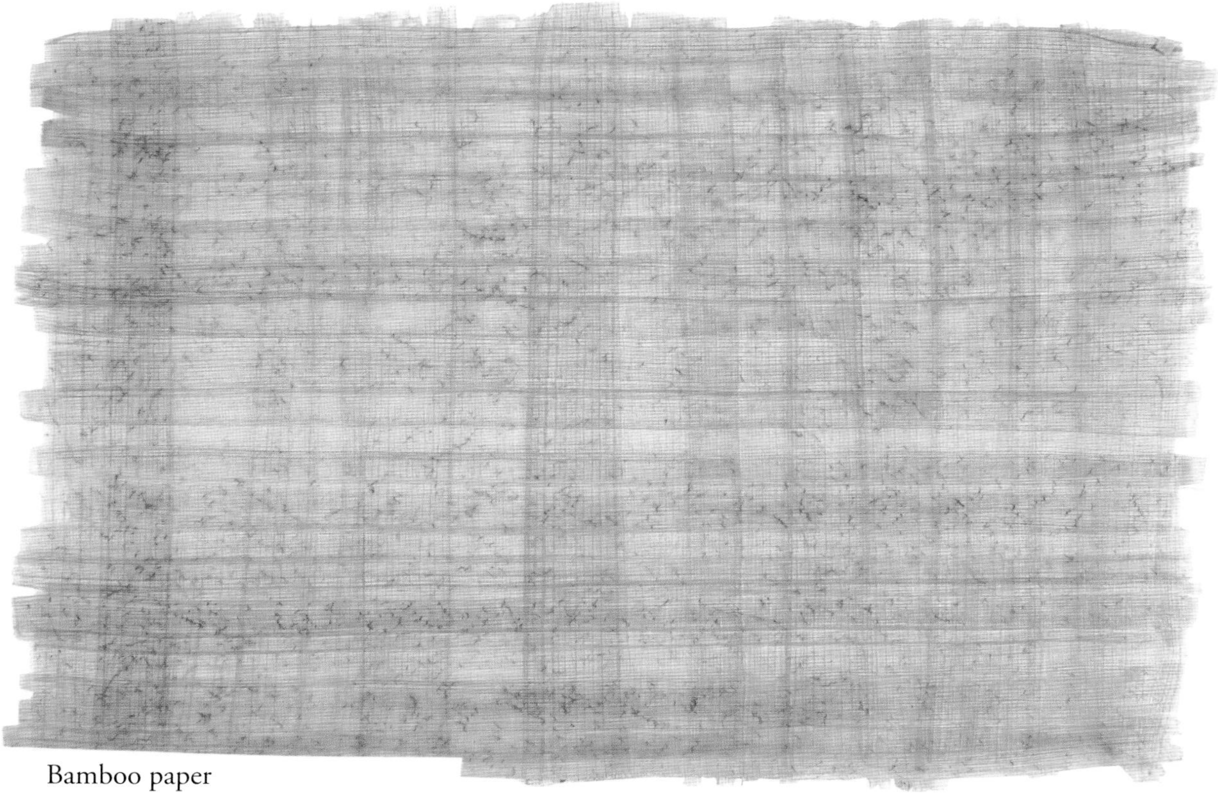

Bamboo paper

Sizing—a substance (like a glue or gelatin) that is added to paper to keep it from absorbing ink. It acts as a protective layer that allows the ink to sit on the surface and dry there, but it also reduces the paper's durability.

All that changed when the western world started industrializing and Canadian Charles Fenerty figured out how to make paper pulp from chopped-up wood. Others refined and patented the process, and machine-made paper was born—just in time for the mass production of books and newspapers to catch on. At that time, more than 100,000 families in Japan were engaged in making paper by hand. One hundred and fifty years later, only a few hundred families still do so. Now most washi paper is made by machine.

Stacks of tree trunks ready to be sent to paper mills

HANDMADE PAPER TODAY

Machine-made papermaking quickly eclipsed the craft of making paper by hand. By the time Dard Hunter—an artisan who was a part of the Arts and Crafts Movement in America and a former member of the Roycroft crafting community—walked into an exhibit on papermaking techniques in London in 1911, there was no longer any paper being made by hand in the U.S.

The exhibit changed Dard Hunter's life. He traveled to Asia to learn everything he could about early traditions of papermaking. He became an expert in the craft, publishing several books on the subject, including a few that he crafted by hand from top to bottom. For his book, *Old Papermaking*, he made the paper at his own mill, using centuries-old equipment and molds, designing his own fonts and then cutting and casting his own movable type, printing the books and binding them according to the age-old traditions. In the process, Dard Hunter opened his own small press, Mountain House Press, and became an active publisher through the mid-1950s. When he published his autobiography in 1958, it was fittingly titled *My Life with Paper*.

Dard Hunter felt that his most important work was the opening of the Dard Hunter Paper Museum at MIT, which was home to the vast array of artifacts he'd collected in his pursuit of the craft of papermaking. The collection was later moved to the Institute of Paper Chemistry in Appleton, Wisconsin. Most of the collection is now held at the Robert C. Williams Paper Museum on the campus of Georgia Institute of Technology.

The craft and traditions of papermaking continue to be celebrated and explored by organizations such as The Friends of Dard Hunter, the biannual magazine *Hand Papermaking*, and active studios such as Carriage House Paper in Brooklyn, New York, and Origamidō Studio in Haverhill, Massachusetts. Origamidō is devoted to fine art origami made from custom, handmade papers that the owners make themselves. Both studios offer workshops on papermaking.

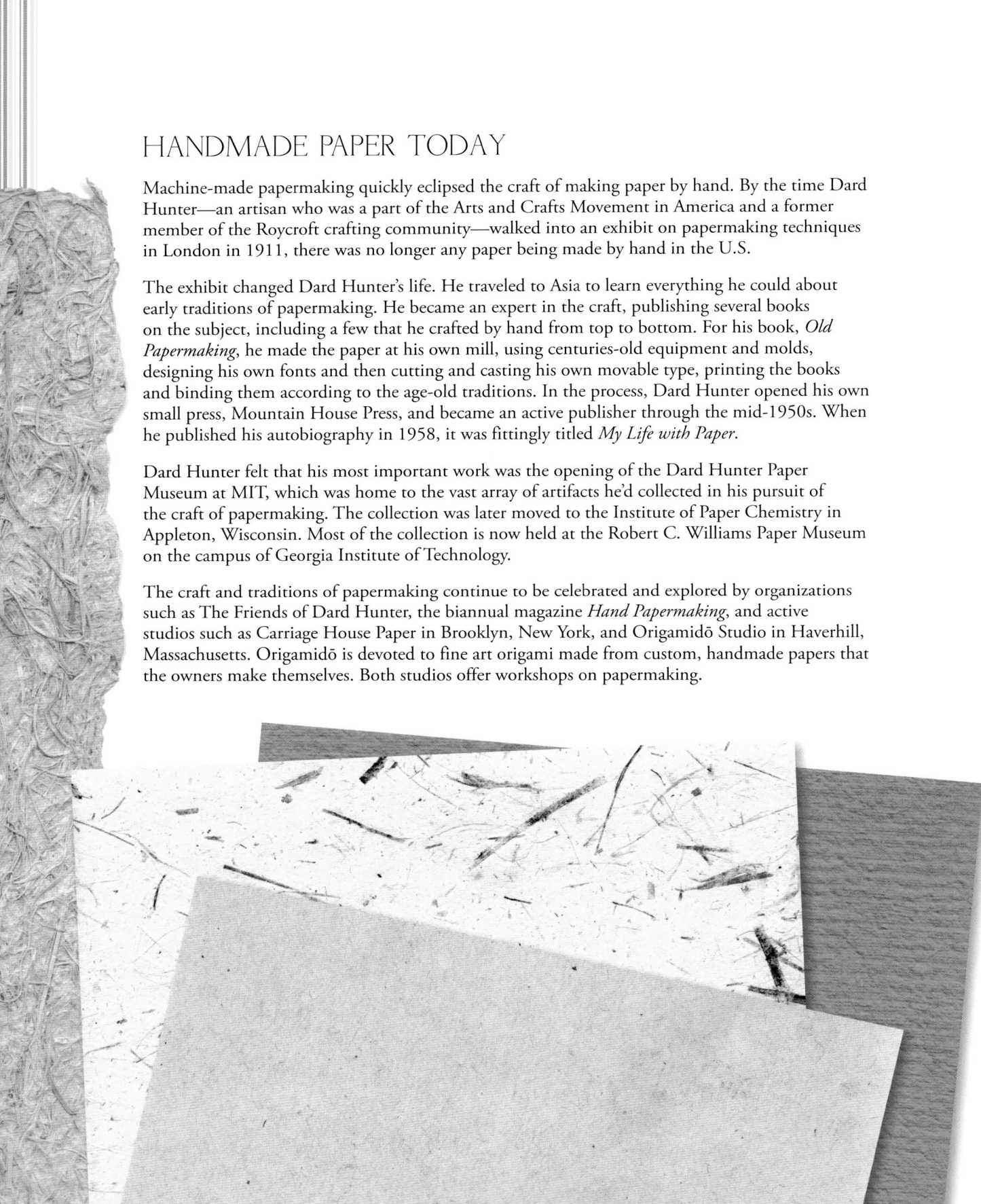

HOW TO MAKE WASHI

Kozo, or the paper mulberry, was the plant used historically in most of the washi handmade by Japanese farmers. Here are the basic steps for making washi from kozo, which are still more or less in use today.

Cut the kozo—This plant can grow 10 feet between annual harvests, with stalks as wide as 4 inches in diameter. When winter arrived, the stalks would be cut into equal lengths and bundled.

Steam the stalks—The bundles were placed in wooden barrels and steamed. Fresh water was then poured over the stalks, enabling the bark to be slipped right off.

Separate the inner bark—In order to end up with the prized inner bark (*shirokawa*), the black outer bark (*kurokawa*) and the middle green layer (*nazekawa*) had to be removed first. The softened bark was submerged in water, then stepped on and rubbed between the feet to remove the black layer. Next, the green layer was scraped away with a knife. The white inner bark remained; this was checked for scar tissue and impurities. Once those were trimmed away, the cleaned white bark was dried in a cool, shaded area.

Bleach the result—The processed bark was placed in a cold running stream to wash away all impurities. It was then left to dry on the bank and bleach in the sun.

Cook the kozo—The dried kozo was cooked in a large tub of alkali solution to break apart the fibers. Traditionally, the alkali was extract from wood ash, but now other substances like slaked lime or lye are used. The alkali dissolves the non-cellulose parts of the bark, resulting in softer paper.

Pick out any dark spots—The cooked fibers were examined for buds, dark spots or scar tissue, which were picked out by hand. Now a bleaching agent can be added, but traditional methods called for water or snow to help with bleaching.

Beat the fibers—The cleaned fibers would be beaten on a stone with a wooden mallet.

Mix the pulp with a sizing/thickening agent in water—To create the pulp mixture to make the sheets, the processed kozo was mixed with water and *neri*, a thickening agent made from pounding the root of the *tororo aoi* plant, to help with sheet formation. These days, western additives are more likely to be used, since tororo aoi powder doesn't store well.

Form the sheet—A papermaker would dip a bamboo screen and scoop the pulp mixture across the surface. This would be done repeatedly until the desired thickness was formed.

Remove the sheet for draining—The sheet would be removed to a special stand where it would drain overnight. It was then pressed for several hours to remove more moisture.

Dry in the sun—The pressed sheets were then moved to individual drying boards and left in the sun to dry completely and bleach further.

KNOW·YOUR·PAPER

Today, washi paper is prized for its softness, translucence and durability by all kinds of artisans. Depending on the additives used in its making, it can be safe for the long-term storage of documents and artwork because it doesn't discolor or deteriorate. It can even be used as a textile!

As you learn more about origami and the particular challenges of folding flowers, you are likely to come across many different terms that refer to washi and other specialty papers from around the world:

Rice paper: Often used interchangeably with washi, rice paper doesn't contain rice; some say the term comes from the translucence of the paper, which can be compared to the translucence of a grain of rice.

Tissue: This refers to the thickness and weight of a sheet of paper. It can refer to kozo paper or commercial tissue paper found in the gift wrap section.

Chiyogami: Washi with stenciled or block-printed designs.

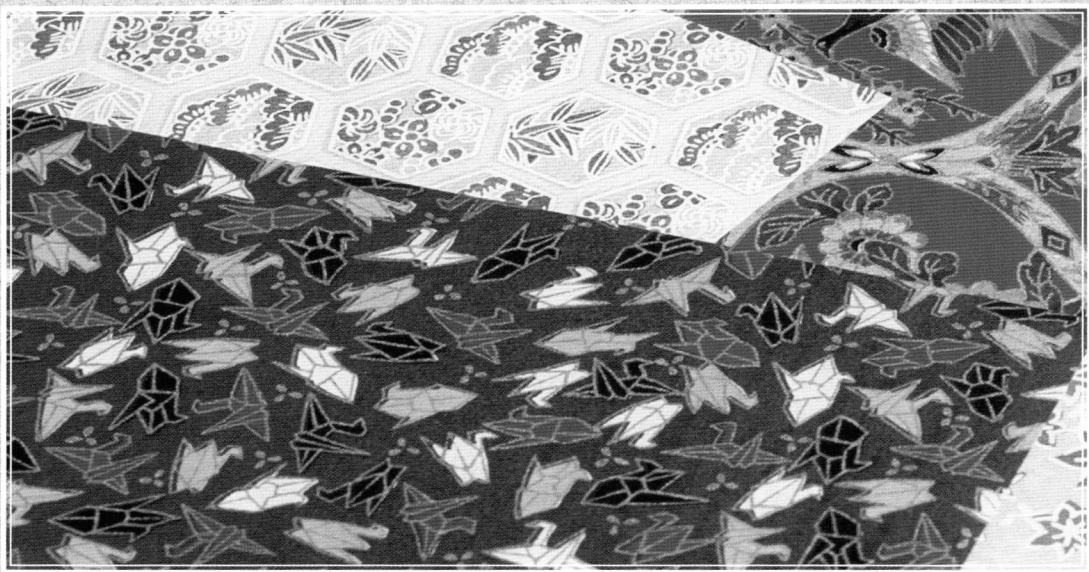

Chiyogami papers

Yuzen: Washi with printed designs inspired by kimono fabrics.

Unryu: This paper is made from mulberry bark with long fibers very visible. It comes from the Japanese for "dragon floating on clouds."

Lokta: A wildcrafted (meaning that is uses materials foraged from their natural habitat) handmade paper from Nepal that is air dried. It comes in beautiful, strong colors.

BACKGROUND ABOVE: Japanese rice paper

A woman making lokta paper by hand

Sheets of lokta paper drying in the sun

THE PAPER THAT'S RIGHT FOR YOU

Luckily, you don't have to buy fancy paper to make most origami flowers.. Just find a paper that results in a softness that echoes the natural look of the flowers you are trying to make. Here is a list of the papers used by the artists who provided models for this book; as you will see, the list covers a lot of different types of paper.

John Blackman: colored fine-quality writing paper

Toshikazu Kawasaki: kami (traditional origami paper)

Robert J. Lang: hanji or watercolor paper

Joost Langeveld: computer paper printed with his own designs and colors

Aldo Marcell: foil gift wrap with tissue paper layered over it

Delrosa Marshall: Thai unryu

Derek McGann: any thin paper (but not too thin)

Alexander Oliveras Avila: recycled paper

Daniel Robinson: handmade origami paper from abaca fiber

David Shall: tissue paper on kitchen foil

EYE ON TECHNIQUES

In a few cases, special techniques were employed to color the paper to the artist's tastes or to adjust the final shape of the finished model.

Dry pastels

Hand Coloring

John Blackman likes to hand-color his flowers for a more natural look. Here's how to utilize his technique to customize the colors on your models:

- Fold the model completely first to identify the areas that need coloring.

- Using dry pastels (not oil pastels, which can stain the paper with oil) in the colors of your choice, rub them on a piece of paper to make small areas of color.

- Pick up some of the desired color with a cotton swab, then rub it on the area, using a little pressure to work it into the paper in the center of where you want it colored.

- Spread the color outward with the cotton swab, trying to avoid creating hard edges of color.

- To color the interior of a flower's throat, twirl the tip of the cotton swab to narrow it before picking up the color. Try to pick up the color on the sides of the swab, not just the tip.

Backcoating

Alexander Oliveras Avila has glued papers of two different colors together so that the lip of his orchid is a different color from the rest of the flower. This process is known as backcoating. Here are the basic steps in a nutshell:

- Purchase the powdered adhesive, methyl cellulose, available at wallpaper stores or specialty paper craft stores.

- Make up a small quantity at a time, according to the directions on the package.

- Clear a large area on a hard surface to work on. Glass or plexiglass is good for this.

- Lay the first piece of paper on the surface. Apply the methyl cellulose with a soft paint brush, working from the center out to cover the paper. The paper should be completely saturated.

- Lay the second paper over the first, matching up the edges as best you can. Then brush the paper from the center out, which will help to eliminate air bubbles. The methyl cellulose will start to seep through this second layer.

- Allow the paper to dry. You can use a fan to direct a breeze over the paper to hasten the drying time.

- When the paper is dry, pull it off the surface, starting from one corner.

For a more complete explanation of the process, visit this website: www.metteunits.com/Backcoat.htm.

Wet-folding

Derek McGann uses wet-folding to give his Hibiscus petals their unique ruffle-y appearance. How does this work? Here is a breakdown of the process:

- Paper owes its stiffness in part to the sizing agent added during the manufacturing process. Not only does the sizing give the paper's surface a protective coating that keeps it from soaking up too much ink, but it gives the paper crispness.

- Water can temporarily dissolve the sizing, allowing the paper to be molded softly in ways that are impossible with dry paper.

- Apply water to the paper: there are several ways to do this, including using damp cloths or a fine mister. When the paper absorbs the water, it will soften enough to shape.

- After the shaping is done, the sizing bonds with the paper molecules once more and the paper dries hard in its new shape.

For an extremely thorough explanation of wet-folding and insight into one artist's technique, visit www.langorigami.com/paper/wetfolding_papers.php.

MAKE YOUR OWN PAPER

If you enjoy origami and papercrafts as much for the paper as you do for the crafting (papergeeks, you know who you are), you might want to experiment with making your own paper. Making paper from scratch—from raw materials like bark, straw and leaves—is an involved process, but making recycled paper is something that you can easily do at home. Here's how:

- Remove the glass and backing from **two wood picture frames** (small is fine). Cover one with a piece of screen from the hardware store and tack in place. The other will be the deckle, which helps to make the shape and size of the paper.

- Search your recycling bin for **used printer paper** (about 50 sheets or so). Tear it up into small bits, around an inch square, and soak them overnight in a bucket of water. You can use **some colored sheets**, if you like, but not too many. You want the colored bits to be accents. Tear up the colored paper and soak it separately.

- Place a handful of the soaked paper in a **blender and add warm water** so it is about ¾ full. Blend until the paper is about the consistency of oatmeal. Continue blending handfuls of paper with water in the same fashion to make the remaining pulp.

- Put the pulp in a **large dishpan** and stir it around with your hands. If you are going to use the paper to write on, add a **packet of plain gelatin** to the mixture (this is the sizing).

- **Blend the soaked colored paper** (if you've used any) for a few seconds. Then **add it to the pulp mixture**.

- **Prepare a drying area**. Lay out plenty of newspaper, and put a disposable dishcloth on top. You are going to leave your paper to dry overnight.

- **Stack the picture frames** so the screened frame is on the bottom and the deckle is on top.

- Give the pulp a good stir. Then **dip the stack into the mixture and bring it to a horizontal position** under the surface. **Pull it straight up**, allowing the pulp to collect on the screen's surface. The water will drain through the screen.

- Carry to the drying area. Lift off the deckle and **flip the screened frame over so the pulp side is down**. Use a sponge to gently blot up the excess moisture, squeezing the sponge out occasionally, until the pulp begins to separate from the screen. At that point, lift off the screen.

- Repeat to make more sheets, if desired. Allow the sheets to dry.

- Stack the dry sheets together and place under several heavy books to flatten them.

SUGGESTED EQUIPMENT AND MATERIALS

In addition to the practice paper of your choice, the following supplies are suggested if you plan to make any of the projects in this book:

- Craft knife
- Floral tape (the colors listed will cover your basic needs for this book)
  - Brown
  - Green
  - White
- Floral wire in a range of gauges (the higher the gauge number, the thinner and more flexible the wire is; floral wire is often coated with a dark green enamel, but you can also buy lengths covered in cloth or brown craft paper)
- Glue
- Monochromatic paper in various colors and textures
- Pots, vases, planters in a variety of sizes and shapes
- Self-healing cutting mat
- Tapestry needle or beading awl (also known as bead reamer)
- Wire cutters
- Wreath form (foam)

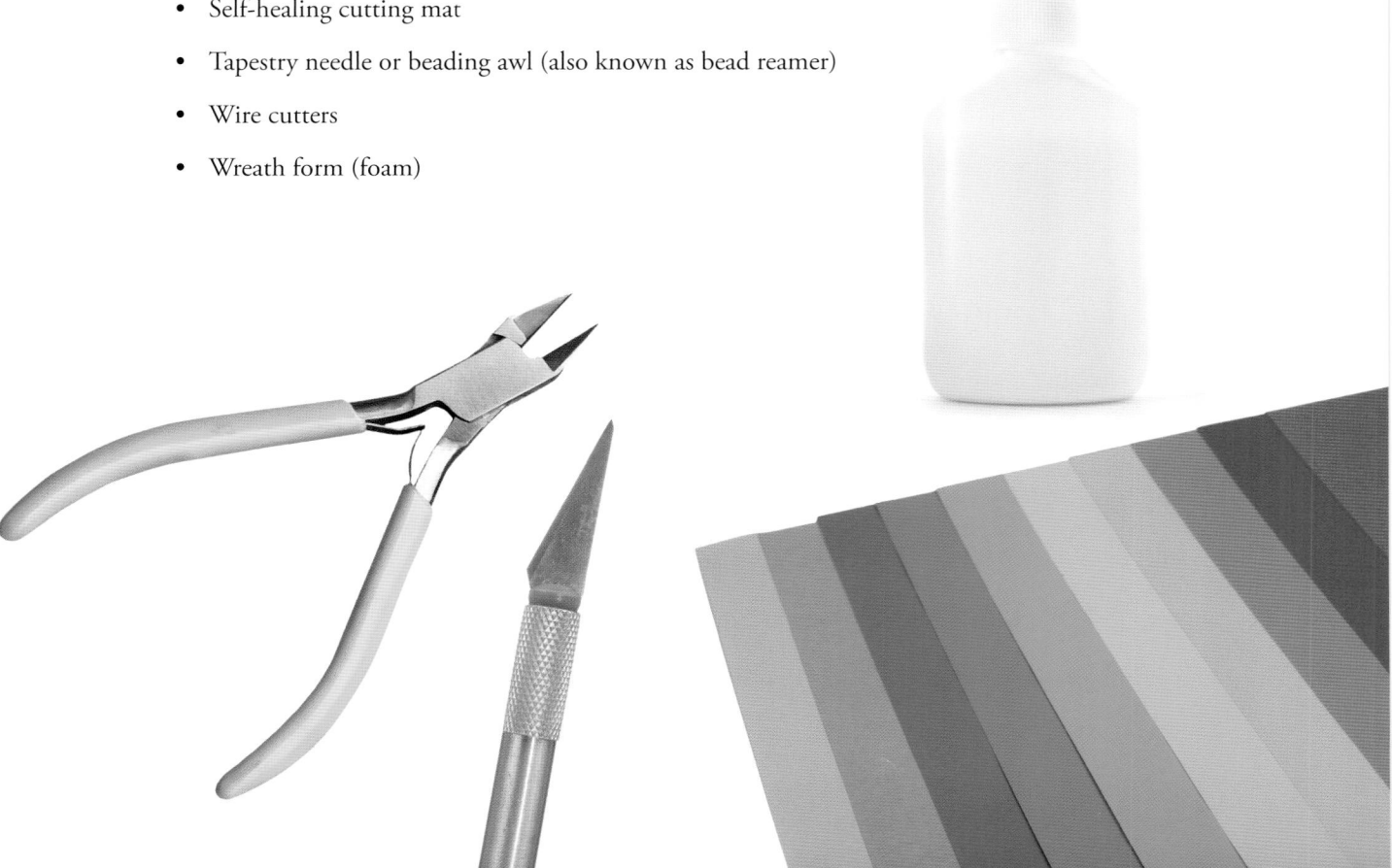

TIPS ON ASSEMBLING FLOWERS

When creating origami flowers, folding is just one part of a larger process. Here are other skills you will need to create beautiful origami flower arrangements.

WIRING

While some of the flowers shown here can be glued onto stems, others need to be wired so they can be attached to other parts or larger arrangements. Even if a flower or leaf has a little stem, attaching wire to it will make it easier to position precisely where you want it.

Floral wire—wire that is used by professional florists to make their arrangements—comes in two basic types: bare wire that is often coated with green enamel and wire that is covered with cloth or paper. This covered wire is handy because it offers a gluable surface that adheres strongly (unlike the protocol for creating many origami models, it is acceptable to glue parts together to make origami flowers). If you choose to work with bare wire, you should wrap the wire with floral tape, especially the areas that will be glued to other parts.

Floral tape comes in many different colors and can be purchased at most craft stores in the floral section as well as online. What is different about floral tape is that it isn't sticky until it is stretched. To use it, unwrap a length and hold about six inches between your hands. Pull the ends gently in opposite directions so it stretches. As it stretches, it will get slightly sticky. Wrap it around a piece of wire on the diagonal. It will adhere to the wire and itself.

To wire leaves without a folded stem: using covered wire (with cloth, paper, or floral tape), glue a length to the back of the leaf to form a rib. Some leaves have a pocket on the back that forms this central rib; if possible, insert the wire into the pocket and glue in place.

To wire leaves with stems, place the wire inside the hollow of the stem and glue in place.

In general, wiring flowers will depend on the shape of the flower. Some flowers can be wired by piercing a hole in the center and inserting prepared wire through the center (see the Bougainvillea flowers on page 36, or the small-flower clusters made for the wreath on page 185), but you will need to make one end of the wire thicker, so it won't be pulled through the hole. In this case, consider wrapping extra tape or paper around the tip to make it bigger, or use pliers to form the tip into a head or eye pin. Other flowers (the Lily on page 64, or the Kawaski Rose on page 90) can be wired by gluing a wire under a fold.

See individual project instructions for more details on wiring flowers and leaves.

FORMING CLUSTERS

Once the elements are wired, it is easy to gather them into a cluster and wrap the stems together with floral tape. You will need to do this to make flowers like the Sweet Pea on page (28), the Stemless Leaves on page (188), or the Bougainvillea flowers on page (36)—or to make other kinds of flowers that are formed from many small blossoms (think of hydrangeas).

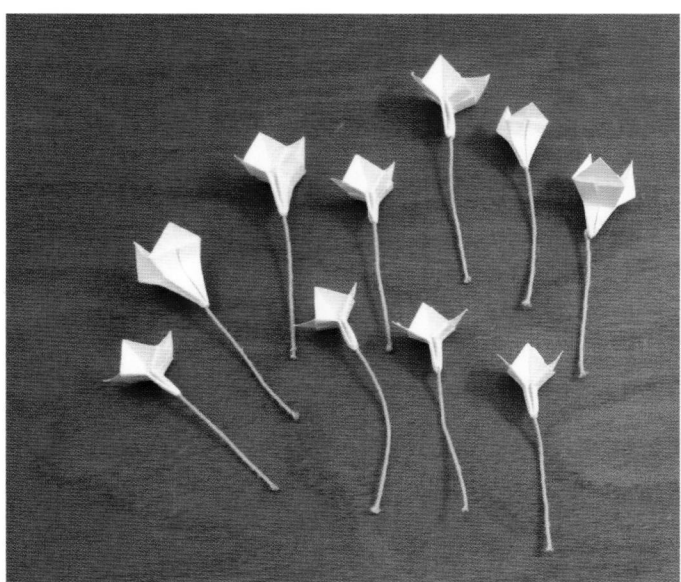

ADDING ELEMENTS VERTICALLY

Some flowers and plants will have a tall central stem, with the flowering part affixed at the tip (and sometimes at varying positions along the length of the stem, too), with leaves in varying positions below the flowers. In this case, you will need to make sure that the central element has a longer wire (stem) than the others; the length will depend on your intended project). Add the other elements to either side of the main piece with floral tape, wrapping with tape down the stem as you go.

SWEET PEA

Designed by John Blackman;
diagrammed by Marcio Noguchi

"I prefer monochromatic paper like high-quality writing paper. Rössler is the brand I like most, but I will use whatever brand gives me the colors I need. I like to give my flowers custom colors with the addition of pigment from dry pastels. I rub a pastel stick heavily onto a piece of scrap paper and sweep up the pigment with a cotton swab. Then I gently rub the pigment-covered swab onto the paper to give it a soft blush."

—John Blackman

John Blackman has been folding paper for over 30 years. He was first exposed to origami when he was a child. A Japanese friend brought it back to his attention when he was in his twenties, and from there it developed into a true passion.

John's preferred choice of subject matter—flowers—reflects his love of plants, gardening and *ikebana*, the Japanese art of arranging live flowers. His work has appeared in numerous books and he has exhibited in multiple group and one-man shows through out the United States. Additional examples of his work can be found on his website at www.origamiflora.com.

A resident of New Jersey, he works in the Internet industry.

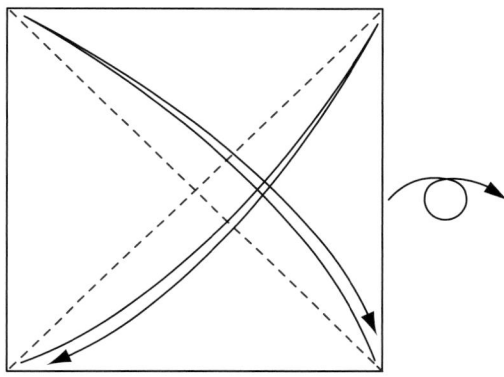 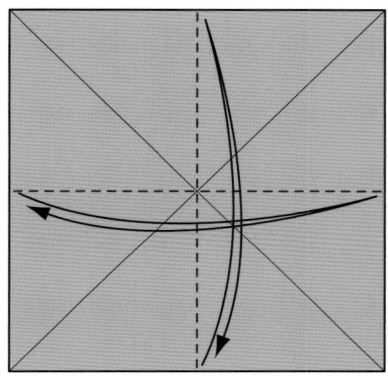

Make the flowers from small squares; 2 inches (7.6 cm) is recommended:

1 With the white side up, fold in half along both diagonals. Unfold. Turn over.

2 Fold in half horizontally and vertically.

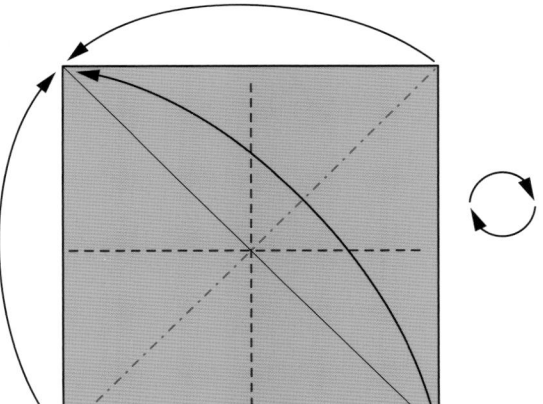 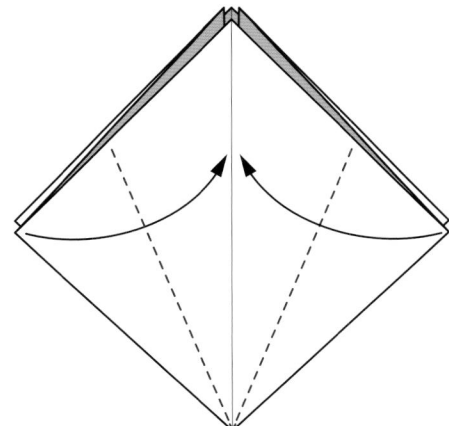

3 Collapse into a preliminary fold. Rotate so the open end points up.

4 Fold the edges to the center crease on the top layer only.

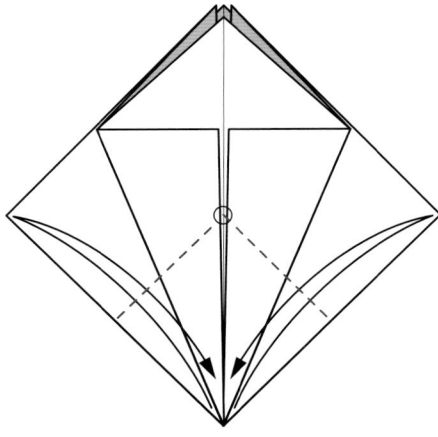

5 Fold the side corners to the bottom corner and unfold.

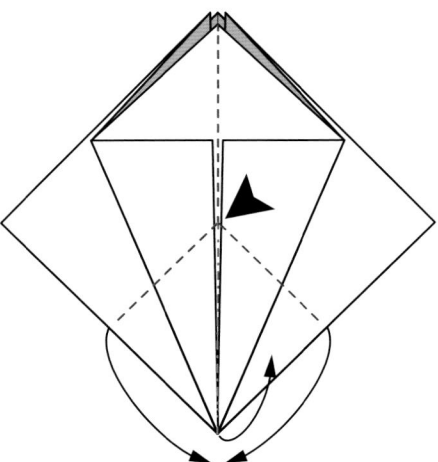

6 Push the center while pulling the bottom corner up, allowing the folded edges to come together. Note: the model will not lie flat from this point on.

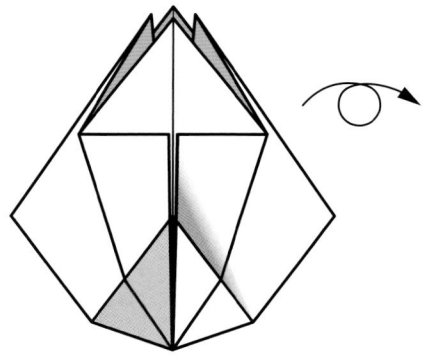

7 Turn over.

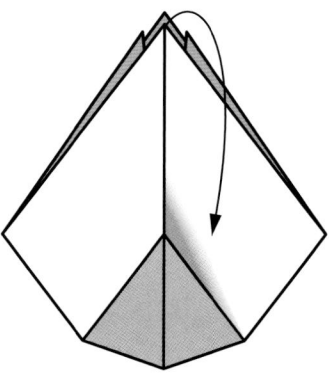

8 Pull down the front-most point.

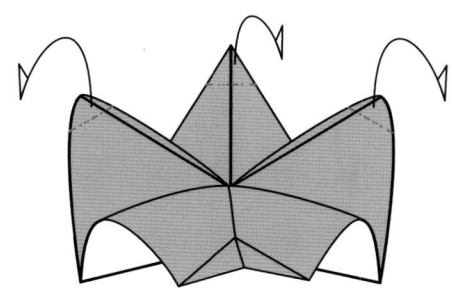

About 1/3

9 Push the center as indicated and pinch hard from the back (pulling the front tip up) to shape the front of the flower.

10 Mountain fold the tips of the other petals. This will help to spread out these petals a bit more.

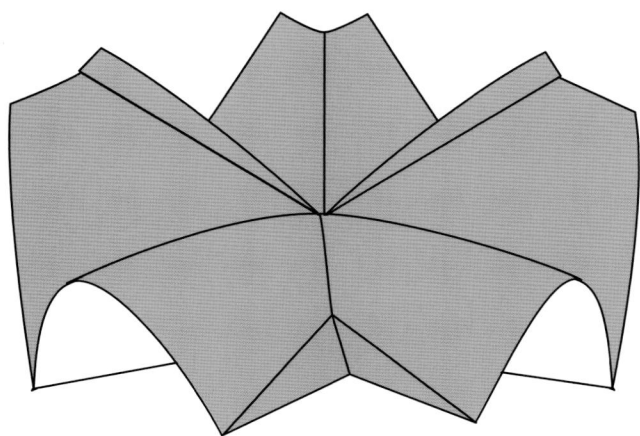

The finished Sweet Pea flower

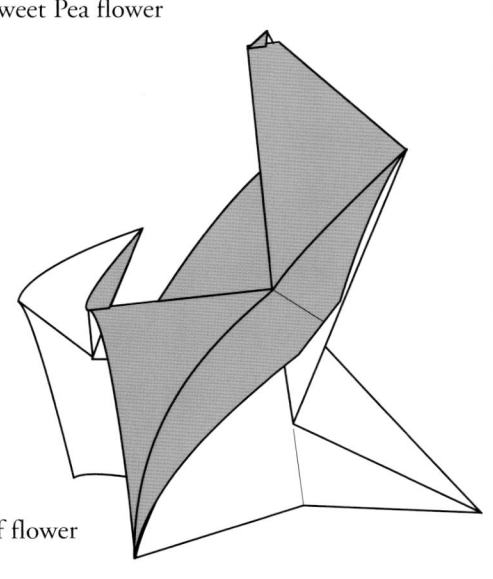

Side view of flower

CALYX

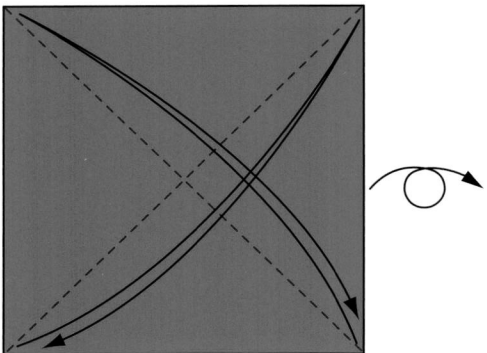 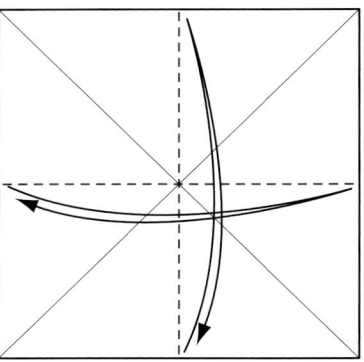

Make the calyx from small squares. They should be half the size of the paper used for the flower. This is a variation of the traditional carnation.

1 With the colored side up, fold in half along both diagonals. Unfold. Turn over.

2 Fold in half horizontally and vertically.

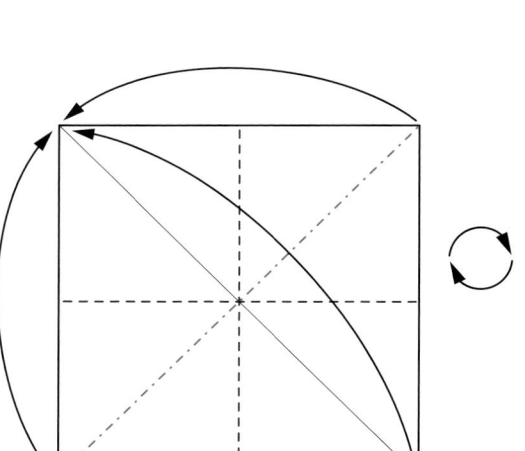 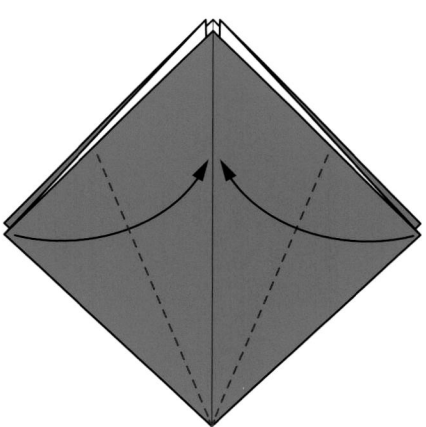

3 Collapse into a preliminary fold. Rotate so the open end points up.

4 Fold the edges to the center crease.

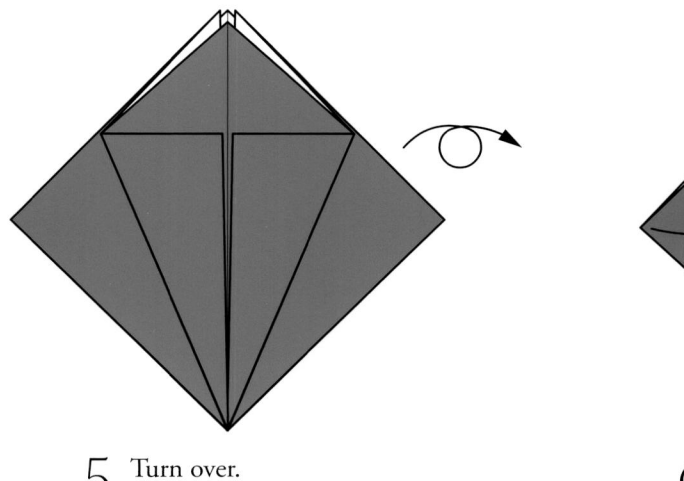

5 Turn over.

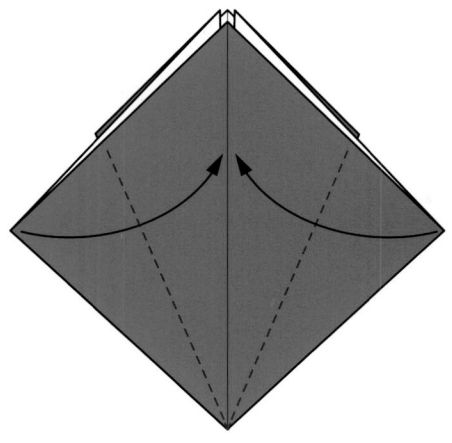

6 Fold the edges to the center crease.

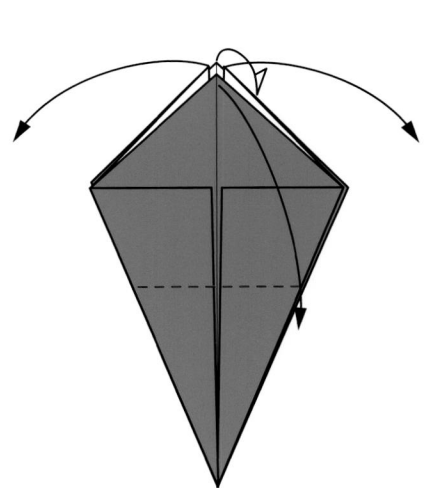

7 Fold the flaps down as indicated to open up the calyx.

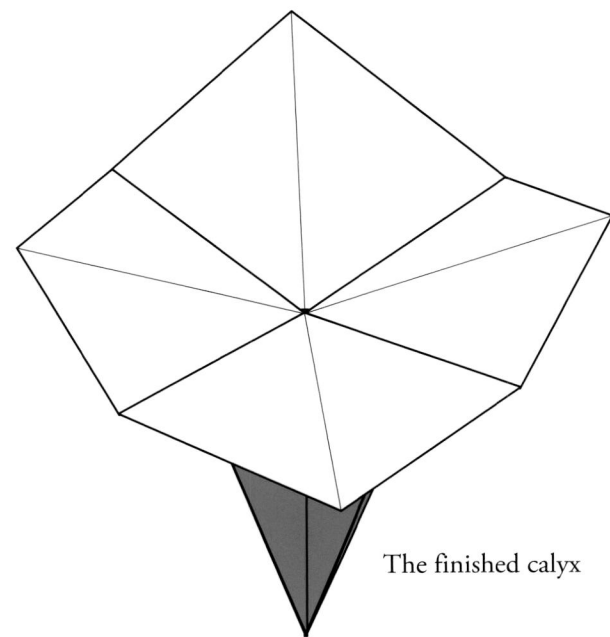

The finished calyx

ABOUT THE
SWEET PEA

Sweet Pea (*Lathyrus odoratus*) is a moderately fast-growing annual, a tendril climber. Bred for its color and fragrance during Victorian times, cultivars produce flowers in shades of pink, blue, purple or white. It is associated with delicate or blissful pleasure.

ASSEMBLY

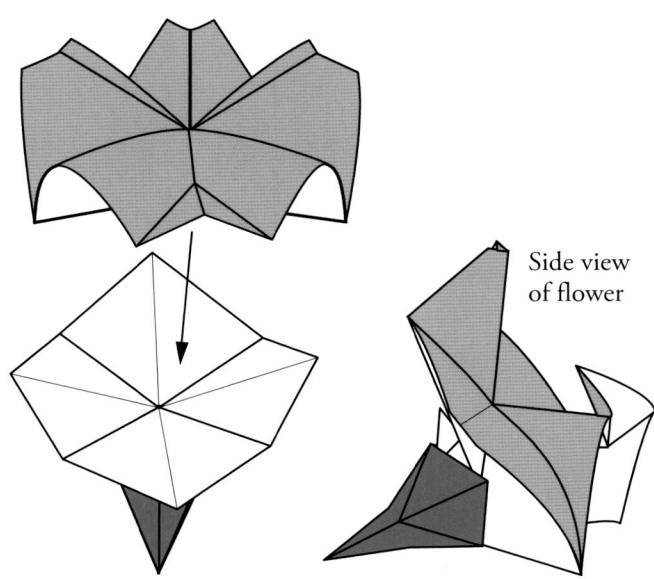

Side view of flower

1 Wire the flowers: glue a length of cloth-covered wire into the fold at the underside of the flower. One of the flowers should have a longer wire than the others.

2 Push a tapestry needle or beading awl from the top of the calyx through the center and out the point of the stem. This will form a hole for the wire on the flower.

3 Add a drop of glue to the pointed tip of the flower's stem. Then thread the wire through the hole in the calyx, drawing the flower tip slightly inside the opening.

4 Repeat steps 2 and 3 to make more flowers with calyxes.

5 Make flower clusters: start with the flower with the longer stem and use floral tape to add flowers along the main stem.

Note: the calyx shown here also makes a nice little flower. If you use it to make a flower, start with the white side up.

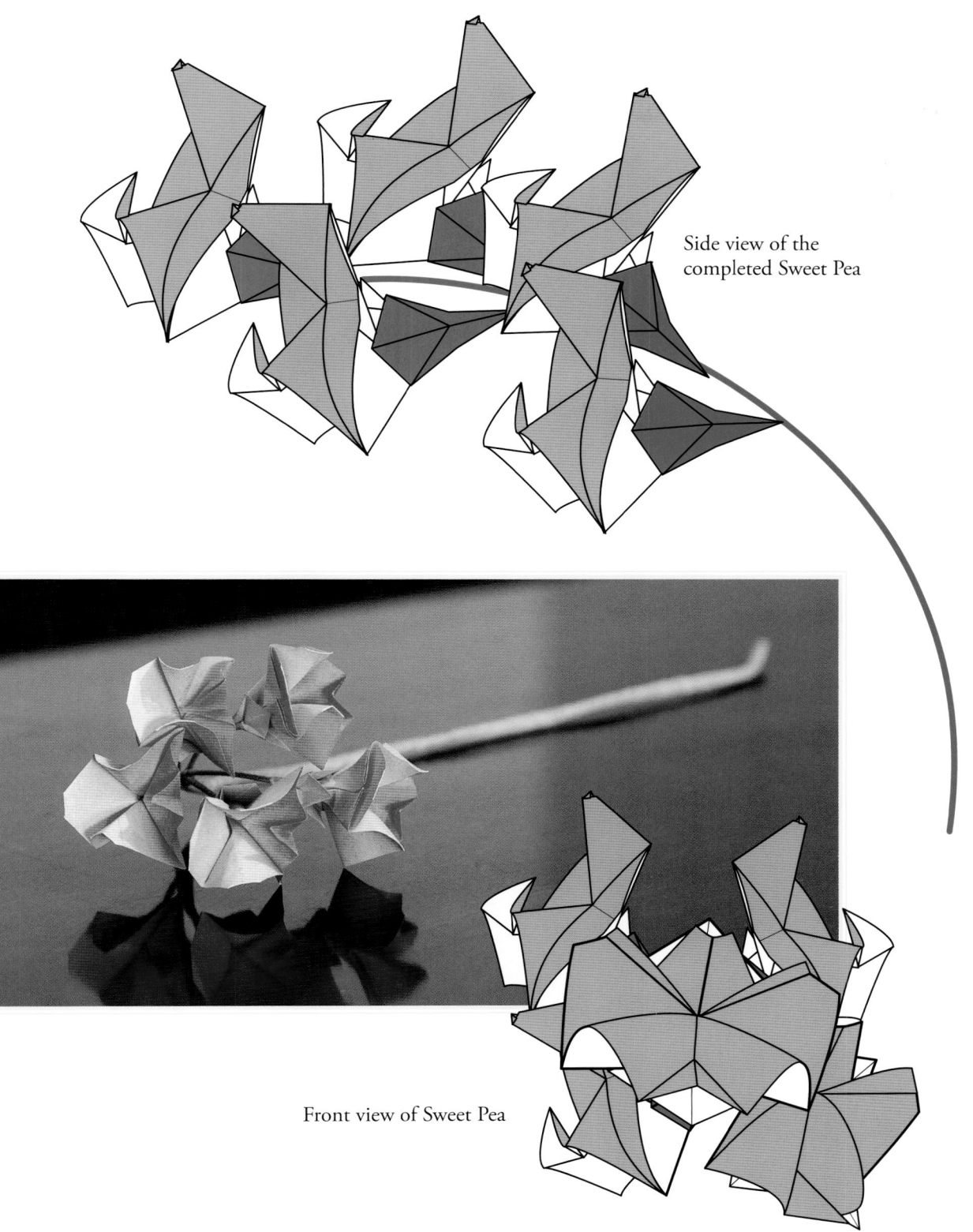

Side view of the completed Sweet Pea

Front view of Sweet Pea

"Bougainvillea plants are made up of three different parts: leaves, bracts and flowers. The bracts are the colorful parts. They aren't a flower, but rather a modified leaf, just like the red foliage on a poinsettia. The flowers are the white structures in the center of a bract. I like to use monochromatic unryu paper for the bracts and leaves of this model, for its softness. I used Thai unryu to make the one shown here."

—Delrosa Marshall

BOUGAINVILLEA

Designed by Delrosa Marshall; inspired by a model by Tomoko Fuse;
diagrammed by Marcio Noguchi

Delrosa Marshall is a retired science teacher from New York City. A colleague introduced her to origami in 1990. She joined OrigamiUSA soon after and has exhibited her work at subsequent annual conventions.

Folding origami flowers allows Delrosa to combine her love of nature with her enjoyment of the challenge and process of folding paper. She has been a co-designer of the annual origami holiday tree at the American Museum of Natural History in New York City several times, and has folded a variety of models (not all of them flowers) for high-end fashion stores such a Hermes, Paul Stuart and Lalique. She has also folded models for two off-Broadway plays, *Animals Out of Paper* and *Moon 2 @ Tryston*.

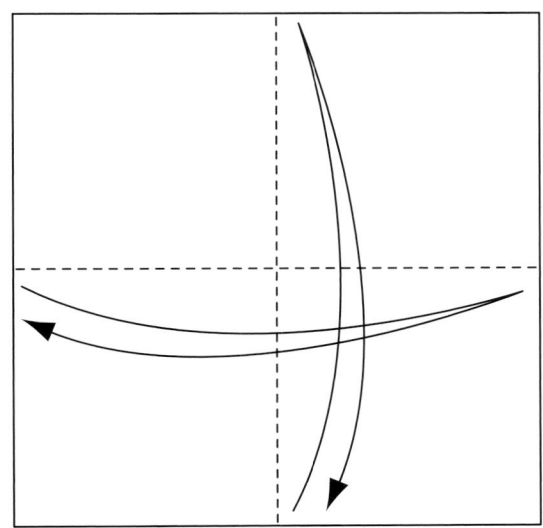

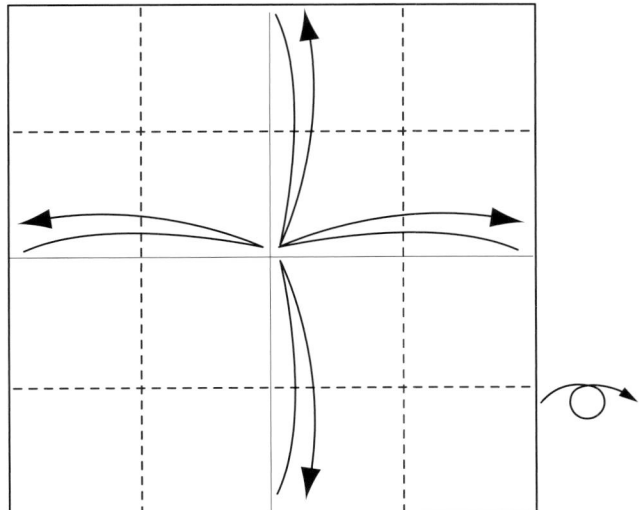

Make the flowers from ¾-inch off-white squares (they are shown in yellow here so you can tell the difference between the front and the back):

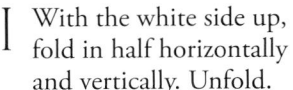

1. With the white side up, fold in half horizontally and vertically. Unfold.

2. Fold the edges to the new creases and unfold. Turn over.

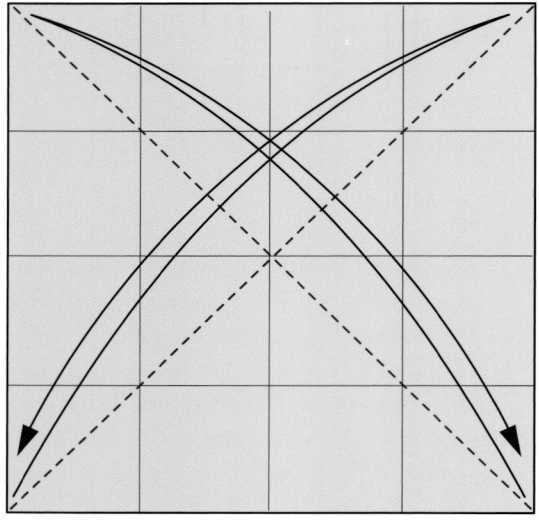

3 Fold in half along both diagonals and unfold.

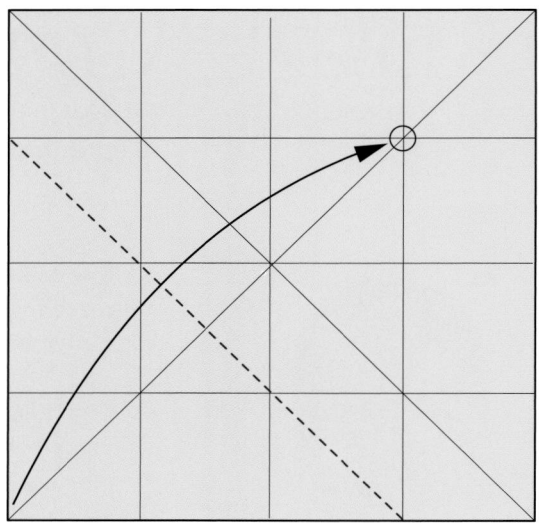

4 Fold the corner to the reference point.

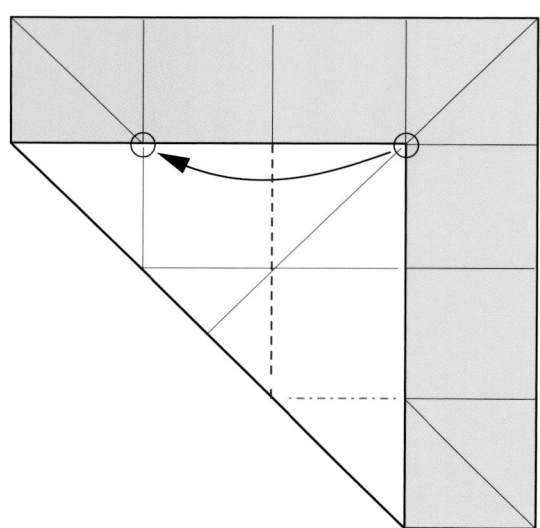

5 Fold the top layer over as indicated. Note: the model will not lie flat.

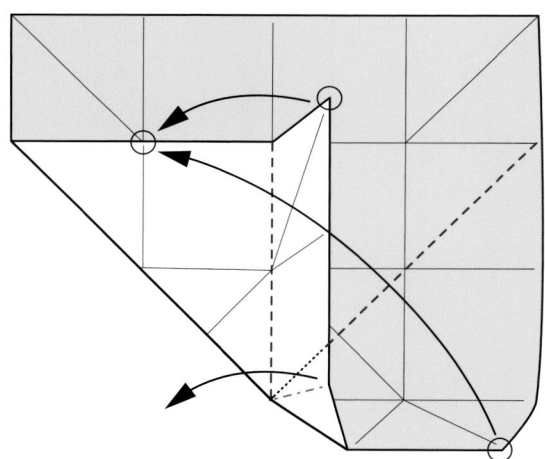

6 Fold the corner over to the reference point as indicated, making the model lie flat.

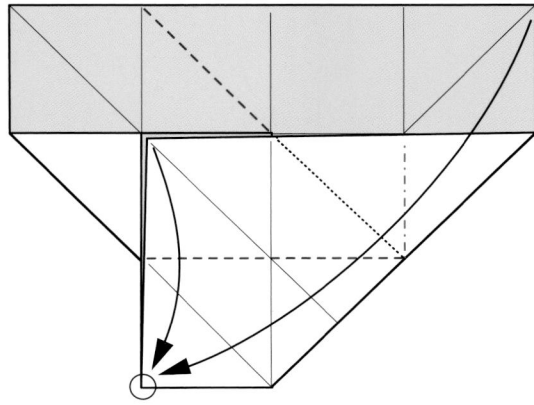

7 Fold the corners down as indicated, similar to the sequence in steps 5 and 6.

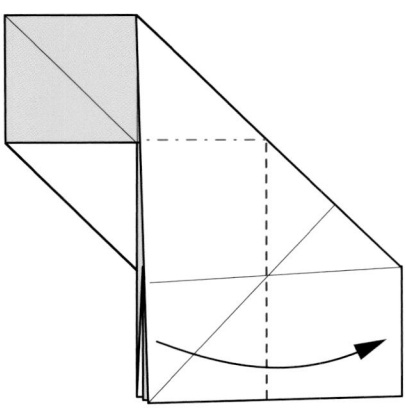

8 Fold over as indicated. Note: the model will not lie flat.

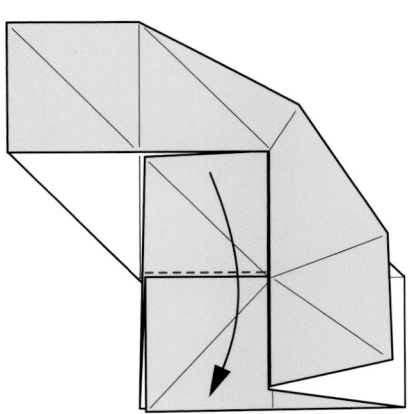

9 Fold the flap down. The model will still not be flat. See next step for details.

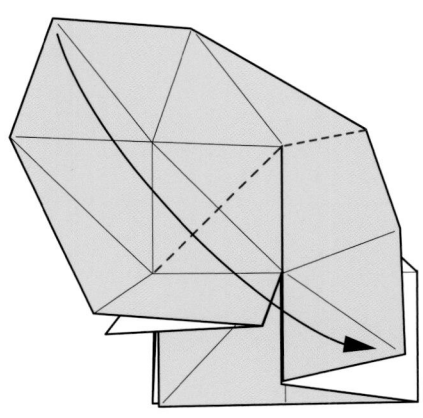

10 Fold the corner down, flattening the model.

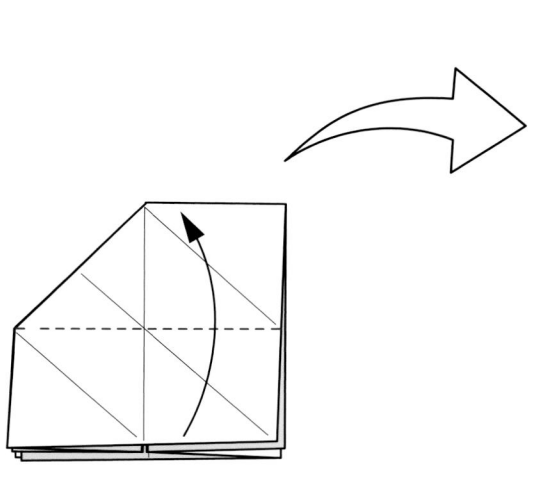

11 Fold the flap up.

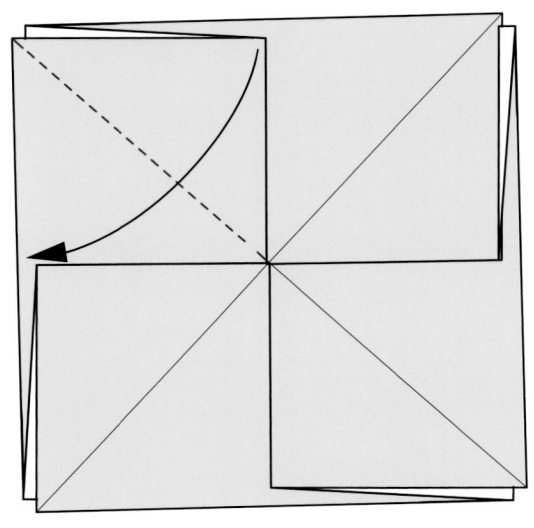

12 Valley fold the flap down.

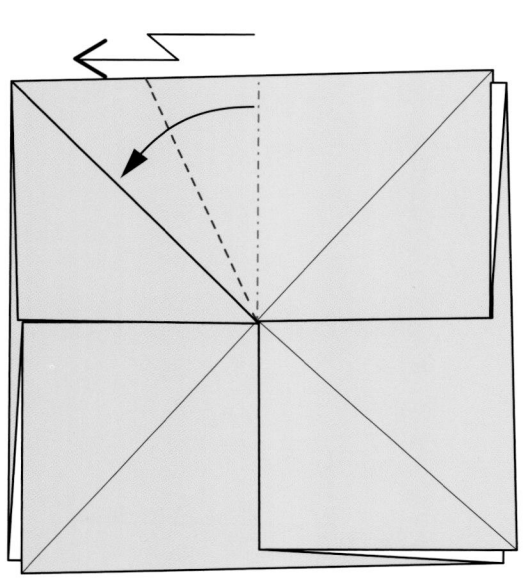

13 Pleat. The model will not lie flat.

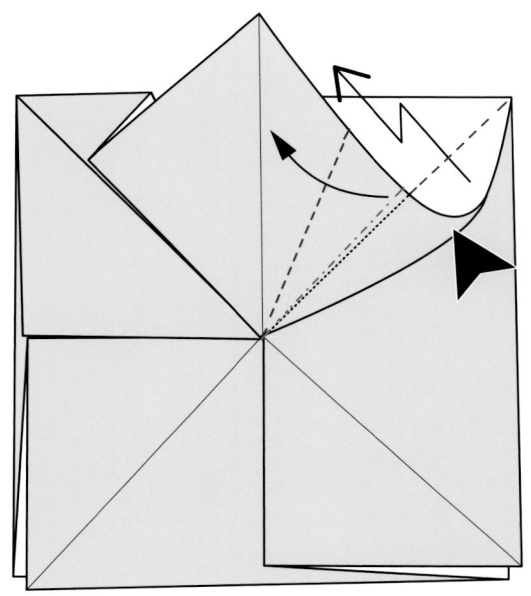

14 Pleat. Squash to make the model lie flat.

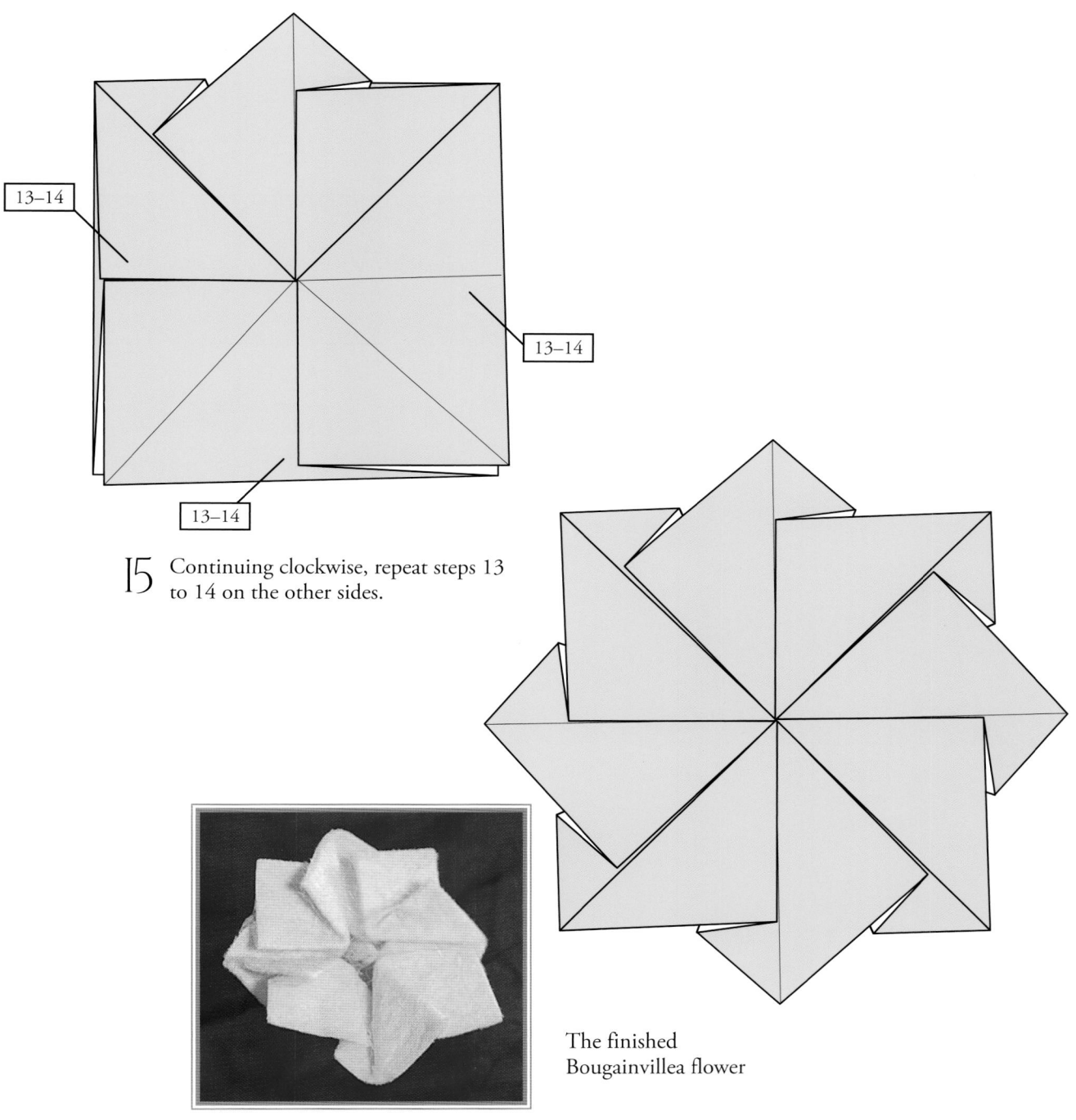

15 Continuing clockwise, repeat steps 13 to 14 on the other sides.

The finished
Bougainvillea flower

BRACTS

Make the bracts from 3⅜ x 11-inch rectangles. They will need to be folded and cut into equilateral triangles. One rectangle will yield four triangles.

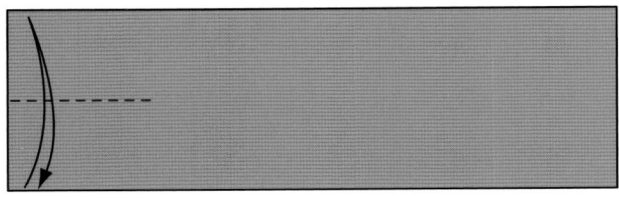

1 Fold in half, creasing closest to the edge.

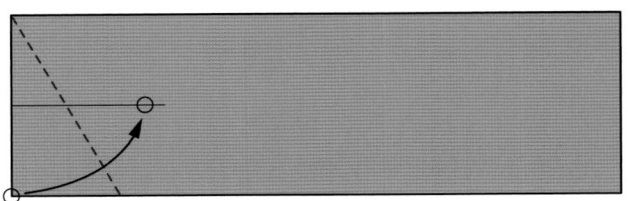

2 Fold the corner to the crease. Unfold.

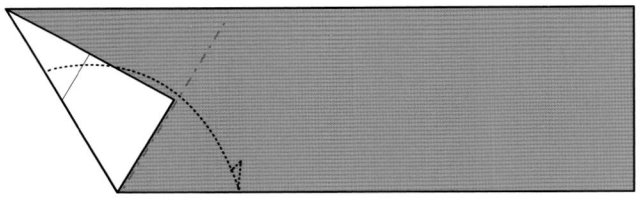

3 Mountain fold the edge to the bottom edge.

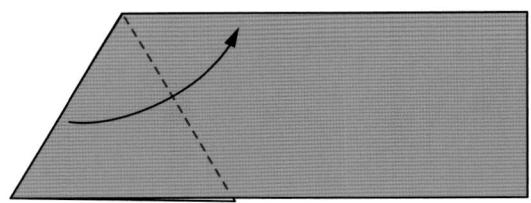

4 Valley fold the edge to the top edge.

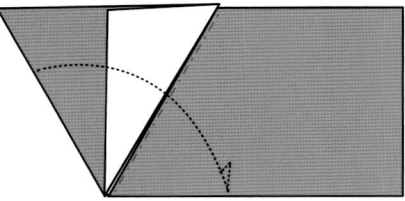

5 Mountain fold the edge to the bottom edge.

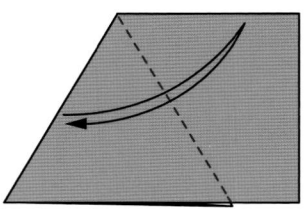

6 Valley fold the top edge to the left edge. Unfold.

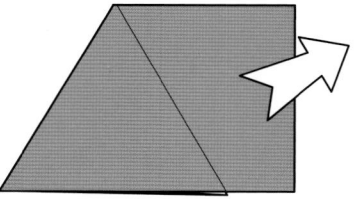

7 Unfold completely.

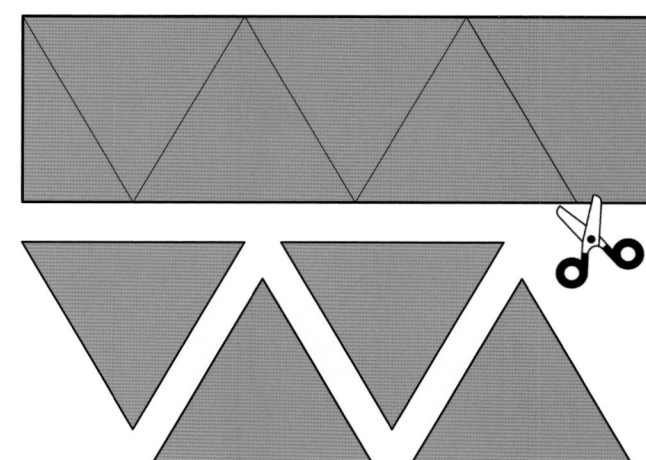

8 Cut the triangles apart.

Fold the triangles into bracts:

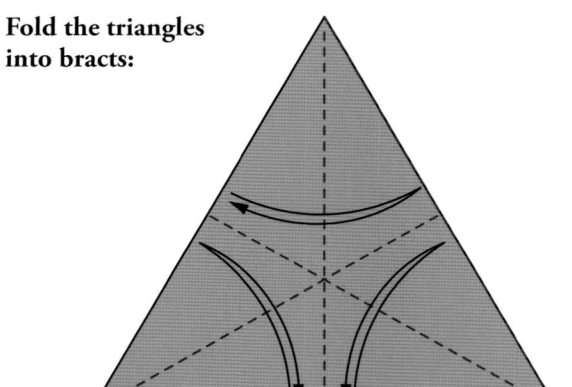

1 With the color side up, fold the angle bisectors and unfold.

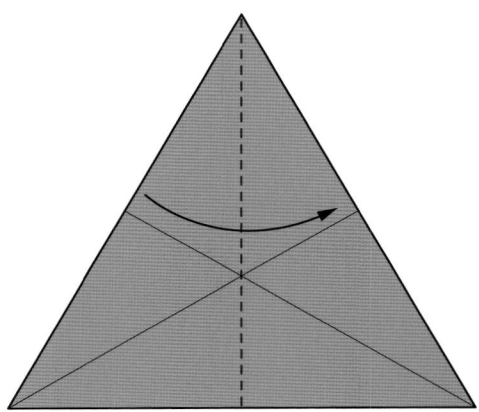

2 Fold in half.

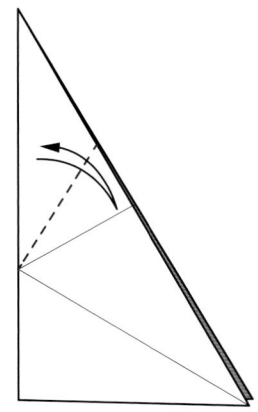

3 Fold the angle bisector. Unfold.

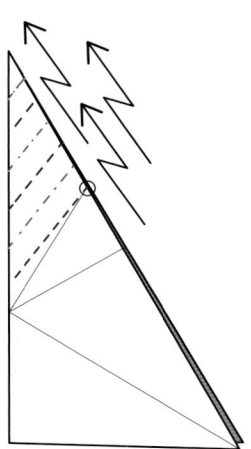

4 Starting at the reference point, create a sequence of parallel pleats. Unfold all pleats.

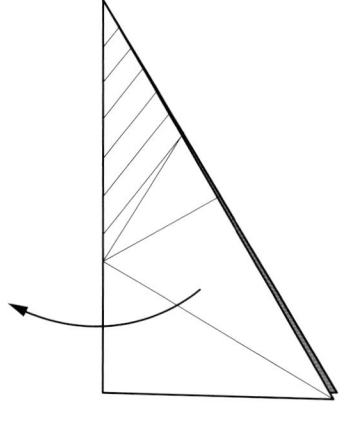

5 Unfold.

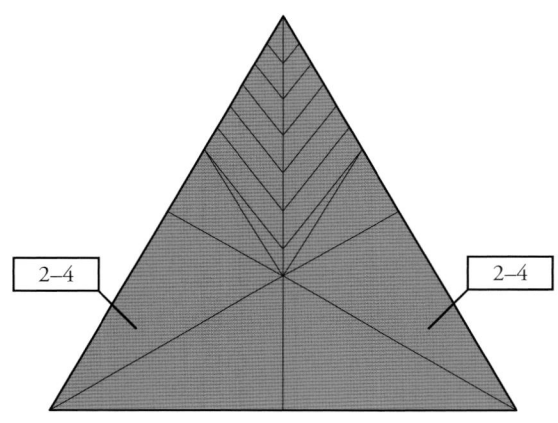

2–4   2–4

6 Repeat steps 2 to 4 on the other corners.

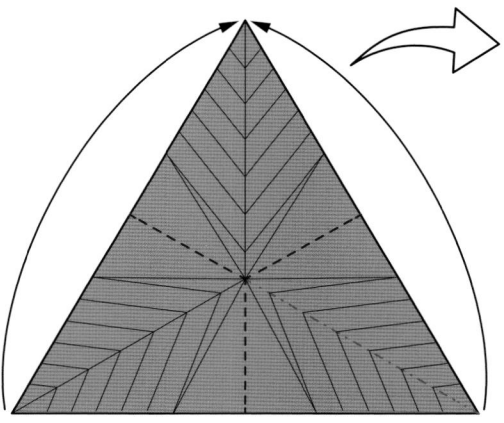

7 Bring all corners to meet at the top.

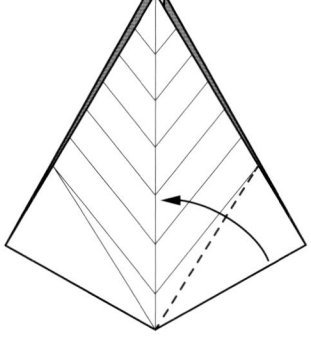

8 Fold the edge to the center crease and crease sharply.

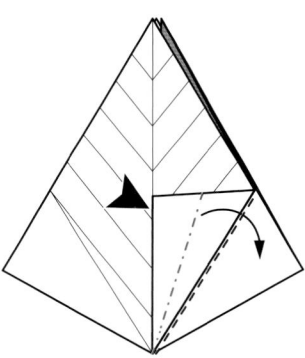

9 Open and squash, creasing sharply.

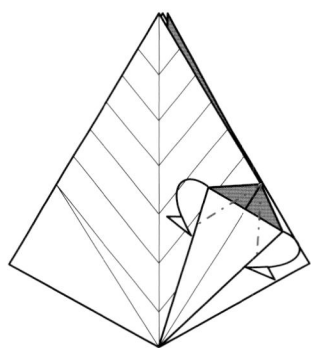

10 Mountain fold the corners sharply.

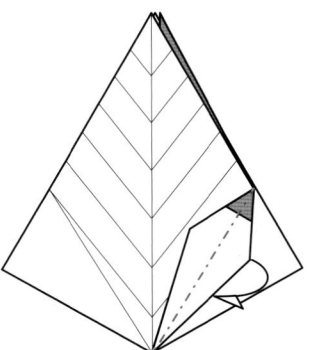

11 Mountain fold the flap to the back, creasing sharply.

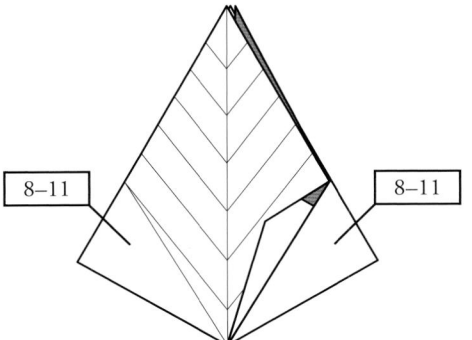

8–11   8–11

12 Repeat steps 8 to 11 on the other flaps.

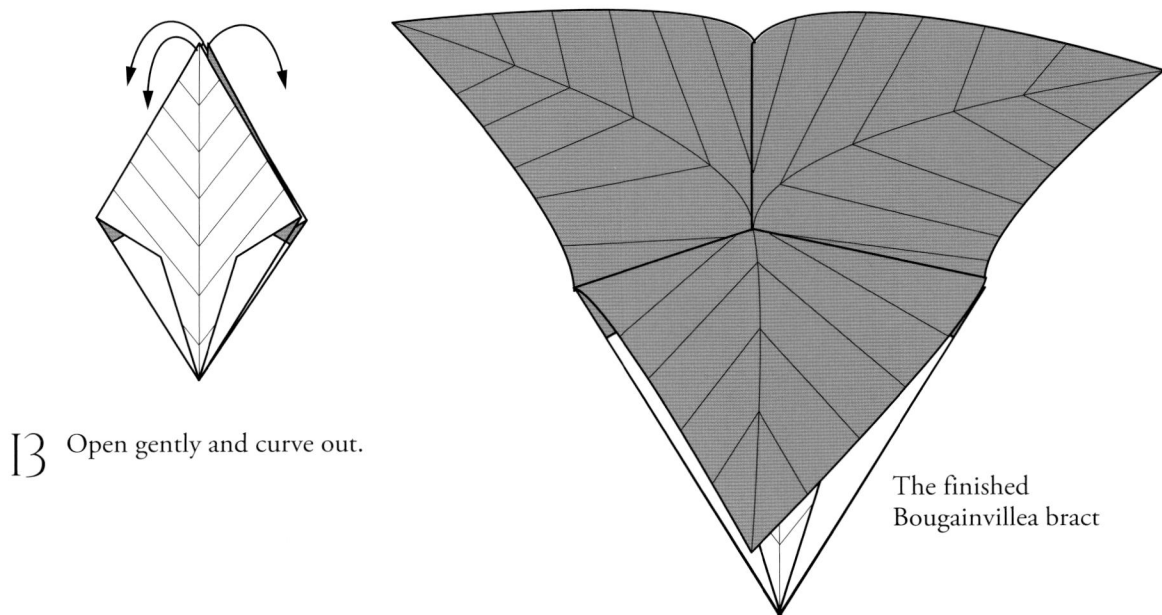

I3 Open gently and curve out.

The finished
Bougainvillea bract

LEAVES

Fold leaves from small squares of green paper, in various sizes from 1 to 2¼ inches (2.5 to 5.7 cm):

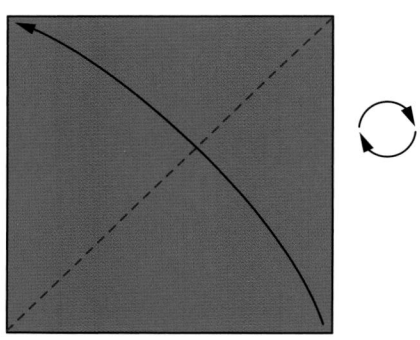

I Fold in half on the diagonal. Rotate.

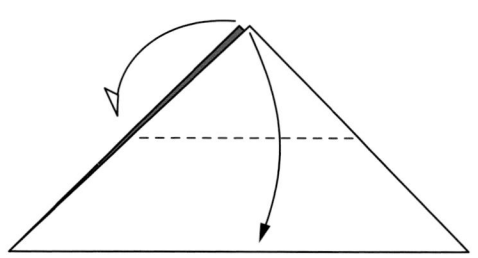

2 Fold the corner down to the crease. Repeat behind.

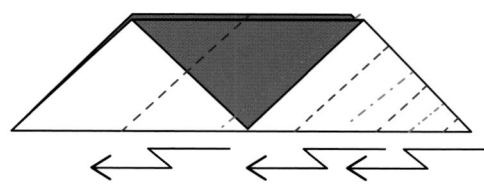

3 Create a sequence of pleats as shown. There are no precise references.

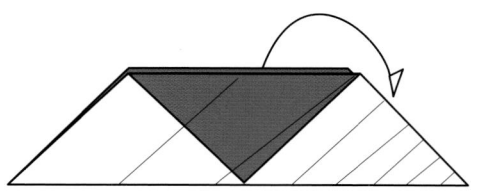

4 Unfold the back.

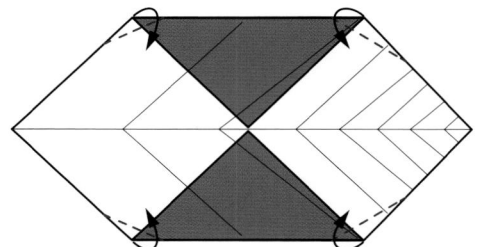

5 Fold the little corners inward to round out the leaf.

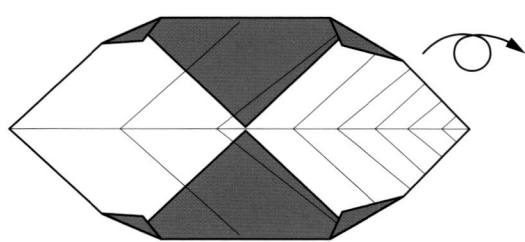

6 Turn over.

The finished Bougainvillea leaf

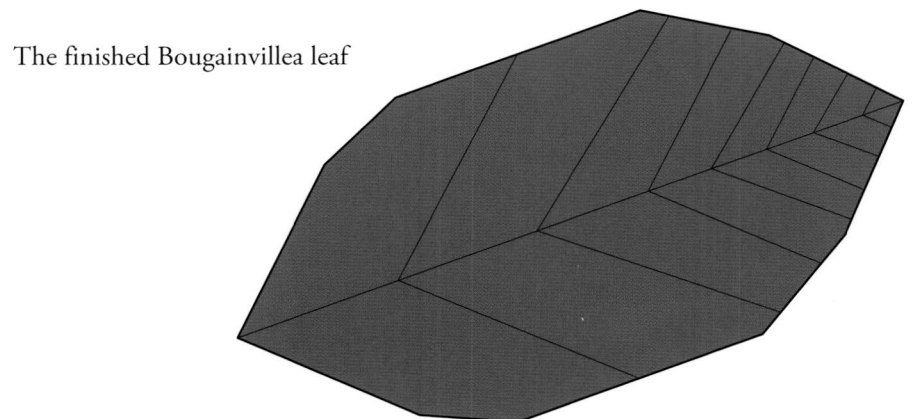

ABOUT THE
BOUGAINVILLEA

Bougainvillea (*Bougainvillea glabra*) is a thorny evergreen vine native to South America. It is known for the brilliant colors (purple, magenta, yellow and more) of the leaf structures called bracts. Some varieties have two different color bracts on the same plant. It is also called "the paper flower" because of the papery quality of the bracts. Bougainvillea is often seen as a symbol of welcome. Hawaiians sometimes use the bracts to make leis.

ASSEMBLY

You will be recreating bougainvillea branches (or vines) from several elements: small branches with leaves only and branches with flowers and bracts plus leaves. First you will be assembling the flowers into bundles that will be glued and taped into a bract. Then the flower-and-bract clusters will be taped onto branches with leaves to fill them out. Make additional branches of the leaves only. Finally, the floral branches and the leaf branches will be taped onto a larger main branch. Plan to make 1–2 leaf branches and 7 floral branches for each main branch. The arrangement shown here consists of 3 main branches and each required 59 leaves plus 25 bracts with flowers.

Supplies and equipment needed to make one main branch:

- Finished bougainvillea flowers, 3 for each bract you intend to use
- Finished bracts, (3–4) per floral branch
- 24-gauge floral wire, covered in white fabric
- Pliers
- Wire cutters
- Floral tape in green and brown
- Thin strips of the same paper used for the bracts
- Glue stick
- Tapestry needle or beading awl
- Finished leaves in an assortment of sizes, made from 1-inch, 1½-inch, 2-inch, and 2¼-inch squares (20 or so are recommended). Make the smaller leaves from a lighter green.
- Flocked floral wire for leaf and floral branches (these come in precut lengths, many to a pack)
- 1 large branch*, trimmed of smaller twigs

*Thin wooden dowels (¼-inch diameter) may be used instead; cut down to the length of your choice (recommended length: 23–30 inches)

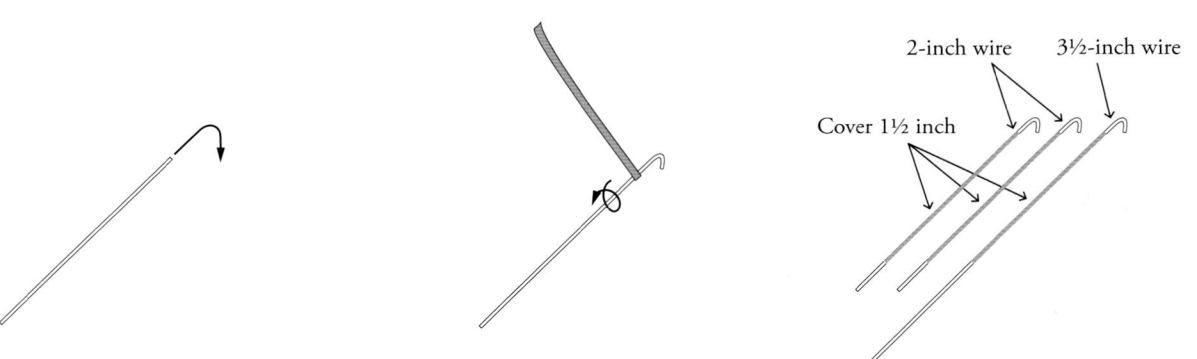

2-inch wire   3½-inch wire

Cover 1½ inch

1   Wire the flowers: for each group of three flowers, cut two 2-inch lengths of cloth-covered wire and one 3½-inch length. Bend the tip down on each wire to form a head pin. Leaving ⅛ inch unwrapped at the top, use the thin strips of bract paper, one side covered with glue from the glue stick, to cover the stem wires for 1½ inches. Leave ½ inch at the ends bare.

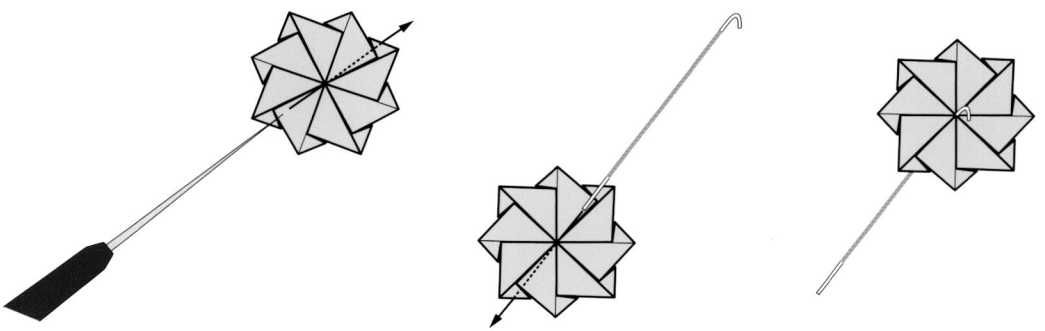

2   Pierce holes in the center of each flower with the tapestry needle or beading awl. Insert the wrapped ends of the wire through the hole and pull through. Only the white head should be visible.

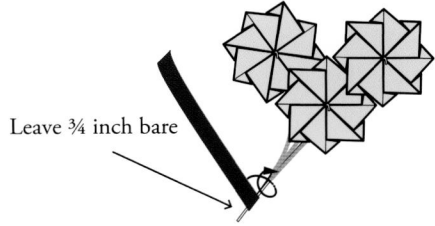

Leave ¾ inch bare

3   Gather the three flowers into a bundle and wrap together with green floral tape. Wrap up to ¾ of an inch from the end of the longest wire. Repeat with remaining white flowers to make additional bundles.

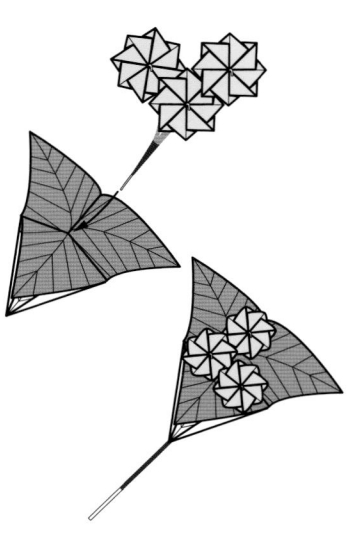

4 Pierce holes in the center of each bract, making sure that the holes are wide enough for the flower stems to pass through. Insert a flower-cluster stem through a hole, so that 1½-inch stems sit above the hole; the green part of the stem should be below the hole. Repeat with remaining bracts and flower bundles.

5 Make the leaf branches: wire the leaves (see "Tips on Assembling Flowers" on page 26). Cut 8- to 11-inch lengths from the flocked wires. Then use brown floral tape to wrap some leaves of different sizes down the length of a flocked wire. Tape almost to the end, leaving the bottom inch bare.

6 Make the floral branches: cut 6- to 9-inch lengths of flocked wires for these. Use brown floral tape to affix two small leaves to the tip of a flocked wire, then tape a couple of flower-and-bract clusters a little further down the wire. Tape almost to the end, leaving the bottom inch bare.

7 Tape the floral branches and the leaf branches to the main branch: first, affix two small leaves to the tip of the branch (or dowel, if you are using) with brown floral tape. Continue taping, adding the floral branches as you tape down the length of the branch and taping one leaf where the floral branch connects to the main one. They shouldn't be even with each other. Then add the leaf branches as you continue the taping. These should also not be even with each other.

The completed Bougainvillea branches

NARCISSUS

Designed by Joost Langeveld;
diagrammed by Marcio Noguchi

"I think this flower looks best made from 6-inch or 8-inch squares. The resulting model is the perfect size to fit into a bud vase. I like to use papers with colors and patterns of my own design, printed on computer paper. Origami paper is much more expensive where I live, so when I started out, I tried printing my own. Now I prefer it that way."

—Joost Langeveld

Joost Langeveld's origami videos on YouTube have been viewed by millions of people. He is the author of eight origami books and has filled so much of his house with his origami creations—everything from flowers and animals to bricks, milk cartons, and even mechanized contraptions—that he has turned the bottom part of it into a museum. When he is not devoting time to folding and creating origami models, he works part time as a computer engineer. He lives in the Netherlands.

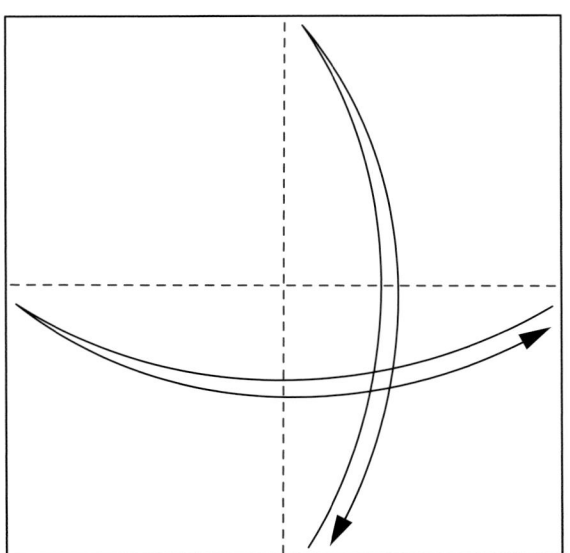

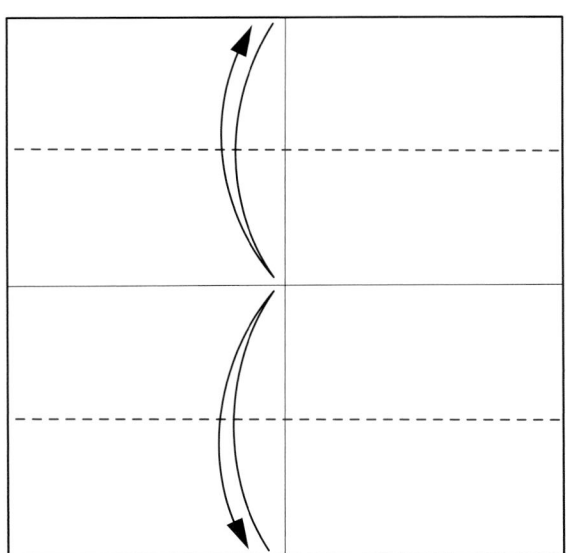

Make the flowers from 6-inch yellow squares:

1 With the white side up, fold in half horizontally and vertically. Unfold.

2 Fold in quarters. Unfold.

ABOUT THE
NARCISSUS

Narcissus is the scientific name for the group of flowers that includes daffodils, jonquils, and paperwhites. They are native to woods and meadows in Europe, northern Africa and western Asia. All varieties are known for a bowl- or trumpet-shaped corona surrounded by a ring of six petals. The flowers range from white to deep orangey yellow. Because it is one of the first flowers to appear in the spring, it symoblizes rebirth and new beginnings.

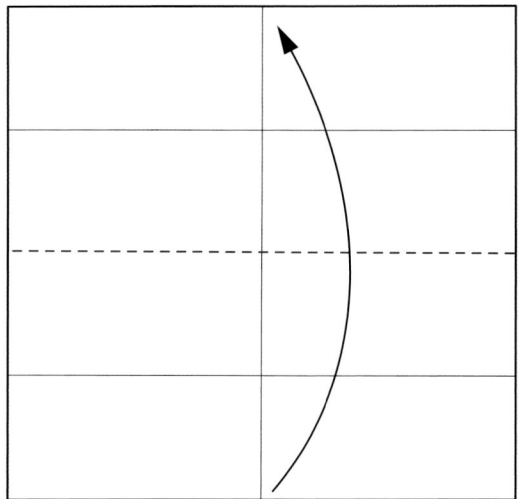

3   Fold the bottom edge to the top.

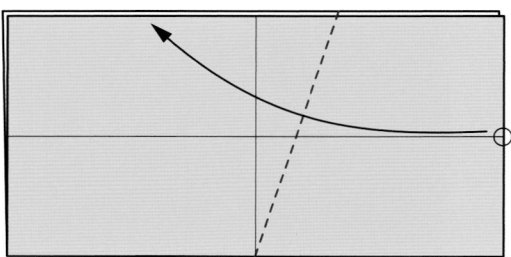

4   Valley fold as indicated, folding the reference point to the top edge.

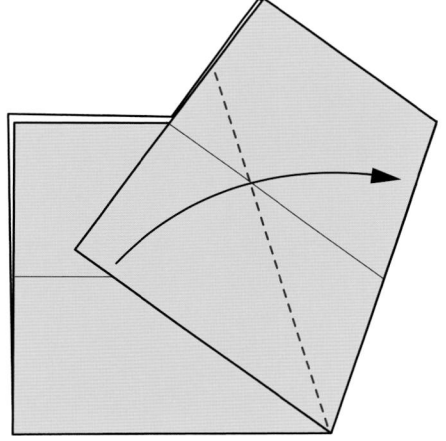

5   Fold the angle bisector, edge to edge.

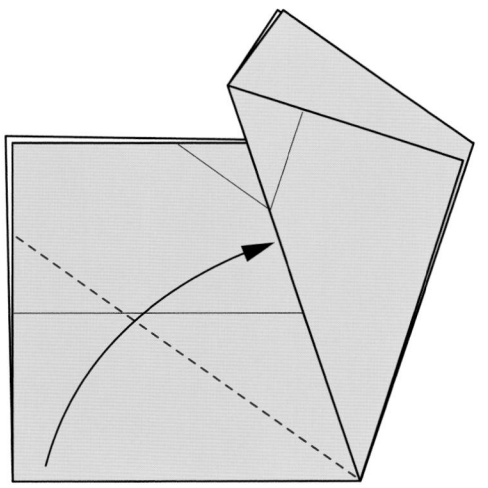

6 Fold the angle bisector, edge to edge.

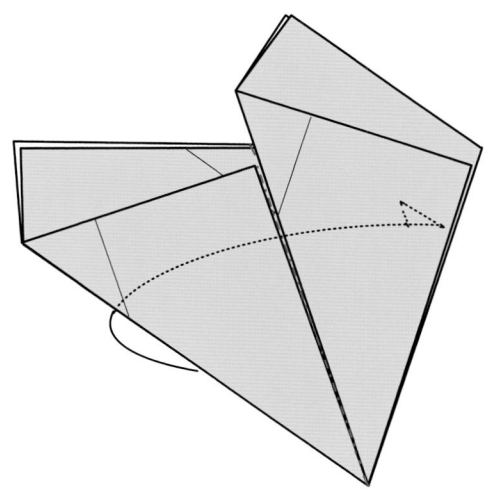

7 Mountain fold the model in half, edge to edge.

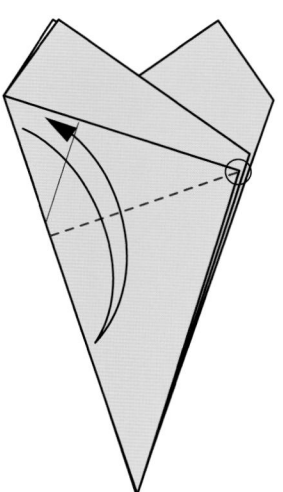

8 Starting from the corner indicated, fold down, aligning edges. Unfold.

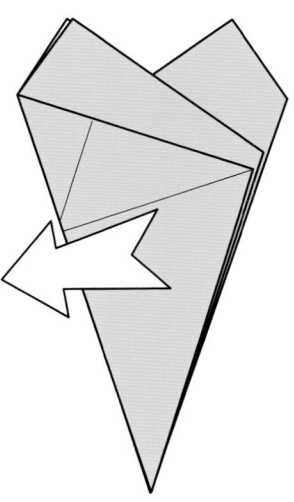

9 Unfold completely.

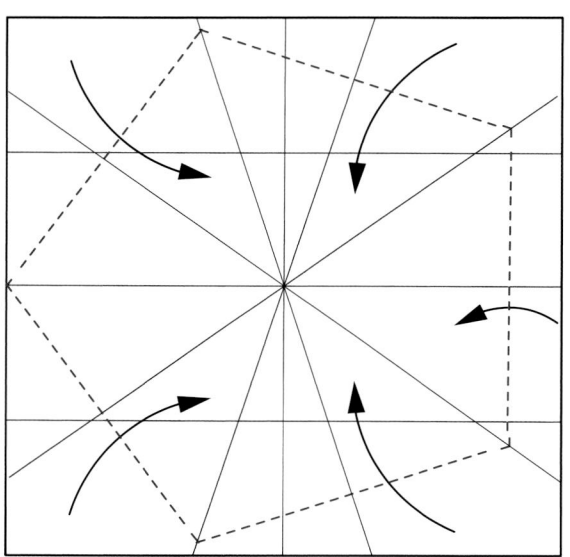

10　Fold flaps inward, forming the pentagon. Note: for a cleaner finish, you can cut the pentagon out.

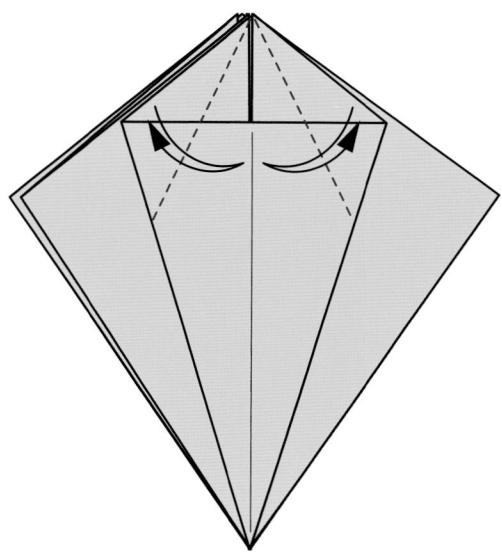

11　Collapse the pentagon on existing creases. Rotate so the open end points up.

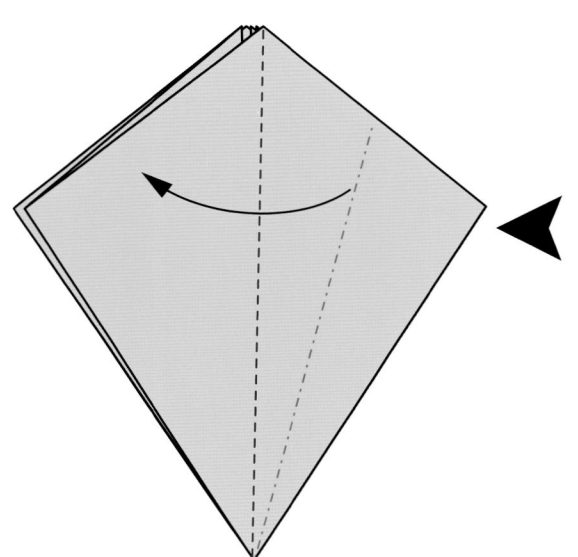

12　Open and squash one flap.

13　Fold the angle bisectors and unfold.

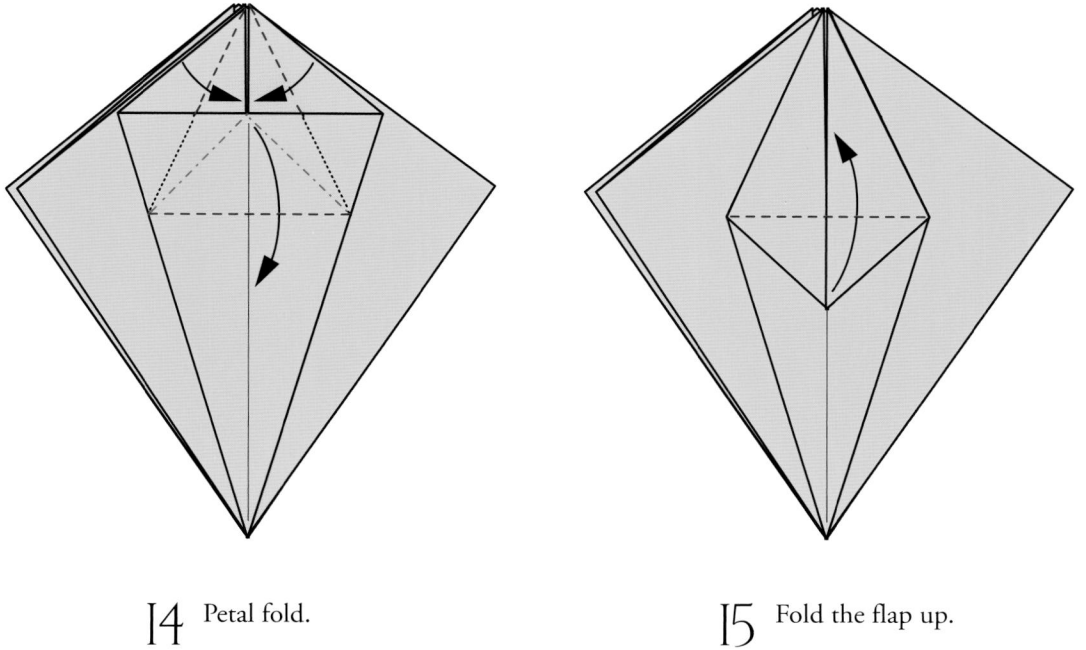

14 Petal fold.

15 Fold the flap up.

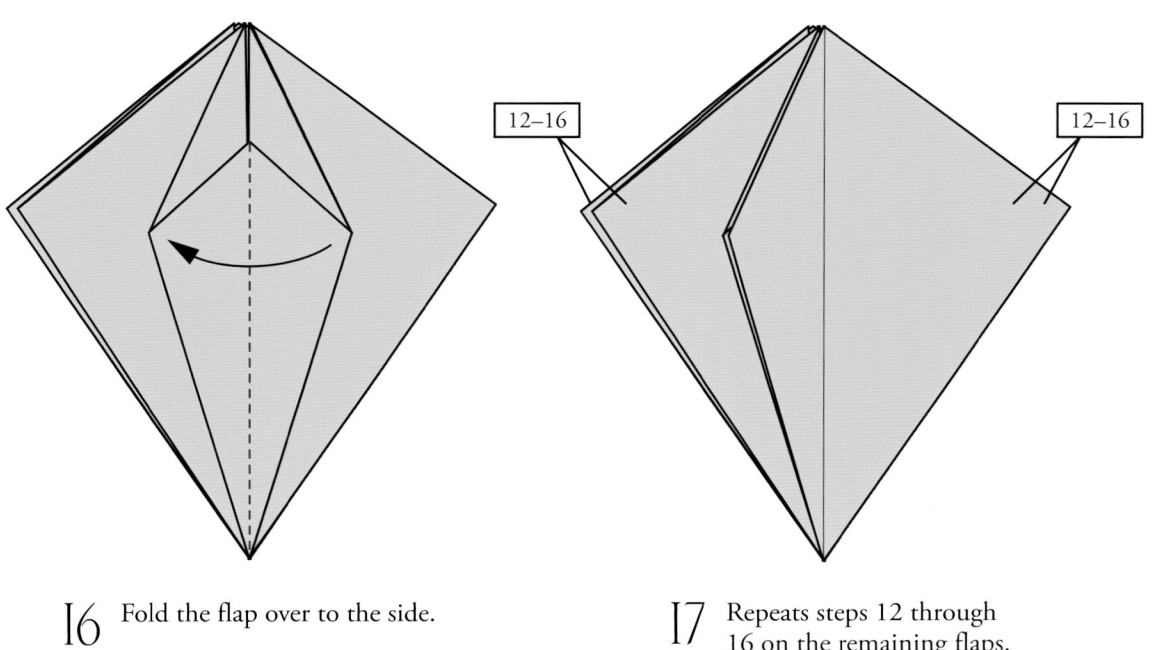

16 Fold the flap over to the side.

17 Repeats steps 12 through 16 on the remaining flaps.

12–16 12–16

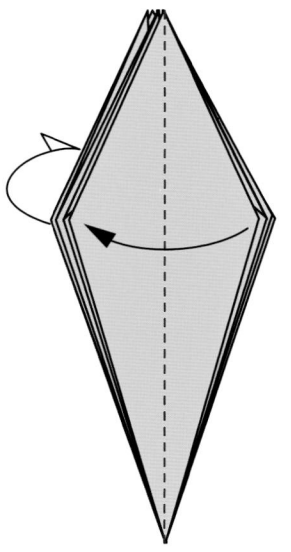

18 Fold one layer in the front to the left. Fold one layer in the back to the right.

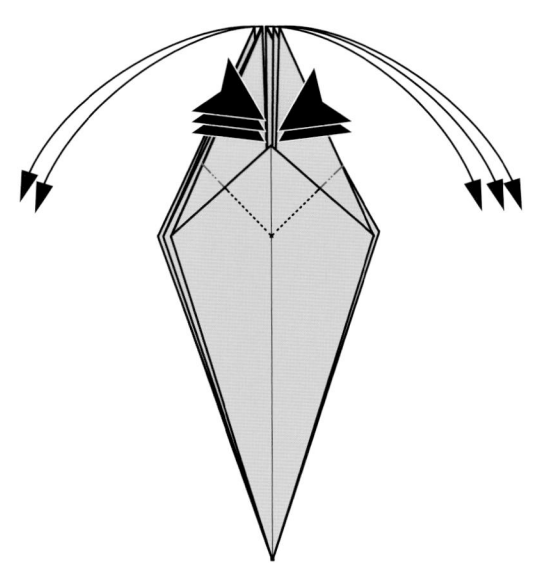

19 Reverse fold the long flaps.

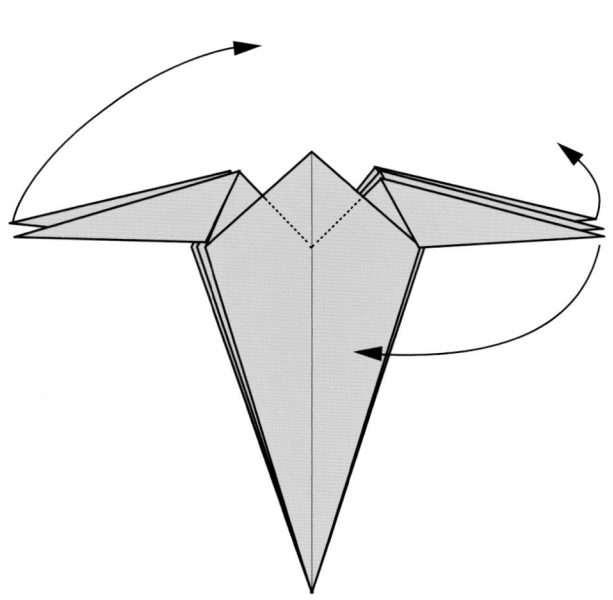

20 Open up the flaps and distribute them evenly so the model is 3D.

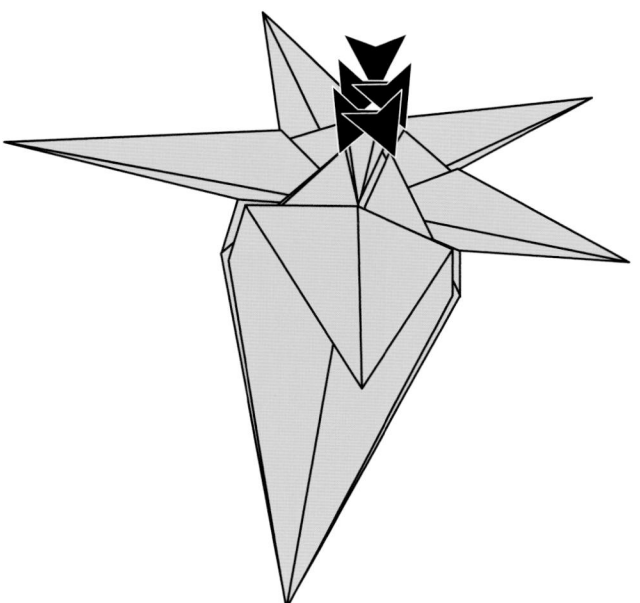

21 Squash all the corners.

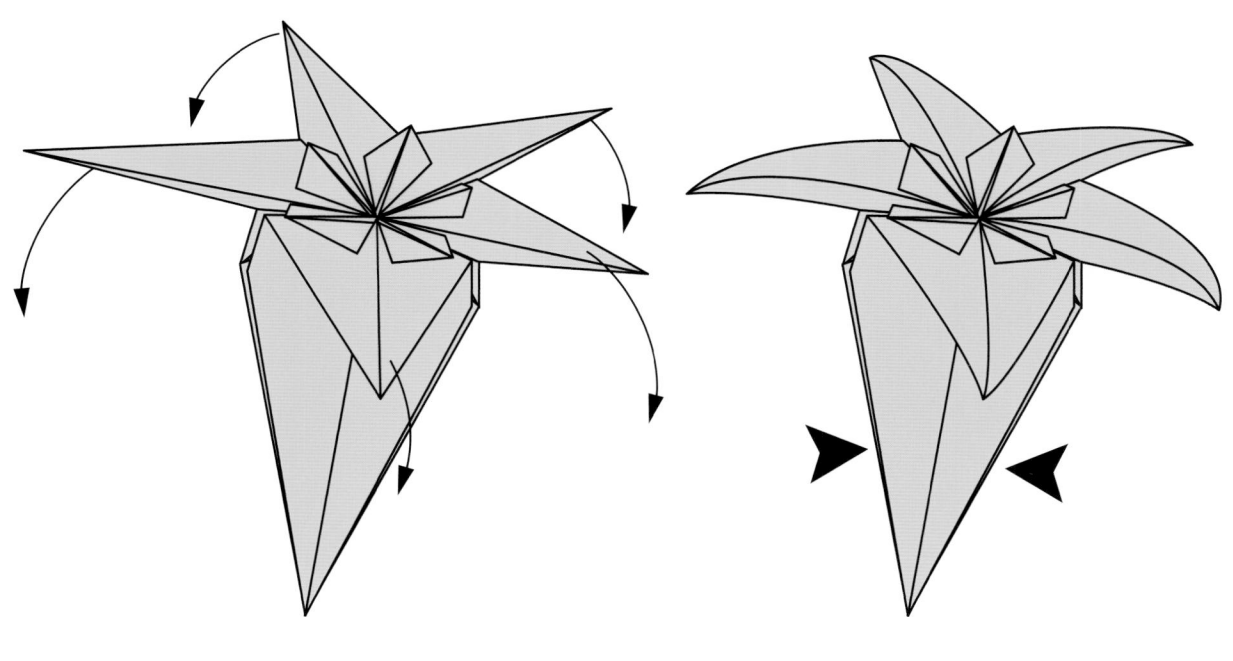

22 Curl the tips of the longer flaps down.

23 Push the sides in to narrow.

The finished Narcissus

STEM AND LEAVES

Use 6-inch green squares for the stem and the leaves.

To make the stem:

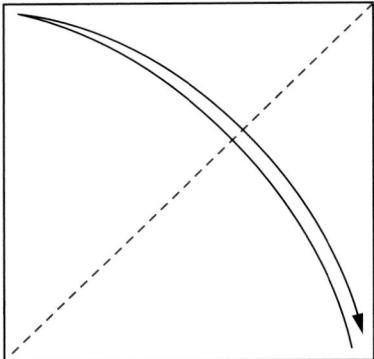

1 With the white side up, fold in half diagonally. Unfold.

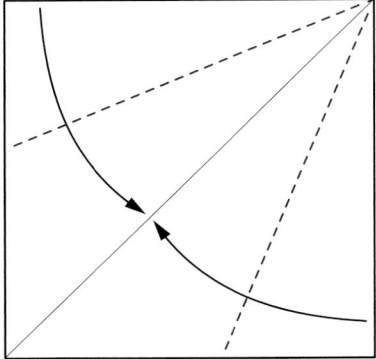

2 Fold the edges to the center.

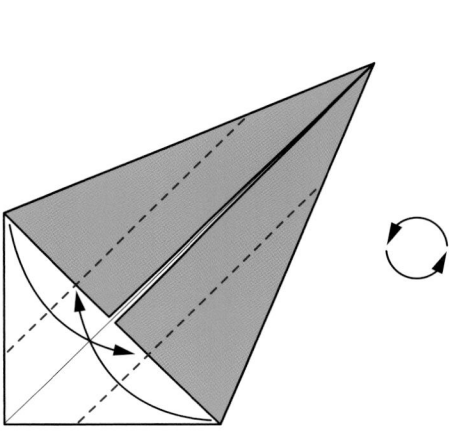

3 Fold the corners in as indicated to form thirds. Rotate.

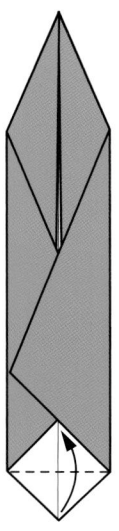

4 Fold the corner up.

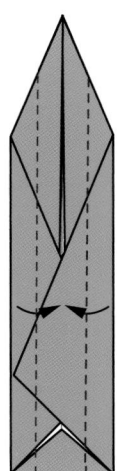

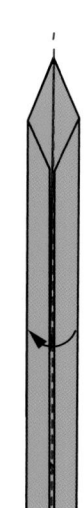

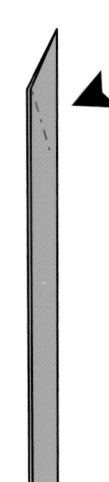

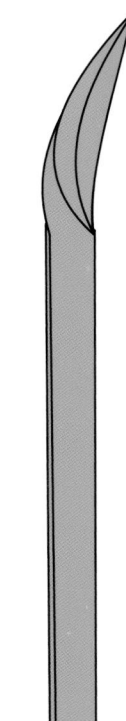

5 Fold the edges to the center.

6 Fold the right edge over to the left edge.

7 Push to flatten the tip, creating a slight curl.

The finished stem

To make the leaf:

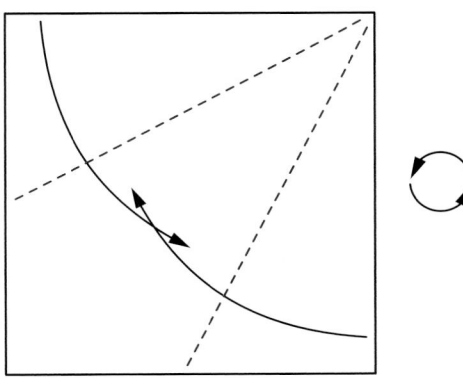

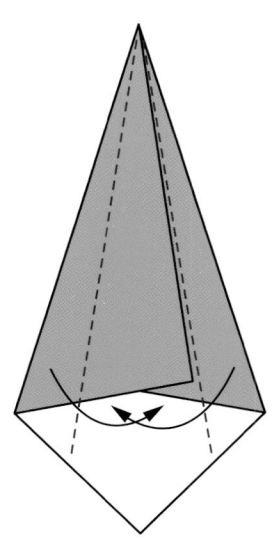

1 Fold the edges inward diagonally. There is no precise reference, but the flaps should overlap a bit. Rotate.

2 Fold edges inward diagonally again to narrow.

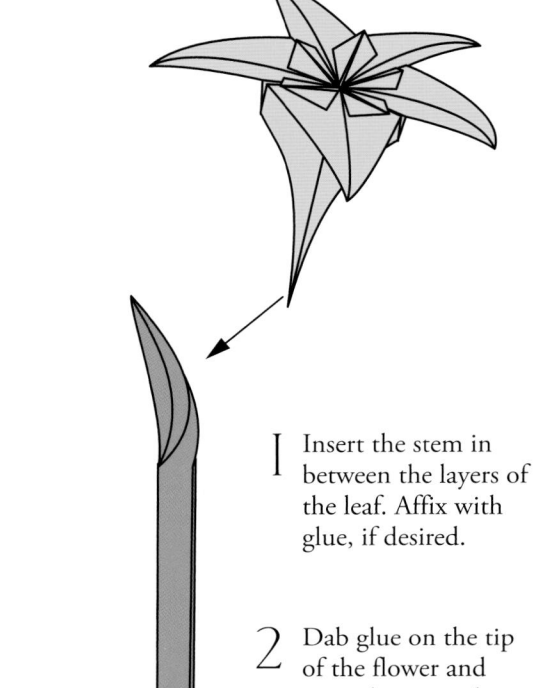

ASSEMBLY

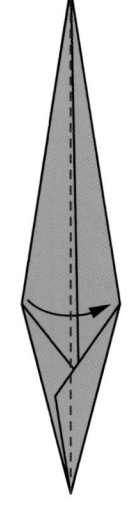

3 Fold the corners inward as indicated.

4 Valley fold the leaf in half.

1 Insert the stem in between the layers of the leaf. Affix with glue, if desired.

2 Dab glue on the tip of the flower and insert between the layers of the stem.

3 Place finished stem (with flower and leaf) in a bud vase.

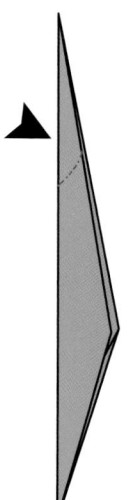

5 Push to flatten the tip, creating a slight curl.

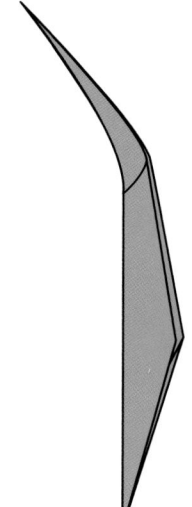

The finished leaf

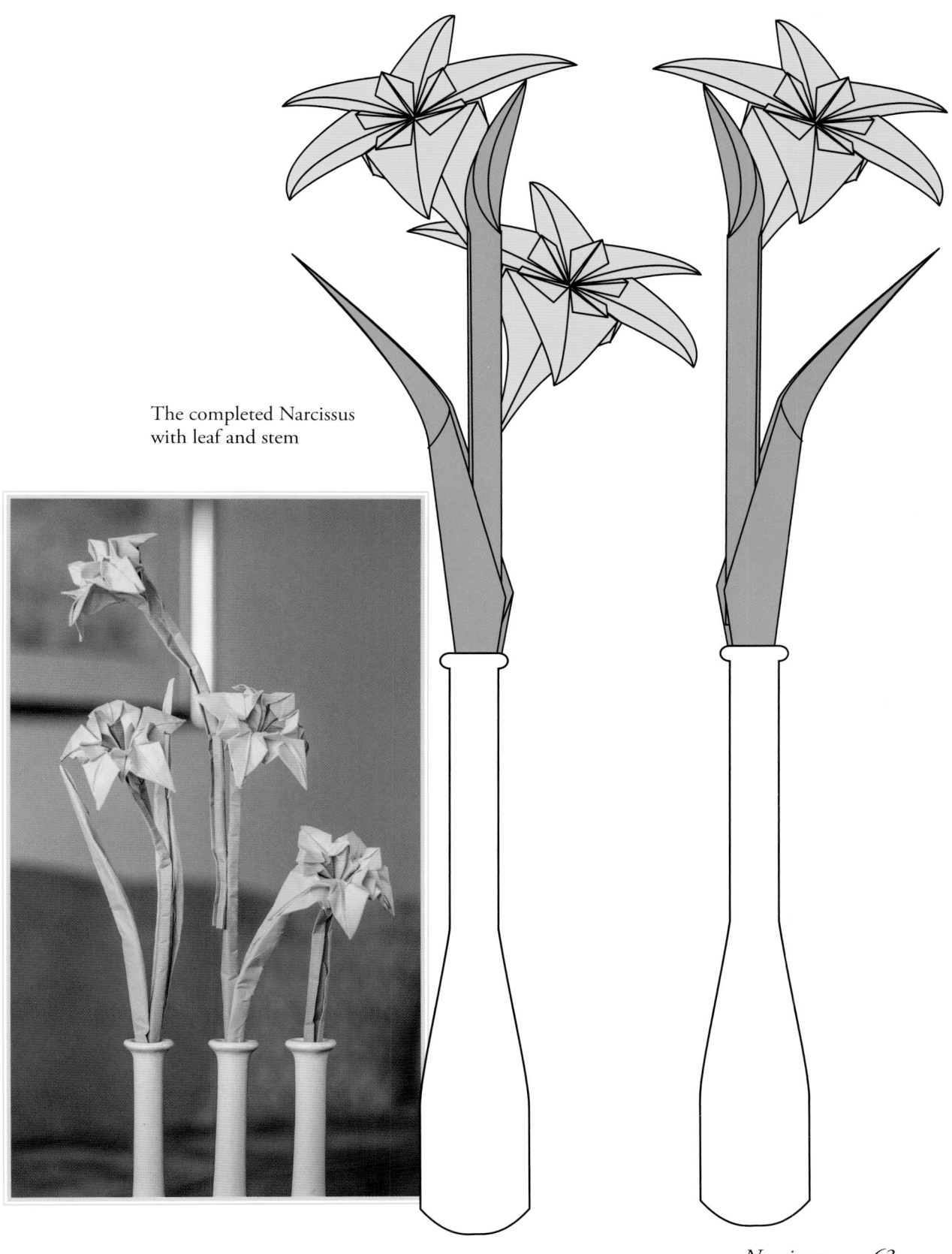

The completed Narcissus
with leaf and stem

LILY
WITH SIX PETALS

Created and diagrammed by David Shall;
inspired by a design by Bill Peck

"To fold a lily blossom of natural size, I advise using a 10- to 12-inch square of paper. My favorite paper for folding lilies—and most of my finished pieces—is prepared by me. I bond layers of art paper or tissue paper to a layer of kitchen foil or foil gift wrap. This method provides a folding medium that enables origami models to survive many, many years of display and handling without losing their shape."

—David Shall

David Shall has been folding origami models since the age of 10. It was a big activity in the Shall family—David, his two brothers, and his father were all devoted folders. A former high school teacher and mental health professional, he has exhibited and taught at US origami conventions, youth programs, and in schools and libraries since the 1970s. He began to develop and create his own designs in the late 1970s and now has more than 60 to his credit. Many of them were collected into a book entitled *Papercopia: Origami Designs by David Shall*; a gallery of these models appears on the book's website, www.papercopia.com.

Currently retired, David Shall lives in Harrisburg, Pennsylvania.

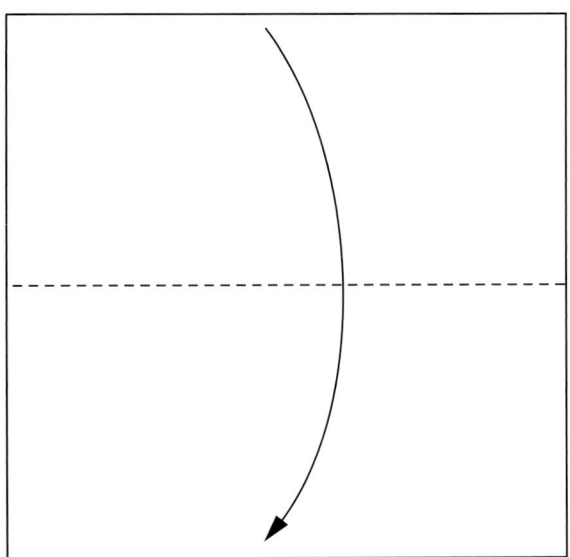

1 With the color side down, fold the top edge to the bottom edge.

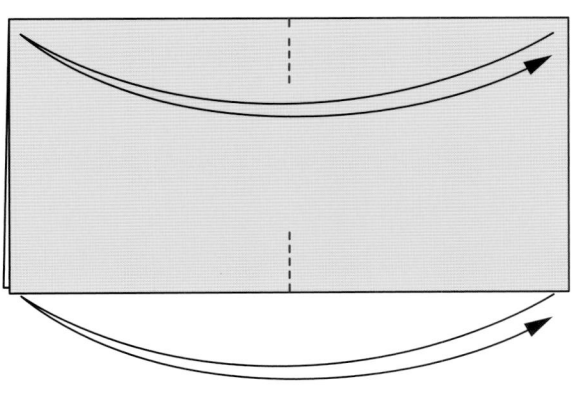

2 Fold the left edge to the right edge and crease at the top and bottom edges. Unfold.

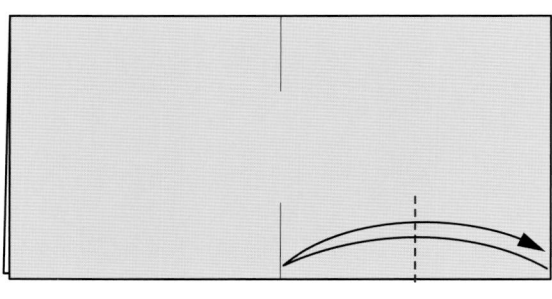

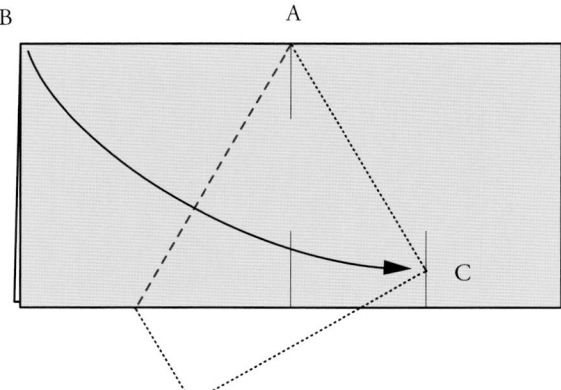

3 Fold the right edge to the center mark and crease at the bottom edge.

4 Begin valley fold at point A as you fold corner B to landmark C.

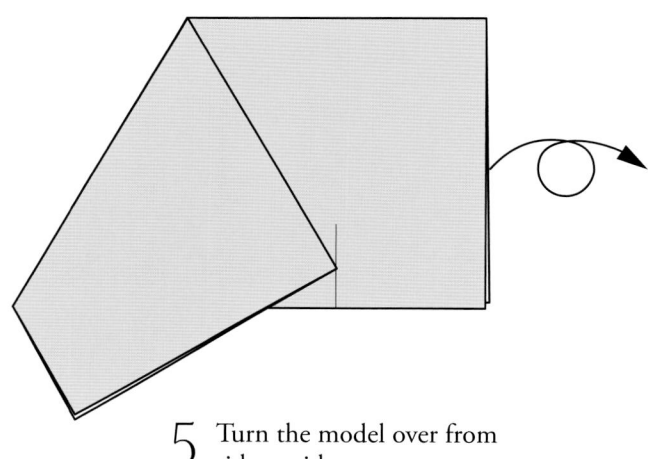

5 Turn the model over from side to side.

6 Fold the top edge over to the right edge.

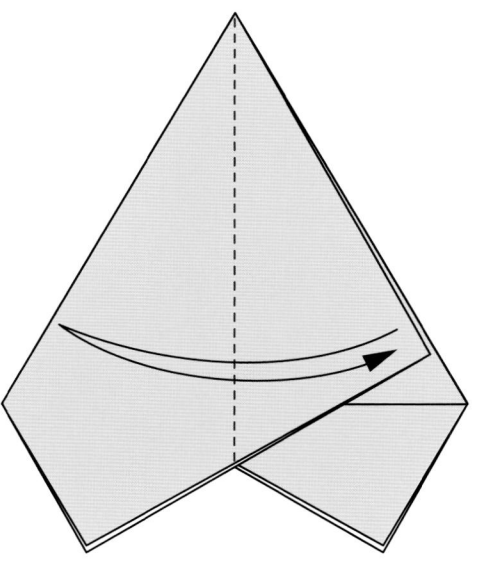

7 Valley fold the top flap over and unfold.

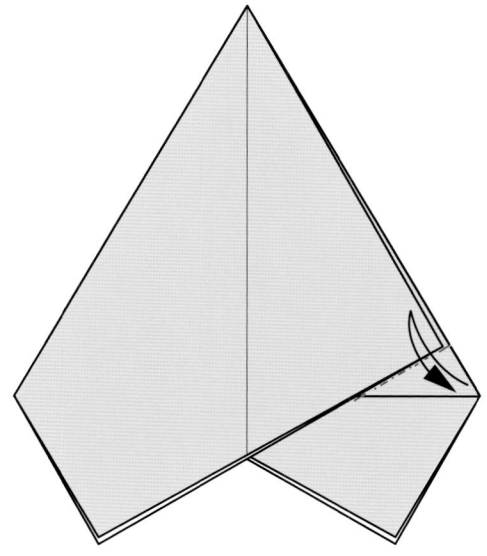

8 Make a landmark, matching edges as shown.

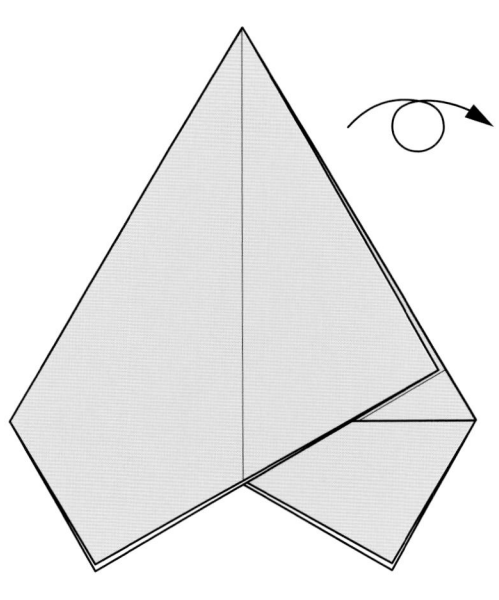

9 Turn over.

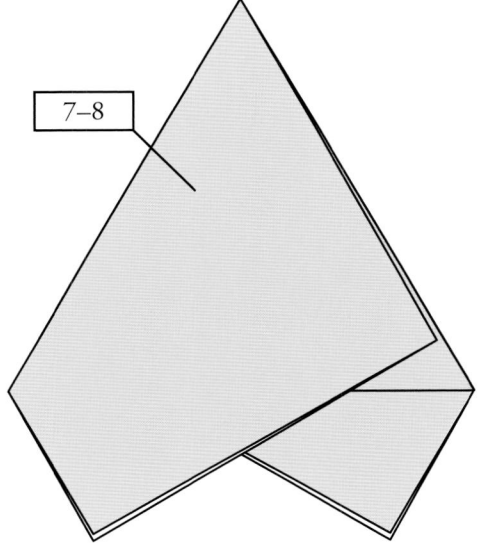

7–8

10 Repeat steps 7 and 8 on this side.

ABOUT THE LILY

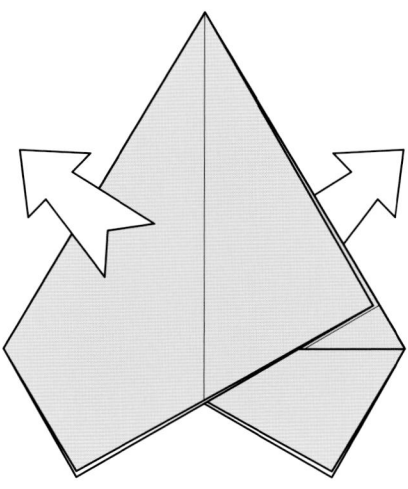

Lilies (scientific classification *Lilium*) have been revered for their beauty for thousands of years. A painted image of one, dating back to about 1580 BC, was found in Crete. In Greek mythology, the lily was identified with the goddess Hera—it was supposed to have formed from the milk of her breast. A symbol of purity and chastity, it later became associated with the Virgin Mary.

11   Open completely.

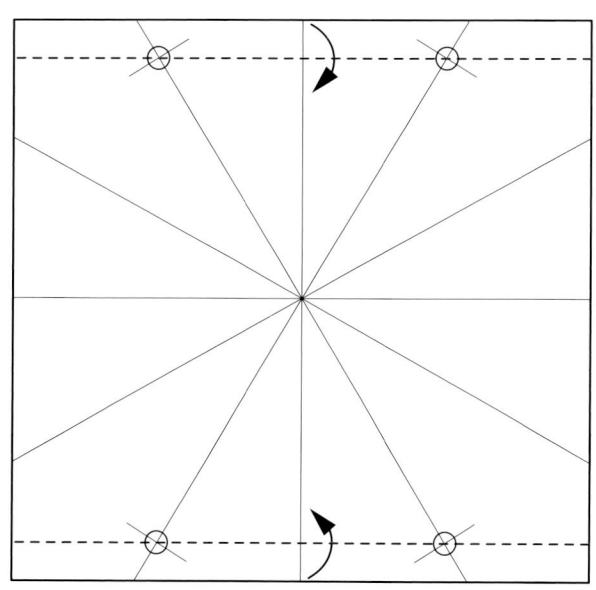

12   Valley fold through the circled intersections of the radii and the landmarks created in steps 8 and 10.

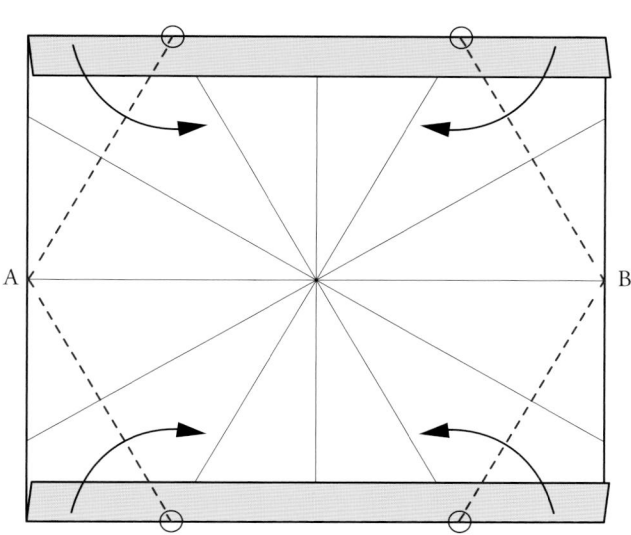

13 Fold the edges to the creasemarks shown to form a hexagon. The fold might not intersect at points A and B, but this is fine.

14 Mountain and valley fold on existing creases as shown. Use folds to form a six-flap preliminary base. Rotate so the open end points up.

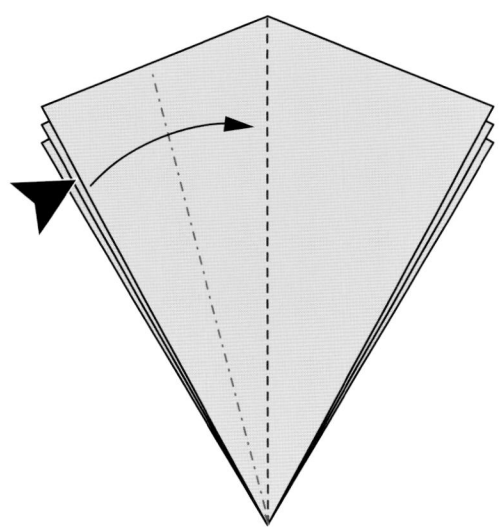

15 Squash fold the top flap.

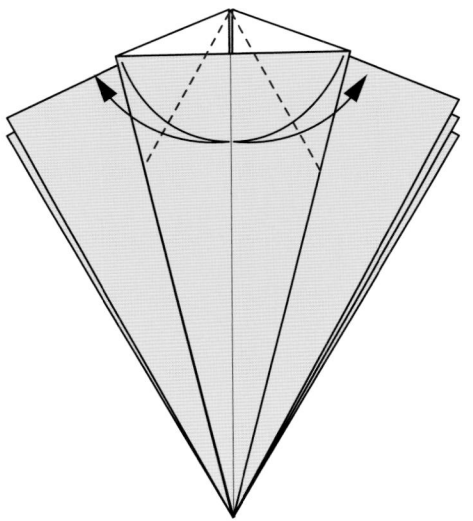

16 Fold the angle bisectors and unfold.

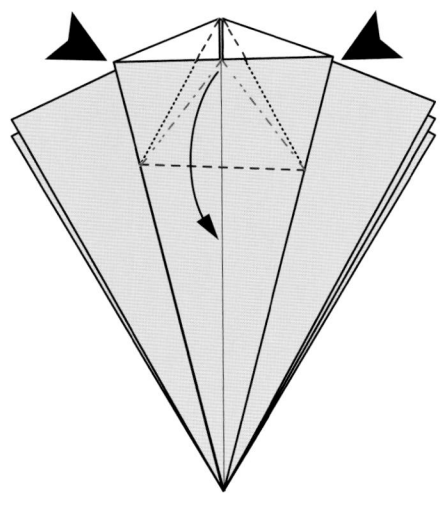

17 Petal fold.

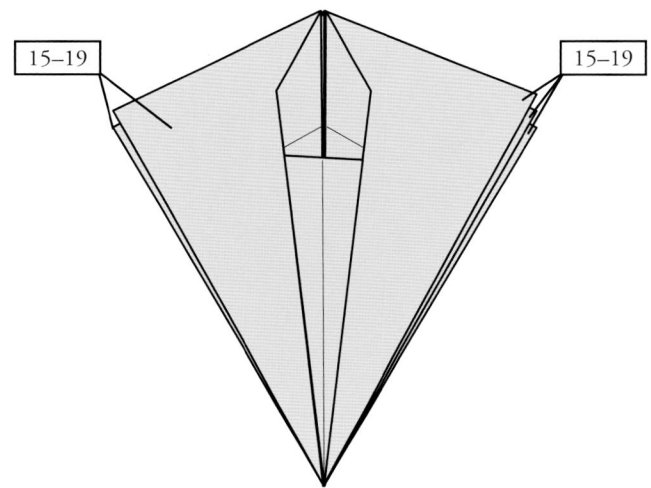

18 Reverse the petal fold and tuck the corner inside.

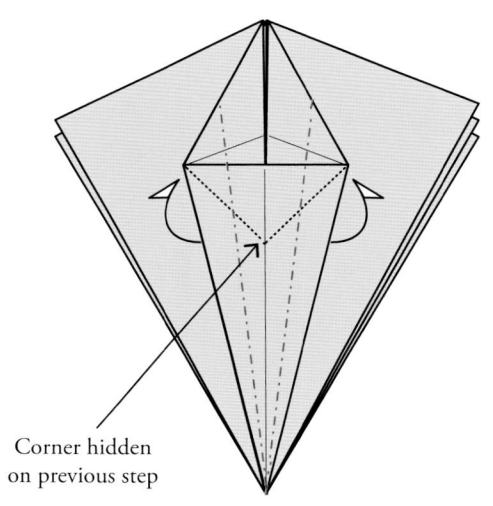

Corner hidden on previous step

19 Mountain fold the angle bisectors to narrow.

15–19

15–19

20 Repeat steps 15 to 19 on the other five flaps.

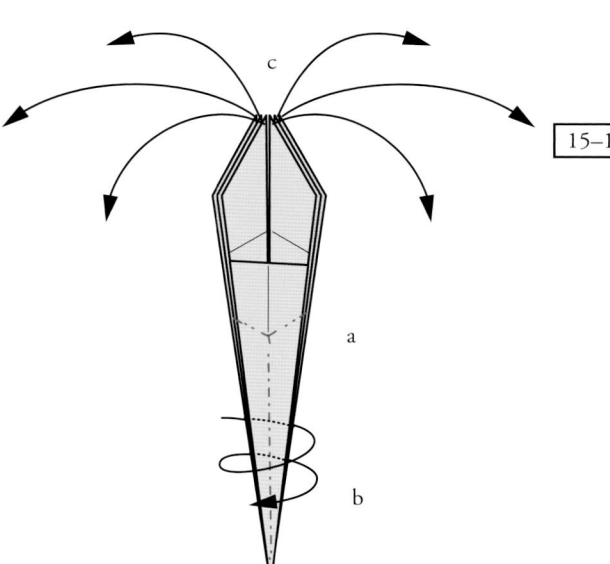

15–19

21 Feel where the inside thickness ends (a), then form a rabbit-ear fold fold to narrow the stem. Twist the stem (b). Open out and shape the petals (c). Curl the petals back. Slightly curl and twist a few petals to make them appear more natural.

The completed Lily

HIBISCUS

Designed and diagrammed by Derek McGann

A high school math teacher from San Antonio, Texas, Derek McGann has been designing his own origami models for the past seven years. Like many people, he learned origami as a child, but did not take it up as a serious pursuit until after college. He began designing on his own after reading Robert Lang's book, *Origami Design Secrets*.

Most of what he fold falls into one of several categories: flowers, for the beauty and elegance of the final product; insects for the challenge of creating extremely thin appendages; and sea creatures for the complexity and variation in the arrangement of their features. Lately, he has developed an interest in folding models inspired by mythical or fantastic creatures, such as the phoenix and the Balrog from Tolkien's Middle Earth. He enjoys the challenge of creating as much detail as possible from a single uncut square of paper, and executing it with as much delicacy and finesse as possible.

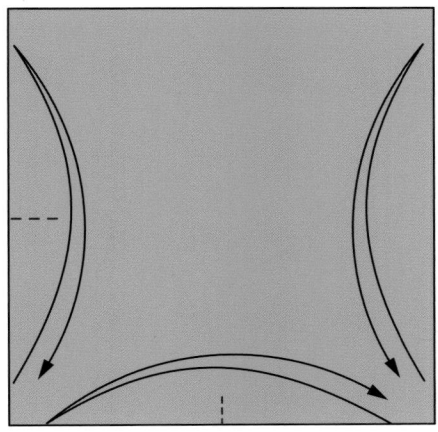

1 With the color side up, fold in half horizontally and vertically, pinching by the edges in three places as shown.

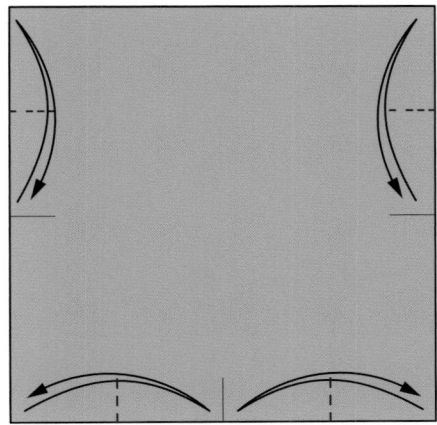

2 Folding edges to the pinch marks made in the last step, pinch by the edges as shown.

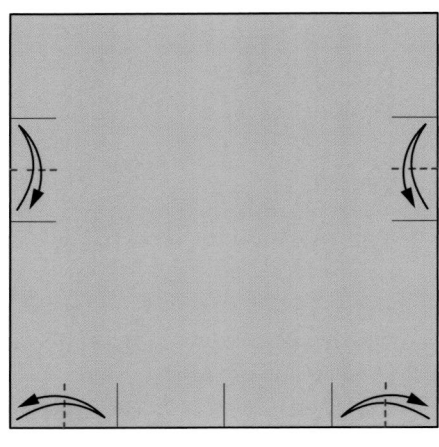

3 Pinch the indicated sections in half by the edges.

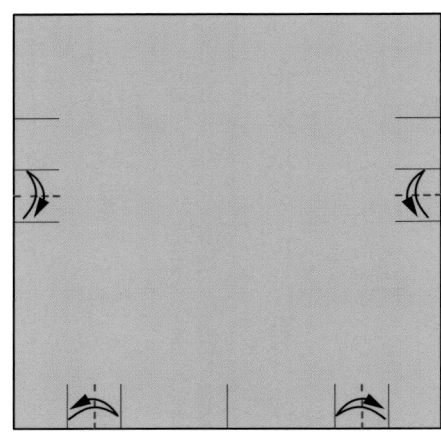

4 Pinch the indicated sections in half by the edges.

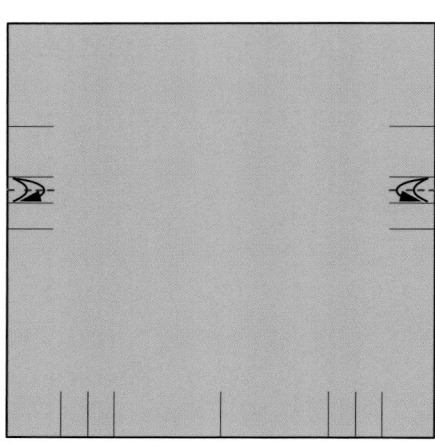

5 Pinch the indicated sections in half by the edges one final time.

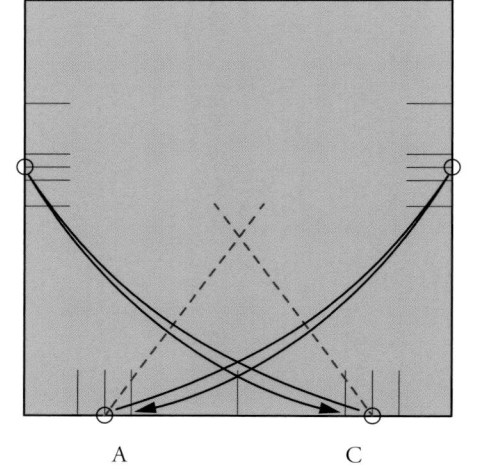

6 Fold point A to point B and unfold (the resulting crease should hit point C). Repeat with points C and D (this crease should hit point A).

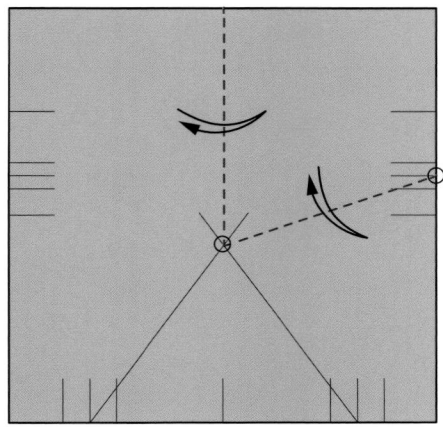

7 Valley fold and unfold to make the radii shown.

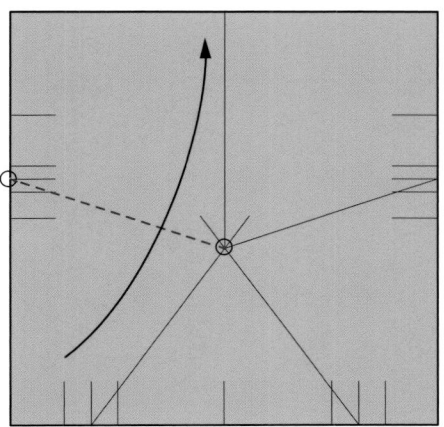

8 Valley fold as shown but do not unfold. Crease sharply to the intersection of the other four creases.

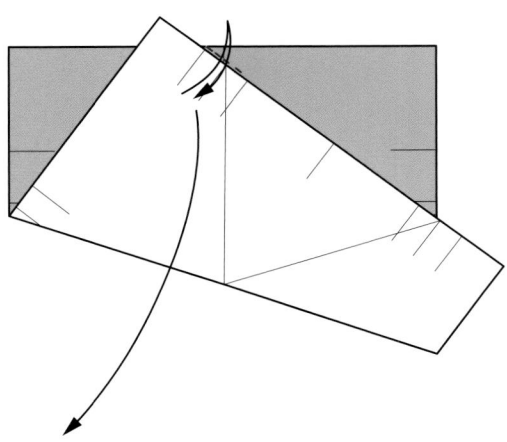

9 Fold and unfold where the raw edge crosses the center line, then unfold the entire flap.

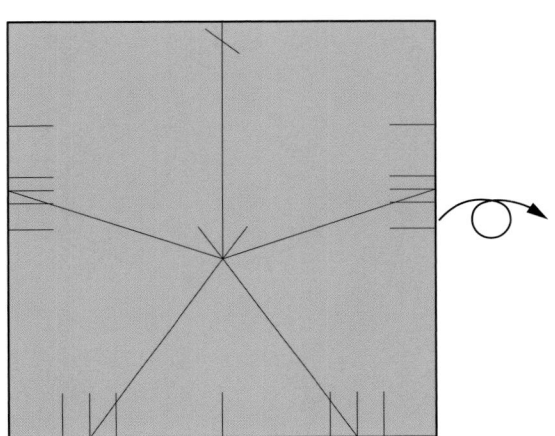

10 Turn over.

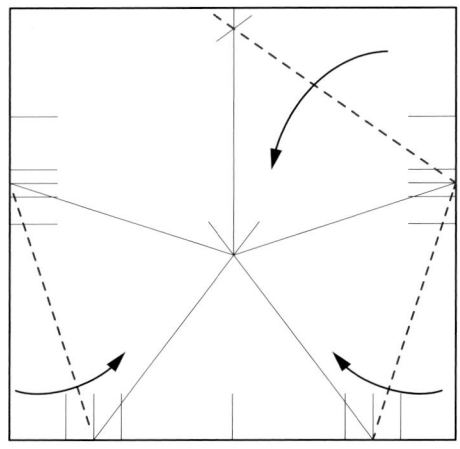

11 Valley fold in three places to form the edges of a pentagon.

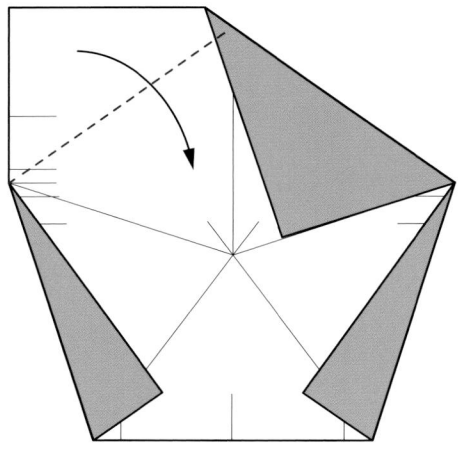

12 Valley the corner as shown to form the final pentagon edge.

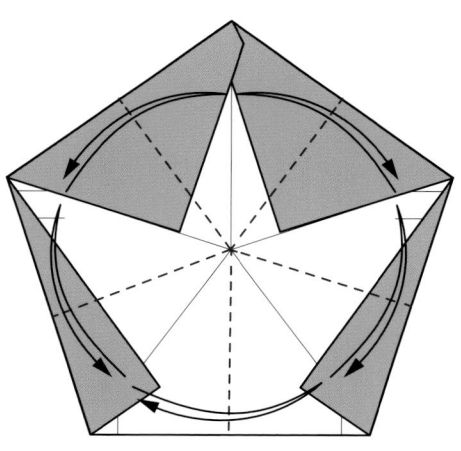

13 Fold and unfold the five angle bisectors.

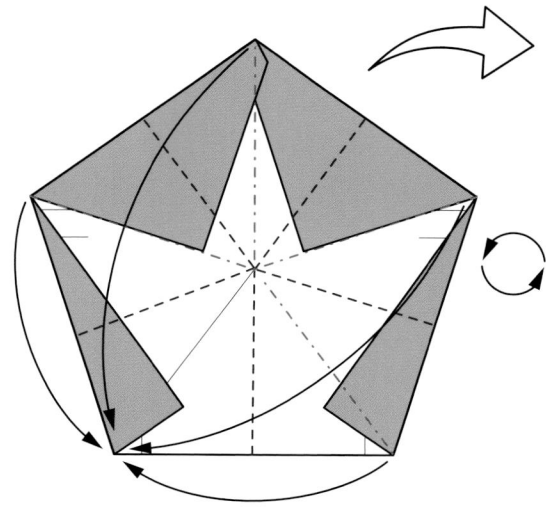

14 Collapse on existing creases.

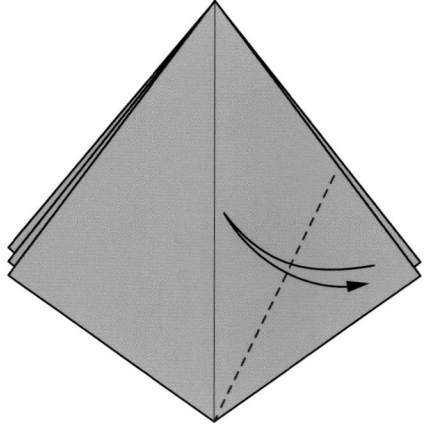

15 Fold the angle bisector and unfold.

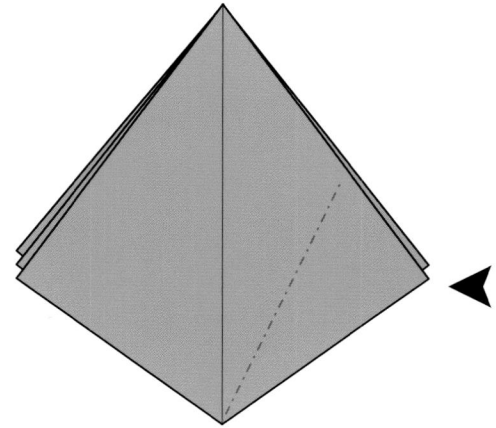

16 Inside reverse fold.

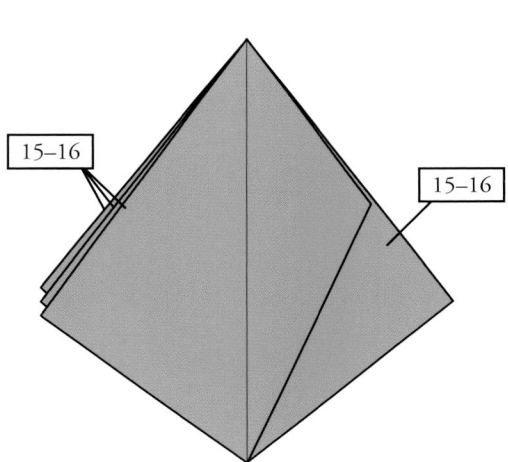

15–16

15–16

17 Repeat steps 15 and 16 on the remaining flaps.

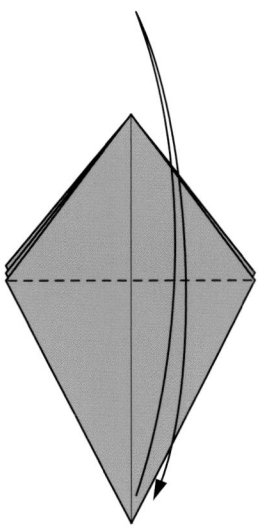

18 Fold the flap up and unfold.

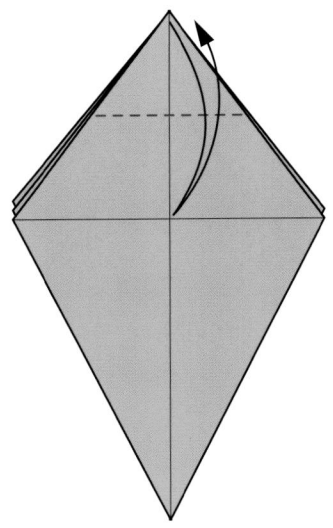

19 Fold the tip down and unfold.

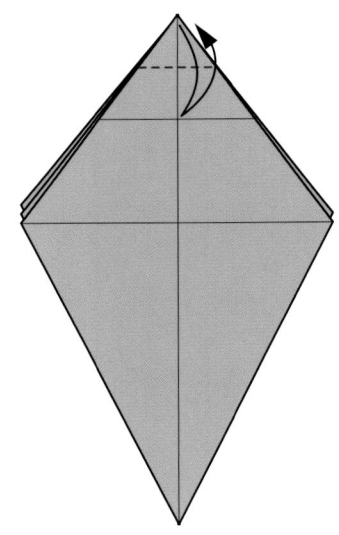

20 Fold the tip to the crease and unfold.

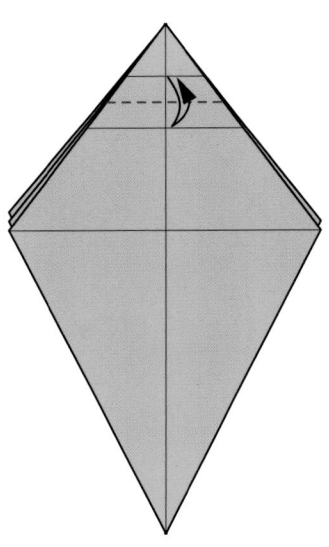

21 Fold crease to crease and unfold.

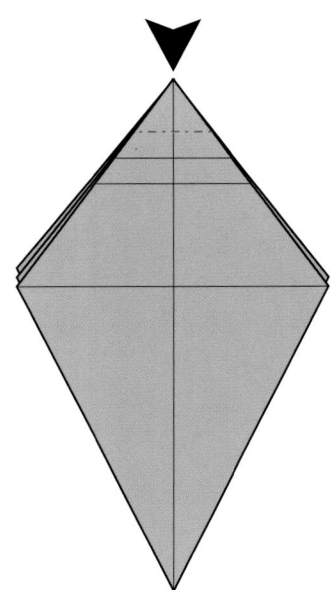

22 Open sink the point on the crease made in step 20.

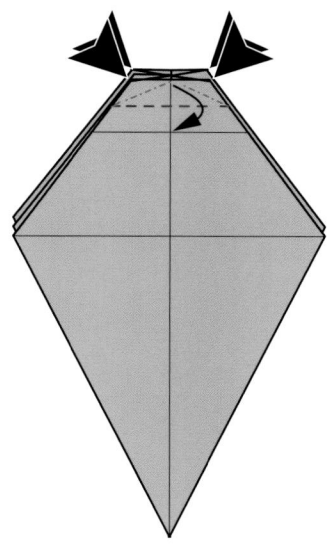

23 Fold the top layer down on the crease while squash-folding the corners. Repeat behind.

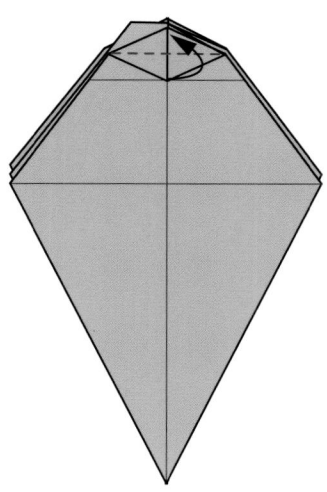

24 Fold the flap up. Repeat behind.

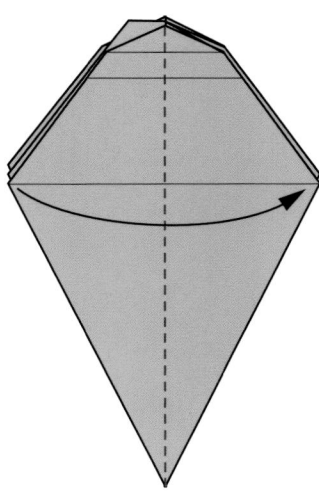

25 Fold the top flap over to the left.

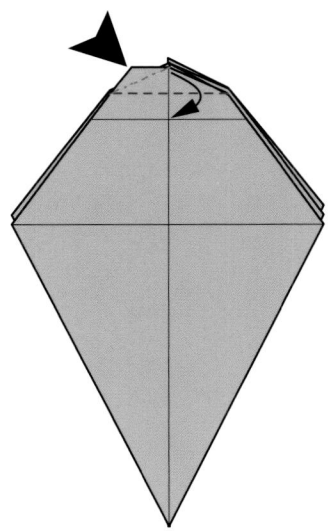

26 Fold the top layer down while squash-folding the corner shown.

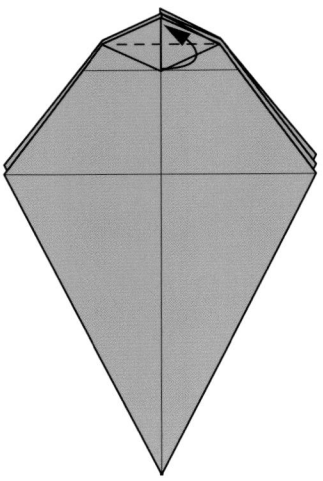

27 Fold the flap up.

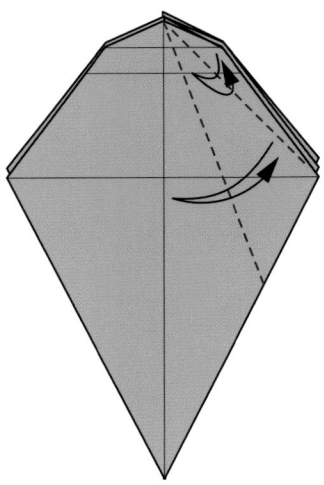

28 Fold and unfold, dividing the angle into thirds.

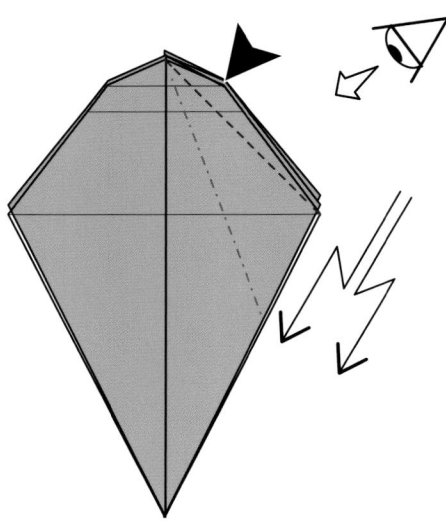

29 Open sink in and out. Step 27 shows a detailed view of the creases inside the sink. Two little corners will end up sticking out.

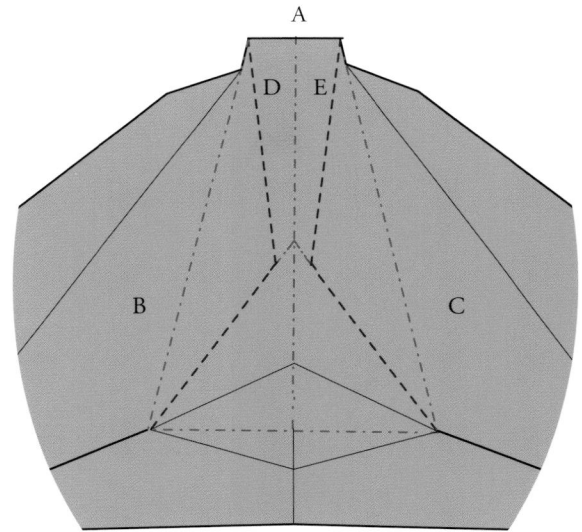

30 Edge A was formed by one of the squash folds in steps 23 through 27. Folds B and C were both formed by the mountain fold in step 29. Folds D and E were both formed by the valley fold in step 29.

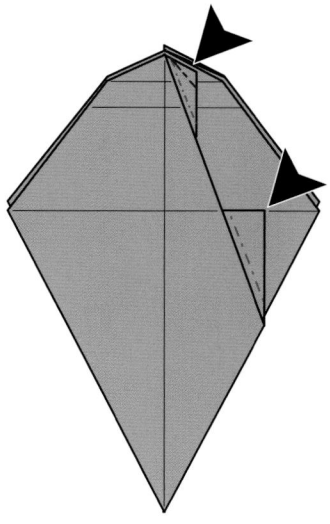

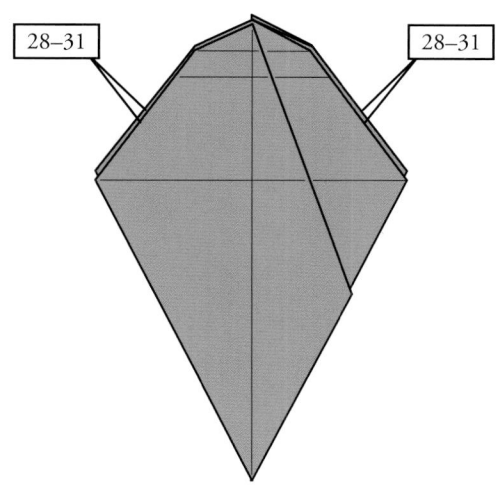

31 Reverse fold the top corner in and out. Reverse fold the bottom corner.

32 Repeat steps 28 through 31 on the remaining flaps.

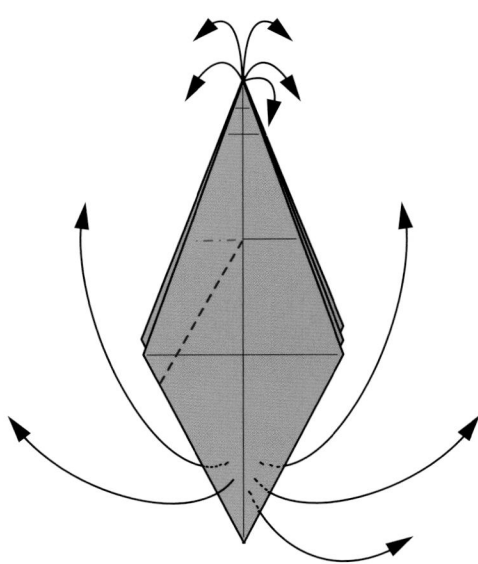

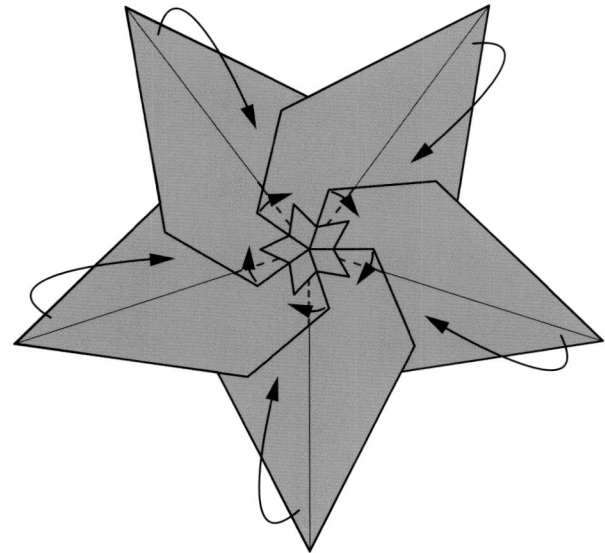

33 Valley folding as shown, fold all the petals out, spreading them symmetrically. Spread out the small points at the top symmetrically as well. From this point on, the model will not lie flat and the view is from the top.

34 Valley fold the five corners near the center. These folds extend up the central column, narrowing it. Bend the petals in toward the central column to make them concave.

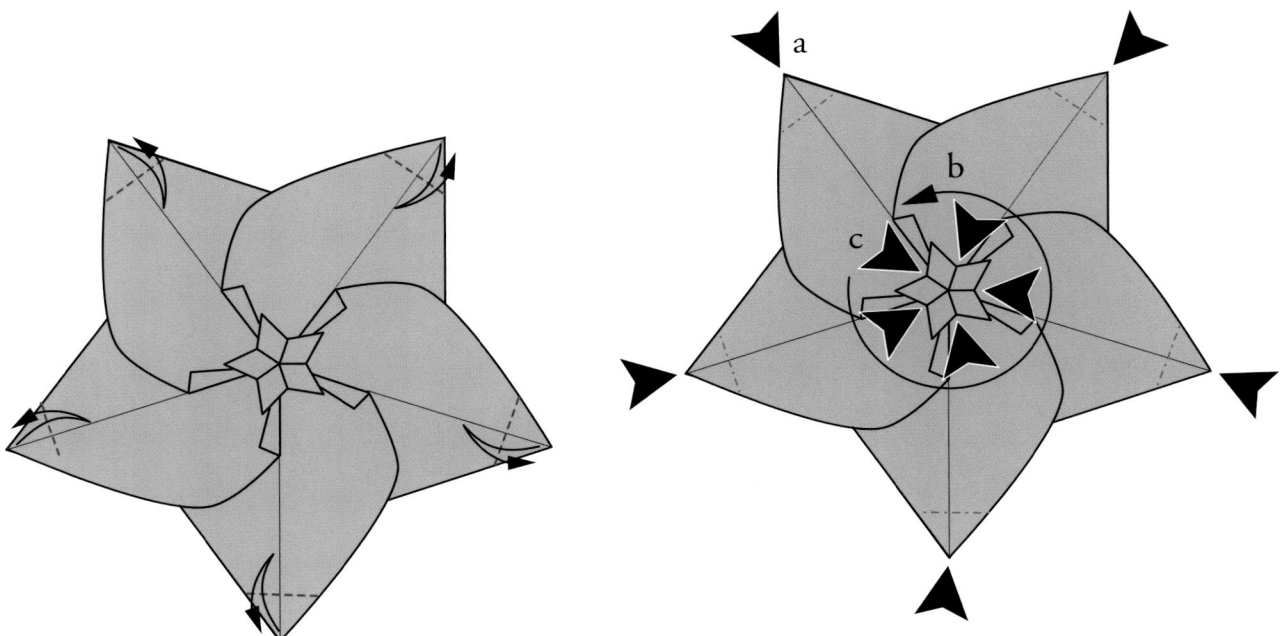

35   Mountain fold the petal tips and unfold.

36   Sink the tip of each petal on existing creases (a). Thin the central column further by twisting it (b). Pinch the base of each small point to form stigmas (c).

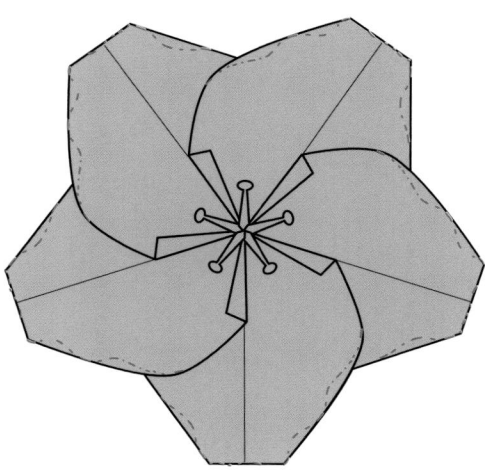

37   Mountain fold the corners of the petals to round them, then ruffle the edges.

"The hibiscus should be folded from paper that is thin, but not too thin. Thick paper will not allow the style or the stigma to be sufficiently thinned, while paper that is too thin will possibly cause some of the petals to be a little see-through. The stem and leaves should be folded from paper that is as thin as possible since a large number of layers accumulate and the stem needs to be narrow. Both should be folded from the same size paper (about 12-inch [30.5-cm] squares) and wet-shaped in the final stages. Since wet paper expands and unfolds, I use a combination of painter's tape (which releases cleanly without tearing the paper) and cotton string before applying water to temporarily constrain the model while it dries. Aluminum foil molds are also useful for supporting the wet paper in the desired position, as well as maintaining soft curvature in the petals, during the drying process."

—Derek McGann

The finished
Hibiscus flower

STEM AND LEAVES

Use a piece of thin, tissue-weight paper to make the stem and leaves:

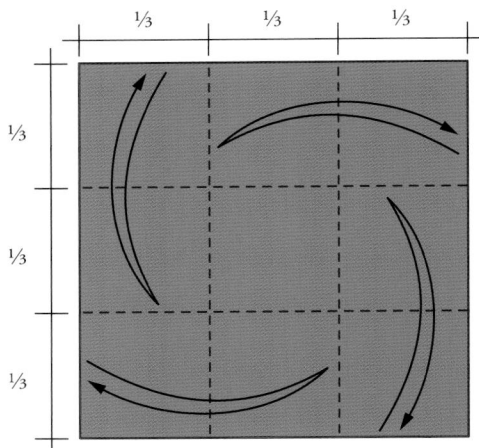

I   Valley fold the paper into thirds horizontally and vertically.

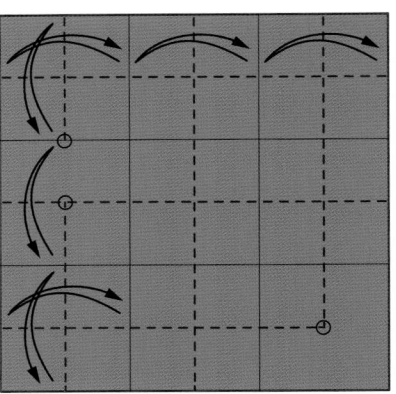

2   Valley fold where indicated.

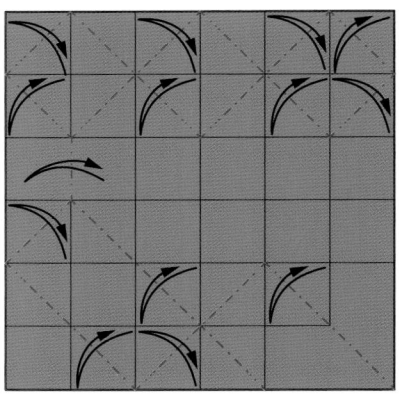

3   Mountain fold where indicated.

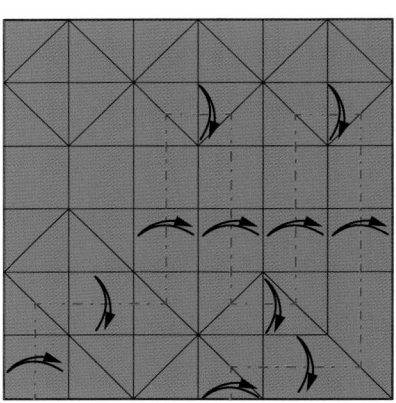

4   Mountain fold where indicated.

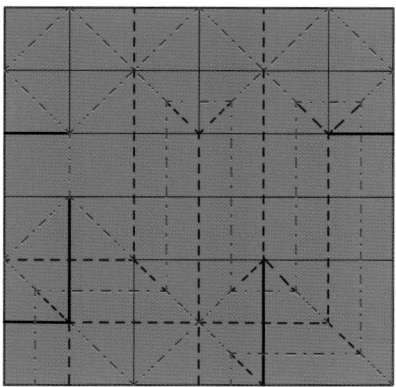

5 Collapse on existing creases. Notice that portion of the diagonal mountain folds are now converted to valley folds. The thick lines indicate hinge creases that show the direction in which the flaps are oriented in the next step.

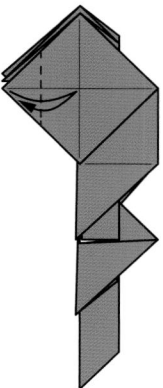

6 Fold the indicated flap in half and unfold.

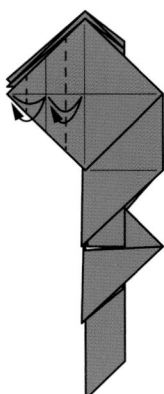

7 Fold the sections indicated in half and unfold.

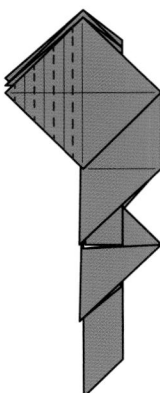

8 Crease between the creases as indicated.

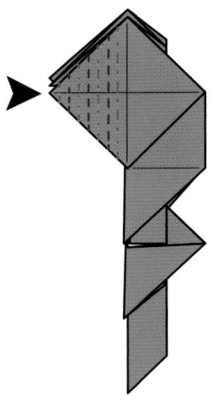

9 Open sink in and out on existing creases.

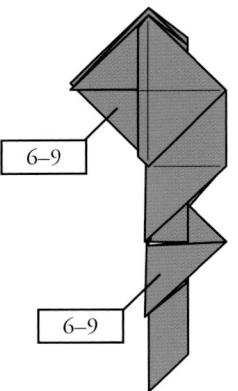

6–9

6–9

10 Repeat steps 6 through 9 on the flaps indicated. A small corner will need to be moved out of the way temporarily on the bottom flap.

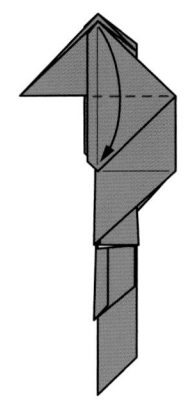

11 Fold one flap down.

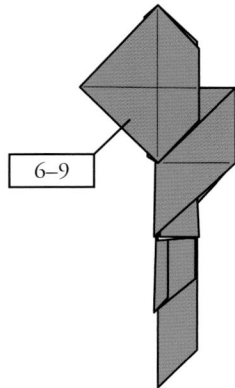

6–9

12 Repeat steps 6 through 9 on the indicated flap.

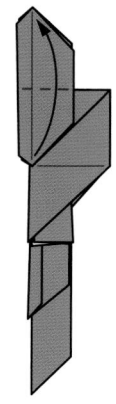

13 Fold the flap back up.

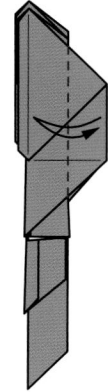

14 Fold and unfold through all layers where indicated.

15   Fold and unfold through all layers where indicated.

16   Crease between the creases where indicated.

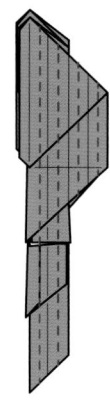

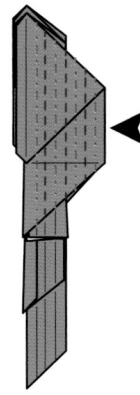

17   Open sink in and out on existing creases.

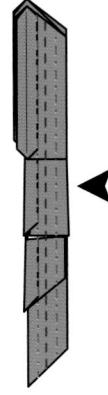

18   Open sink the remaining portion in and out on existing creases. This is an intricate, time-consuming step; the ridge created by the mountain fold in step 4 defines a connected region that must be sunk all at once.

ABOUT THE
HIBISCUS

There are hundreds of species of *Hibiscus* (the scientific name for the genus as well as the common name), flowering members of the mallow family. Native to tropical and subtropical regions around the globe, they are often cultivated for their large, showy flowers. The red hibiscus is the flower of the Hindu goddess Kali; it is used as an offering to the goddess and Lord Ganesha in Hindu worship. A single flower, when worn by a Tahitian woman tucked behind the ear, indicates that the wearer is available for marriage.

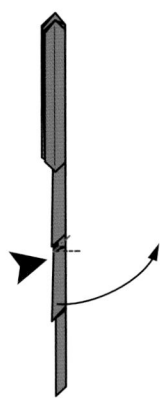

19 Squash fold the indicated flap to the right.

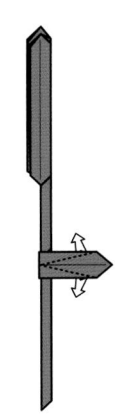

20 Pull the paper of the top-most group of pleated layers out. The valley folds shown apply to hidden layers. The visible layer remains uncreased.

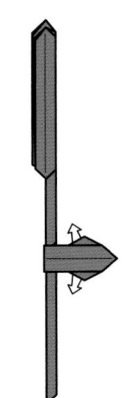

21 Pull more pleated layers out in a similar fashion.

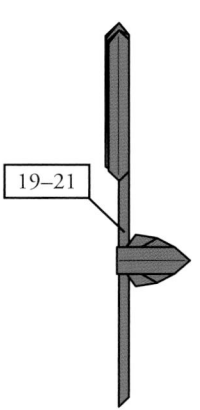

22 Repeat steps 19 through 21 on the indicated flap to make another leaf.

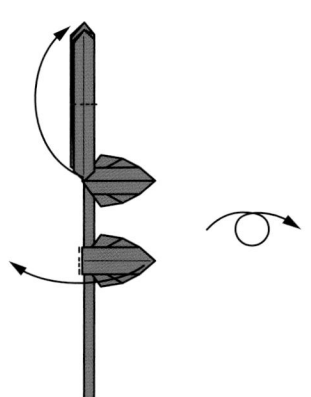

23 Fold one flap up. Fold the indicated leaf to the left (hidden layers will need to be squashed slightly to accomplish this). Turn over.

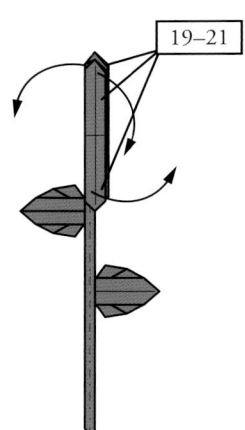

24 Repeat steps 19 through 21 on three more flaps. Do not fully complete the squash folds—the front top flap should point straight out, the bottom flap should point back and to the right, and the middle top flap should point back and to the left. The back-top flap (folded up in step 23) should remain pointing up and be mountain folded along with the stem.

The finished stem
with leaves

ASSEMBLY

The top flap (pointing up) of the
stem should be inserted into the
flower's central column before
twisting it in step 32 of the flower.

The completed Hibiscus
with stem and leaves

KAWASAKI ROSE

Designed and diagrammed by Toshikazu Kawasaki

While this model can easily be folded from 15-cm (6-inch) squares of paper, the particular model shown in this photo was folded by the master himself from kami paper squares of about 25 cm (9.8 inches). It is from the personal collection of the illustrator and diagrammer Marcio Noguchi.

Toshikazu Kawasaki is an artist and mathematics professor in Japan. He was inspired to pursue origami after seeing a photo of a white swan designed by Akira Yoshizawa, the man considered by many to be the father of modern origami. Toshikazu Kawaski is famous for his series of roses that feature a structure with petals that fold out from the center, a move called "twist folding." This rose is from that series. He also discovered and proved that with any given flat point in an origami model, the sum of alternating angles is always equal to 180°, an idea now named for him: Kawasaki's theorem. He recently became the first doctor of mathematics to present a paper on origami. It is called "Theory of Deformated Bird Bases."

Use one piece of paper to fold the flower:

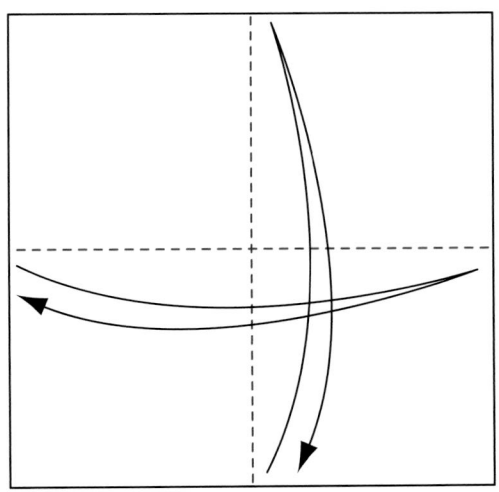

I With the paper white side up, fold in half vertically and horizontally. Unfold.

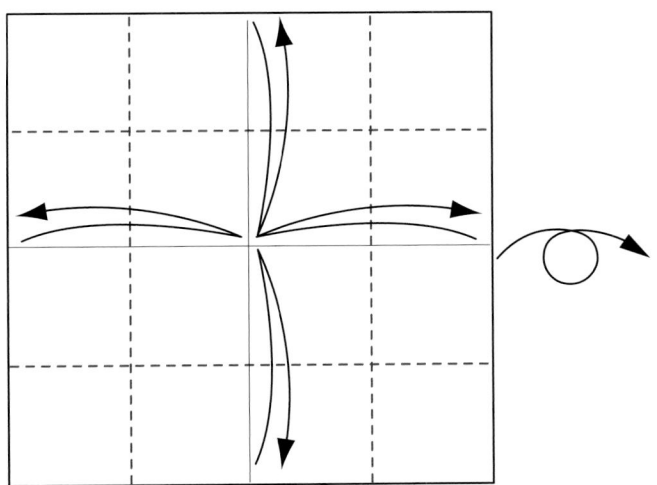

2 Fold the edges to the center crease and unfold.

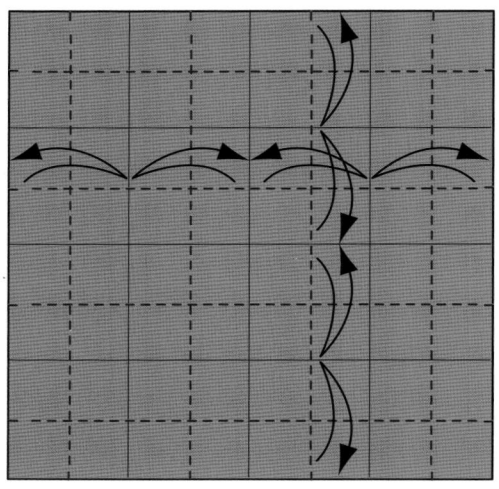

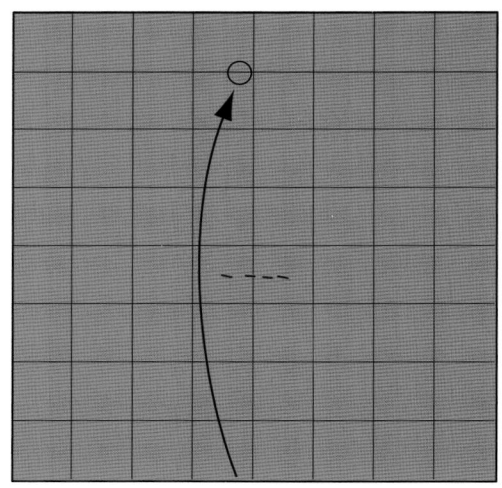

3 Fold edges to the new creases and unfold. Fold creases to creases as shown and unfold as well.

4 Bring the edge to the crease shown and pinch as indicated.

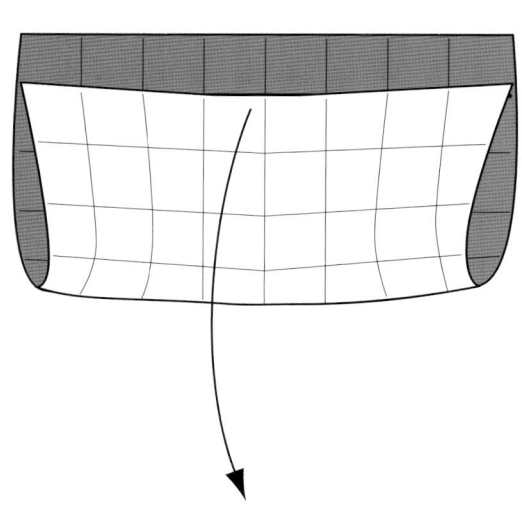

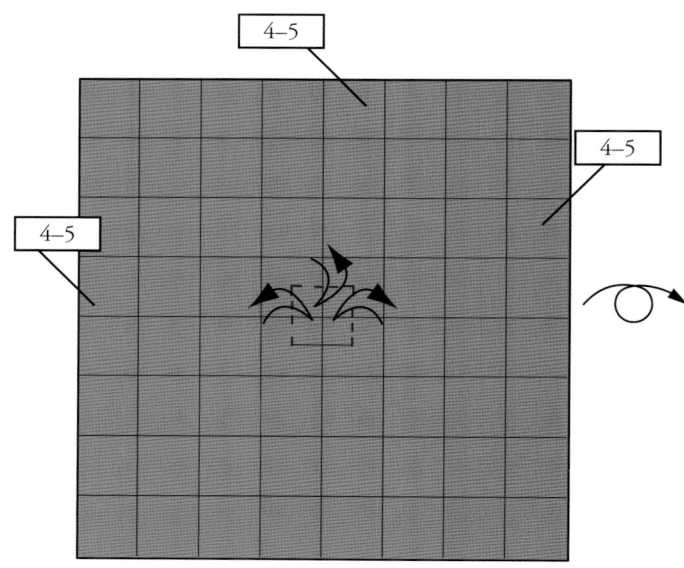

5 Unfold.

6 Repeat steps 4 and 5 on the remaining sides of the square. Turn over.

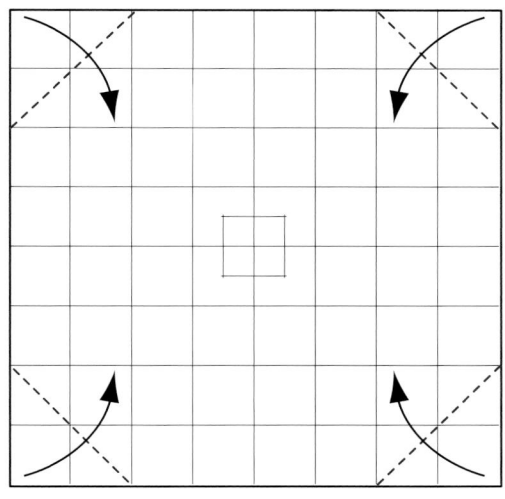

7   Fold the corners in on the diagonals shown.

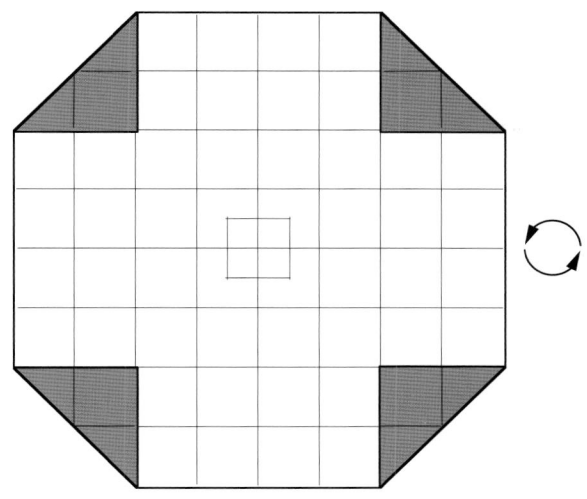

8   Rotate.

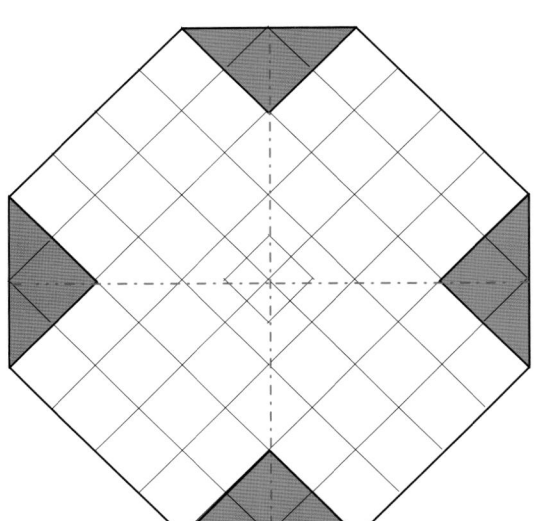

9   Mountain crease as shown and unfold.

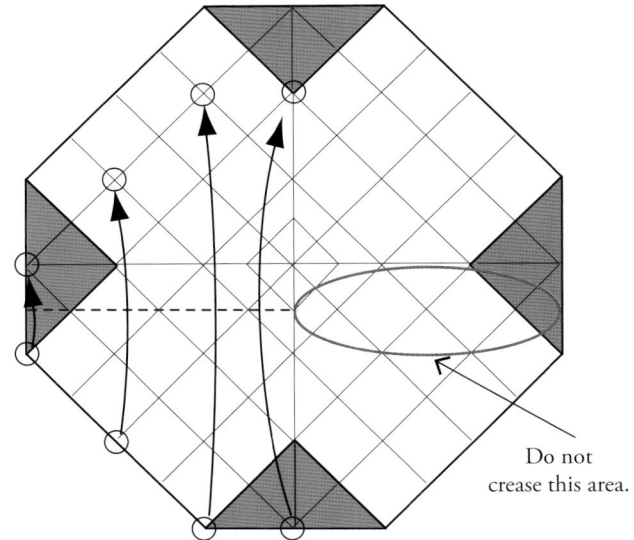

Do not crease this area.

10   Bring the edge to the crease as shown, matching reference points, and crease only where indicated.

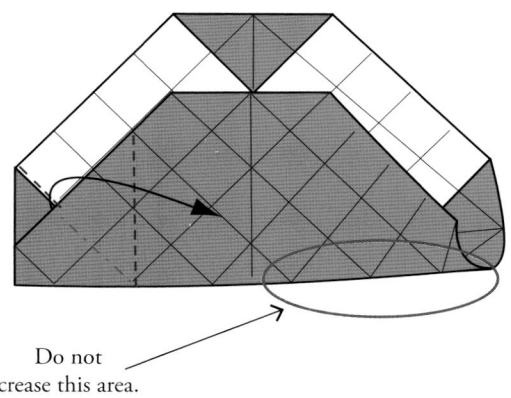

Do not
crease this area.

II Open and squash.

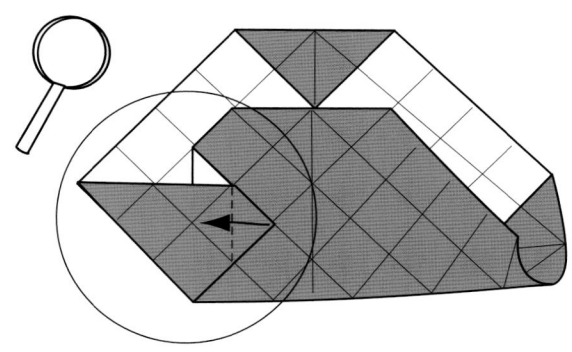

12 Fold the corner over.
Detailed view is next.

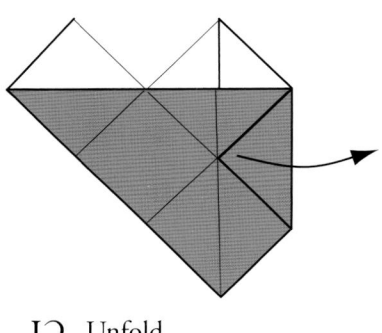

13 Unfold.

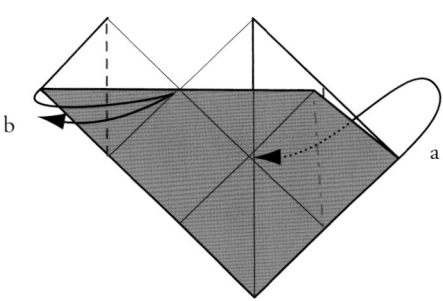

14 Reverse fold (a), then fold the
corner shown and unfold (b).

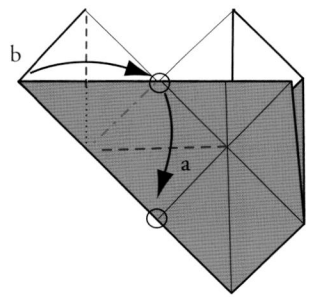

15 Valley fold as indicated (a), then
swivel using the crease formed
in the previous step (b).

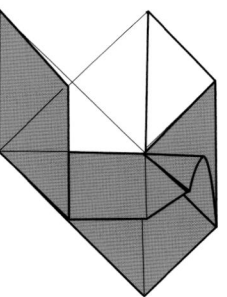

16 Unfold back to step 15.

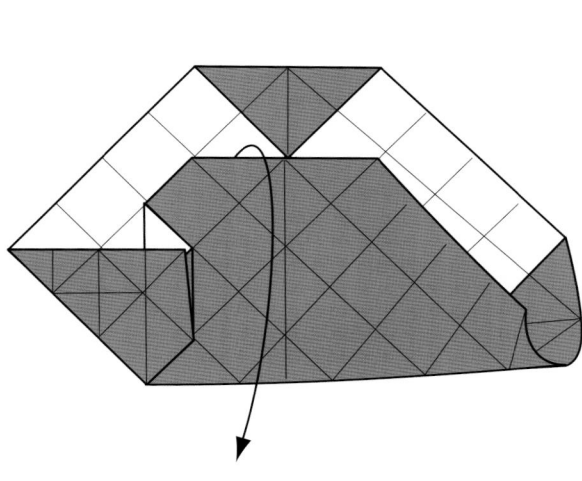

17 Open.

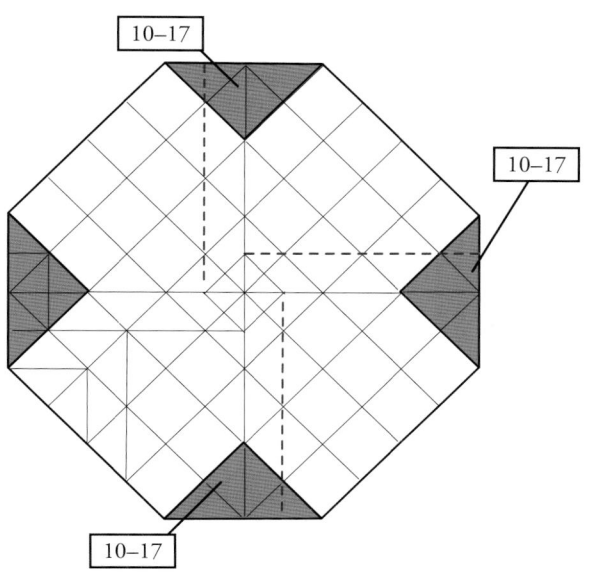

10–17

10–17

10–17

18 Repeat steps 10 to 17 on the remaining sides.

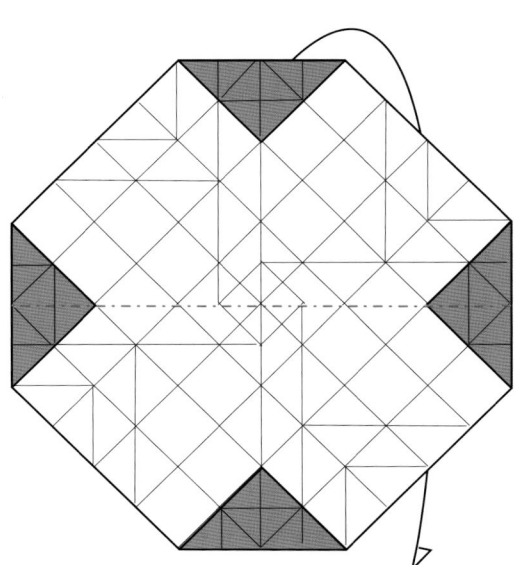

19 Mountain fold in half.

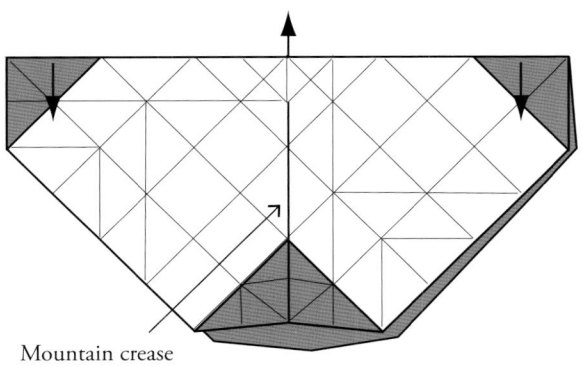

Mountain crease

20 Hold the corners as indicated. Push the center up while bringing the sides downward.

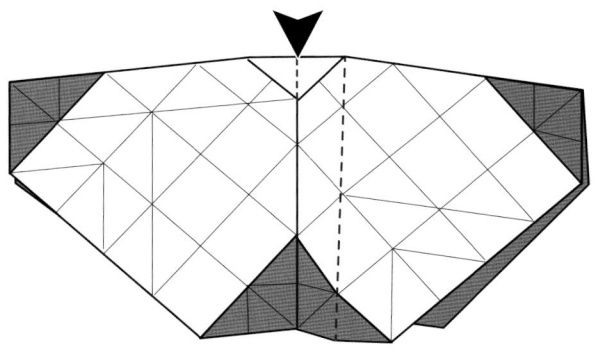

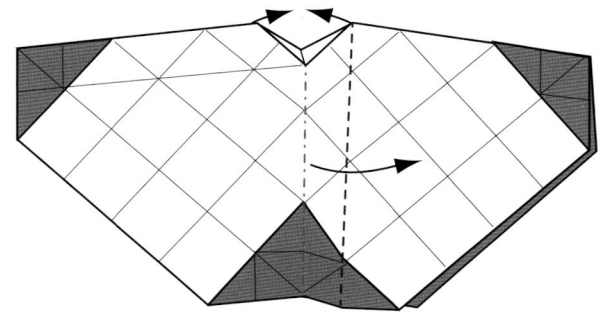

21 Push the center, creating a square with the mountain creases.

22 Pleat the front to the right and the back to the left. This will cause the square at the center to fold in half.

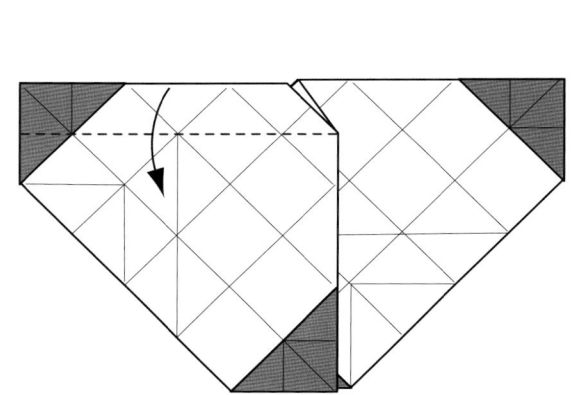

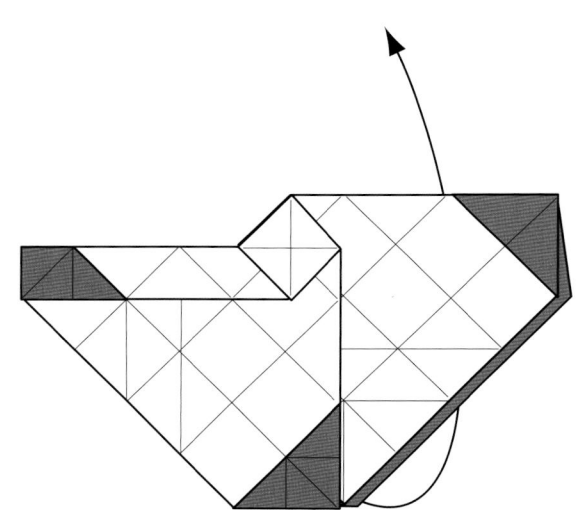

23 Fold the edge down.

24 Open the back.

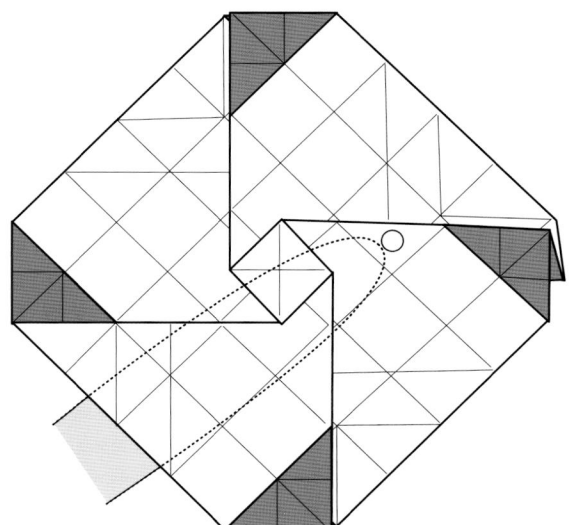

25 Insert your finger into the pleat.

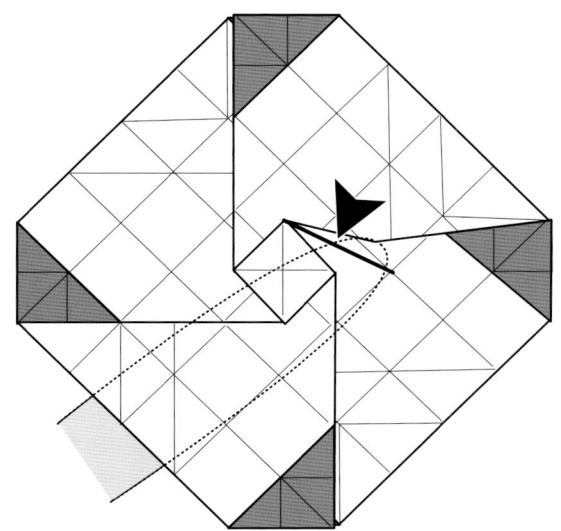

26 Use your other finger to flatten the model by pushing lightly.

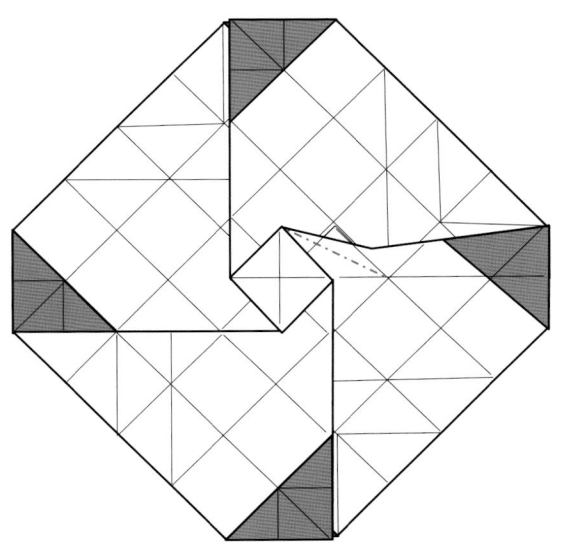

27 Mountain crease from corner to corner as shown by pinching.

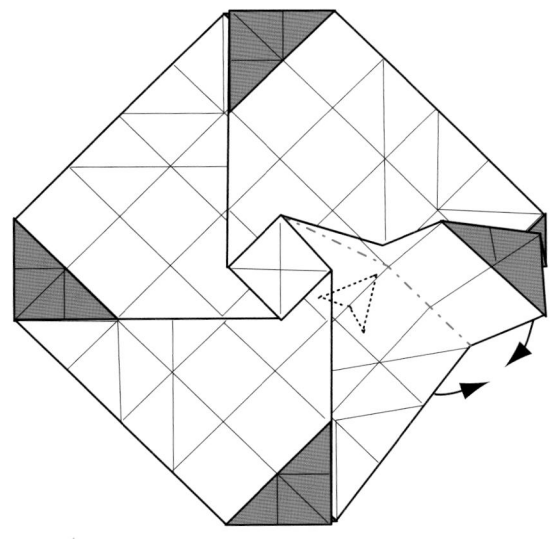

28 While pushing up from the back to flatten the area, extend the mountain crease to the edge.

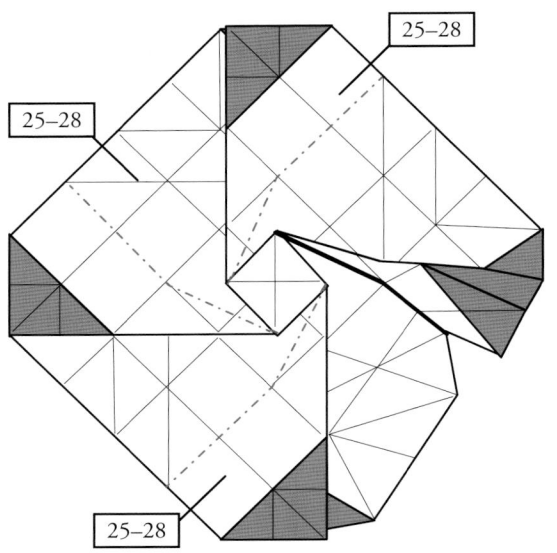

29 Repeat steps 25 to 28 on the remaining sides.

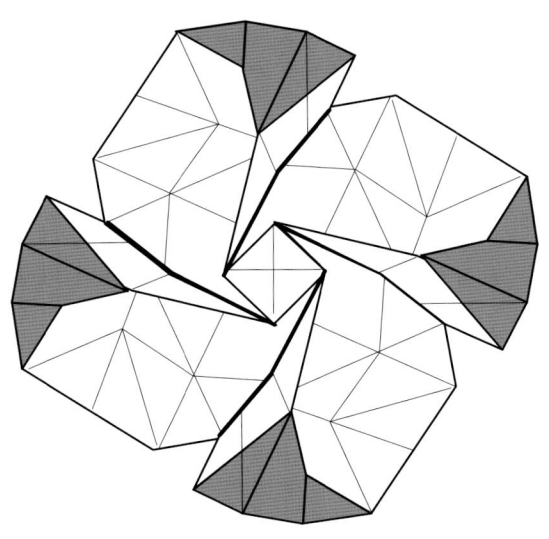

30 It will look like this.

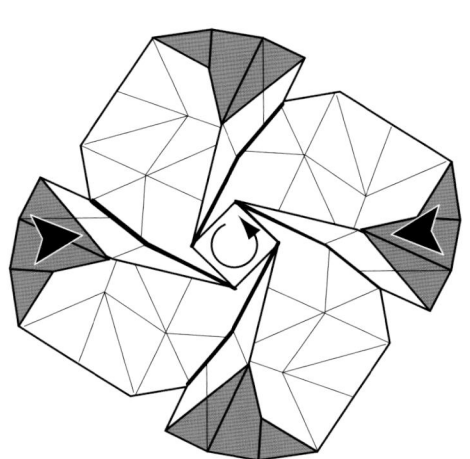

31 Using both hands, fold the sides inward so they curve around the center counterclockwise.

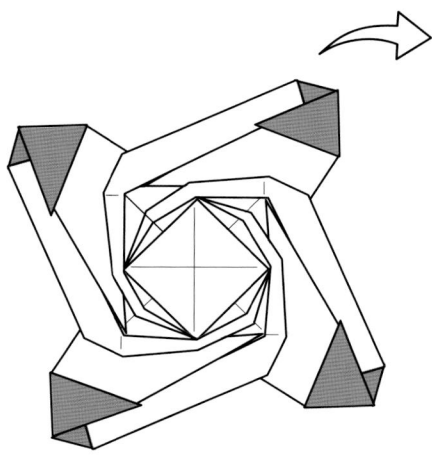

32 Magnified view is next.

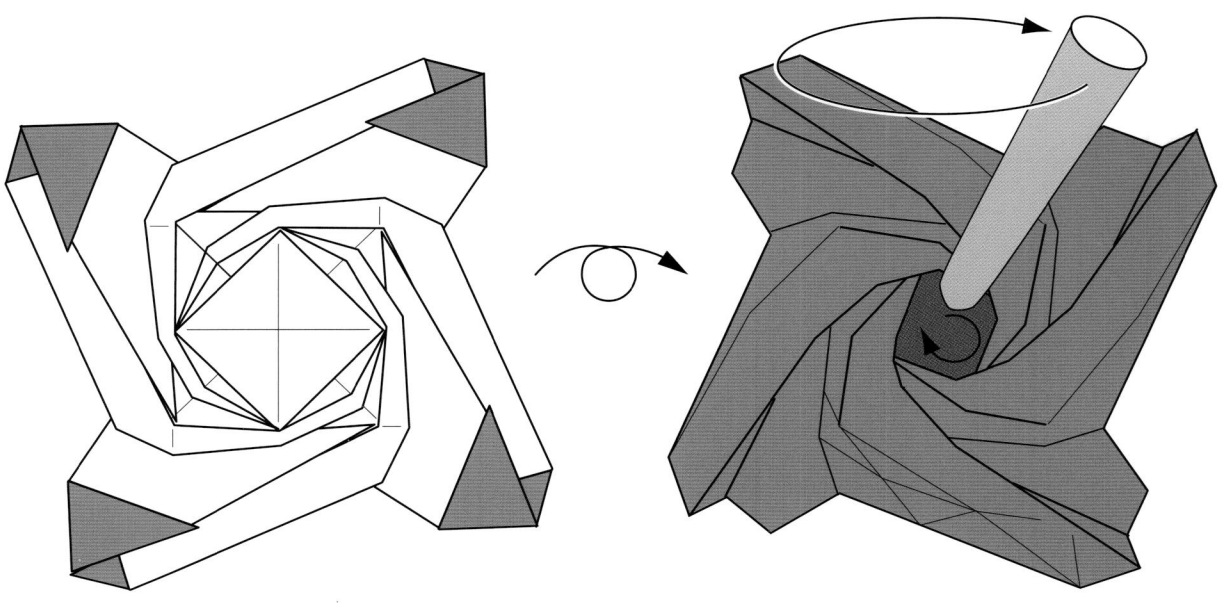

33 It will look like this. Turn over.

34 Using a pen or another thin cylinder, smooth out the internal edges.

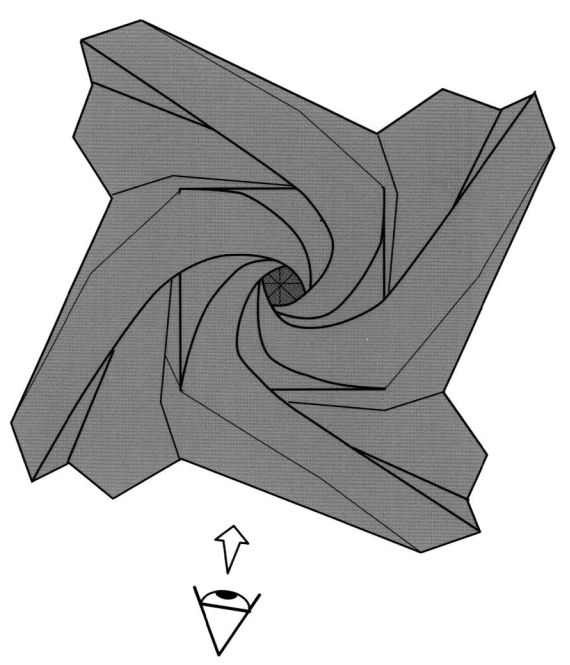

35 View from the side next.

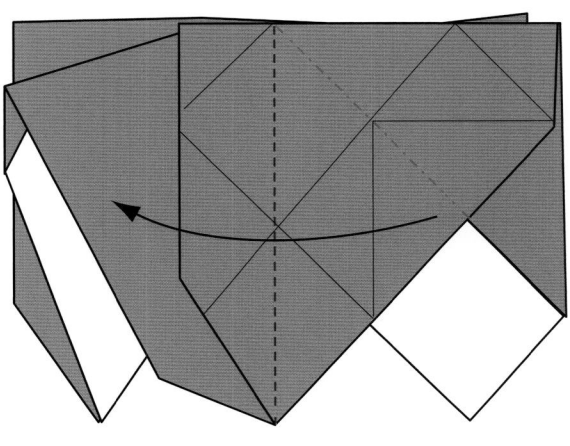

36 Follow the same sequence of folds as in step 11: open and squash.

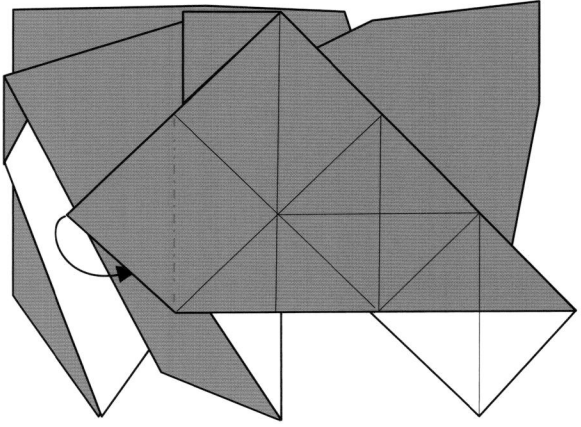

37   Inside reverse fold.

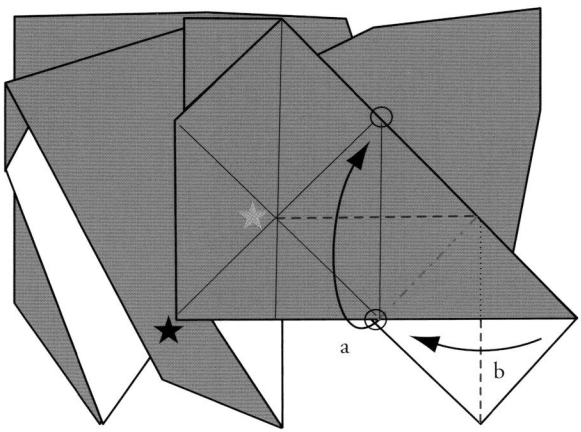

38   Follow the same sequence established in step 15: Valley fold the edge up (a), then swivel using the crease formed in the previous step (b).

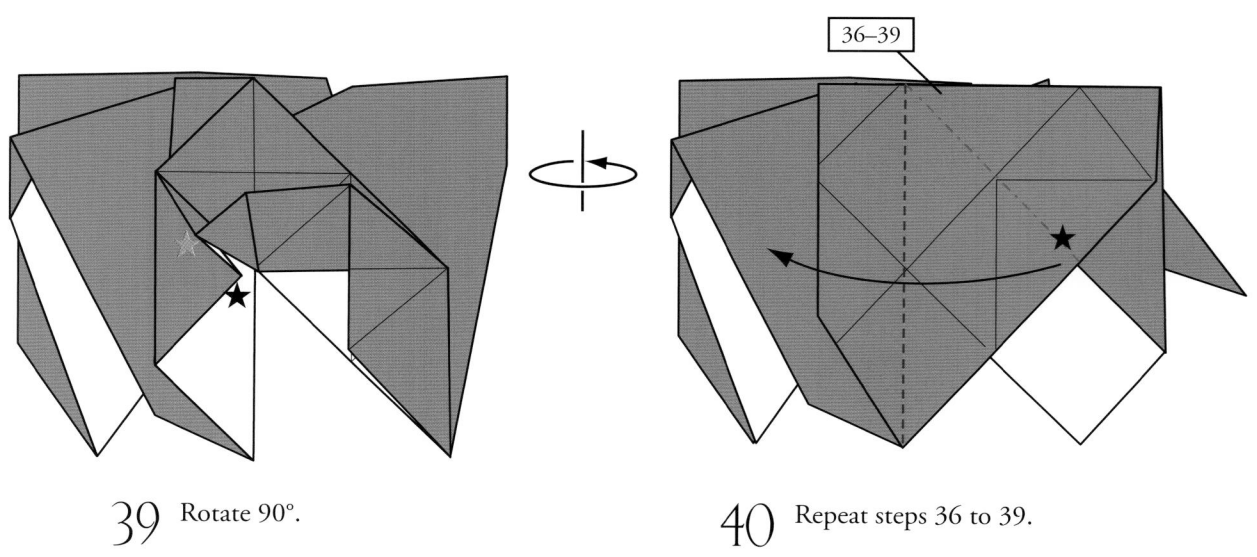

39   Rotate 90°.

40   Repeat steps 36 to 39.

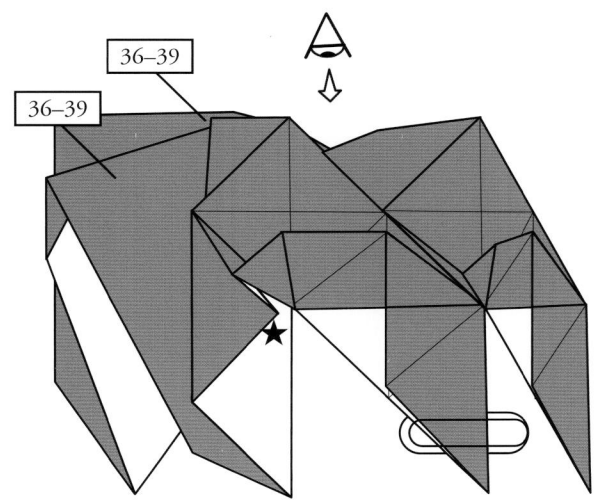

41 Repeat step 36 to 39 on the remaining flaps. Tip: Use a paper clip to keep the flaps from opening. View from the top next.

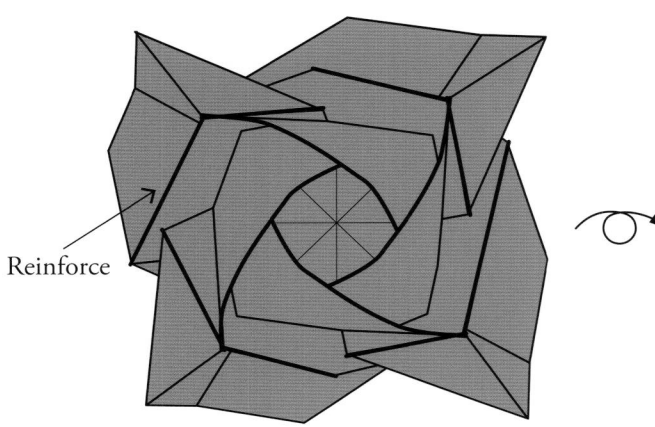

42 Reinforce the creases indicated by the thick edges. Turn over.

Reinforce

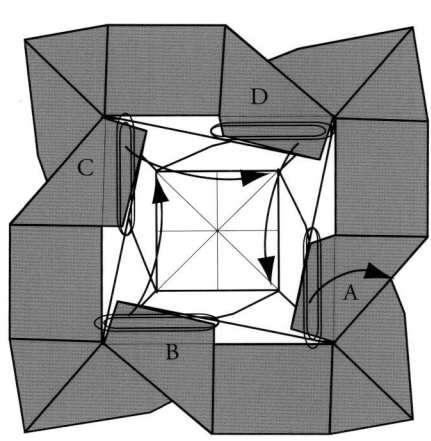

43 Fold triangle A out, then B, C, and D, in that sequence.

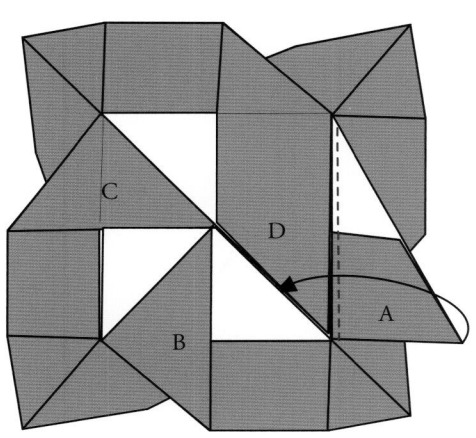

44 Fold triangle A to the inside.

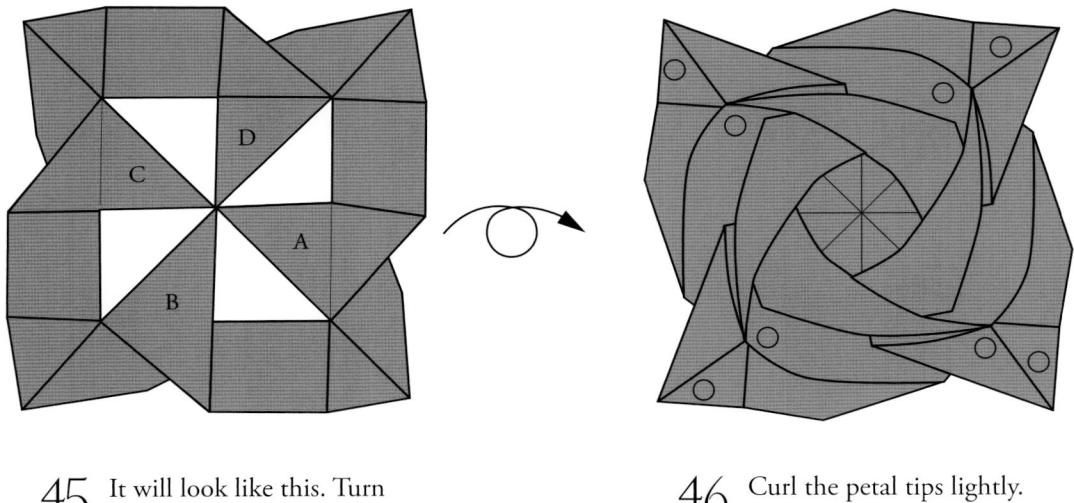

45 It will look like this. Turn the model over.

46 Curl the petal tips lightly.

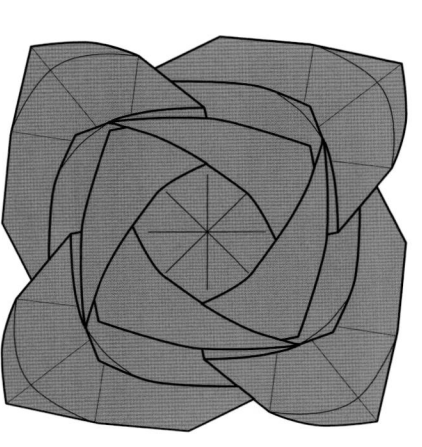

The finihsed Kawasaki Rose

LEAVES

Use another sheet of paper to make the leaves.

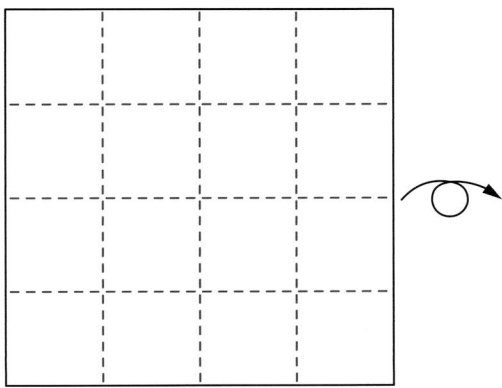

1 Make valley creases shown. Turn the paper over.

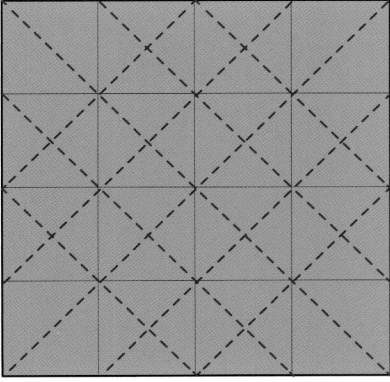

2 Valley crease the diagonals shown.

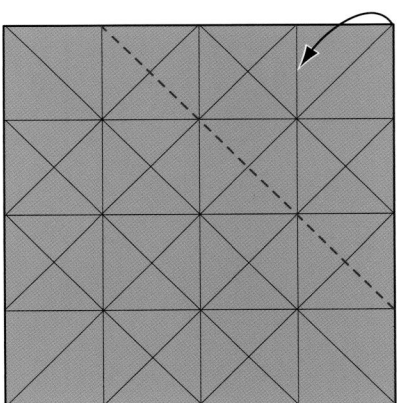

3 Lift the corner using the valley crease indicated.

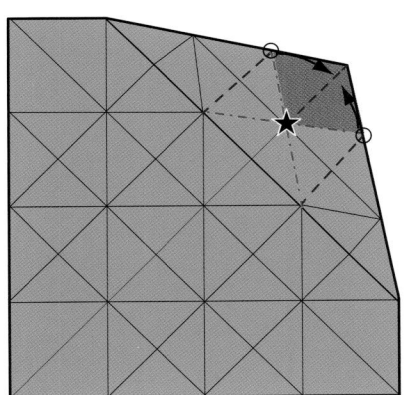

4 Fold the corner square in half diagonally, bringing the reference points together.

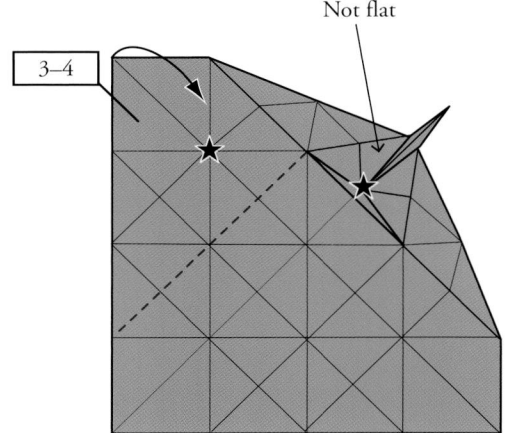

5 Repeat steps 3 to 4 on the opposite corner.

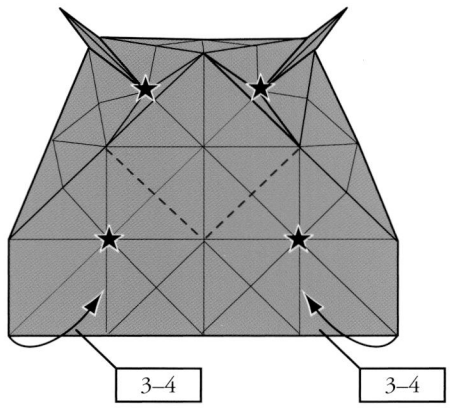

6 Repeat steps 3 to 4 on the remaining corners.

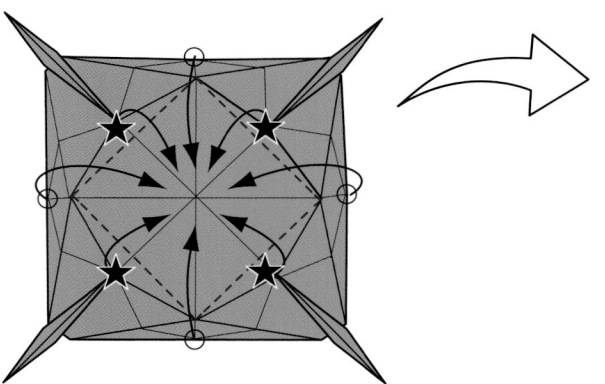

7 Valley fold as shown, bringing the points indicated to the center.

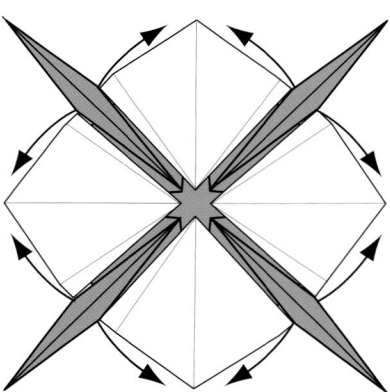

8 Open the flaps that are standing up, flattening the model.

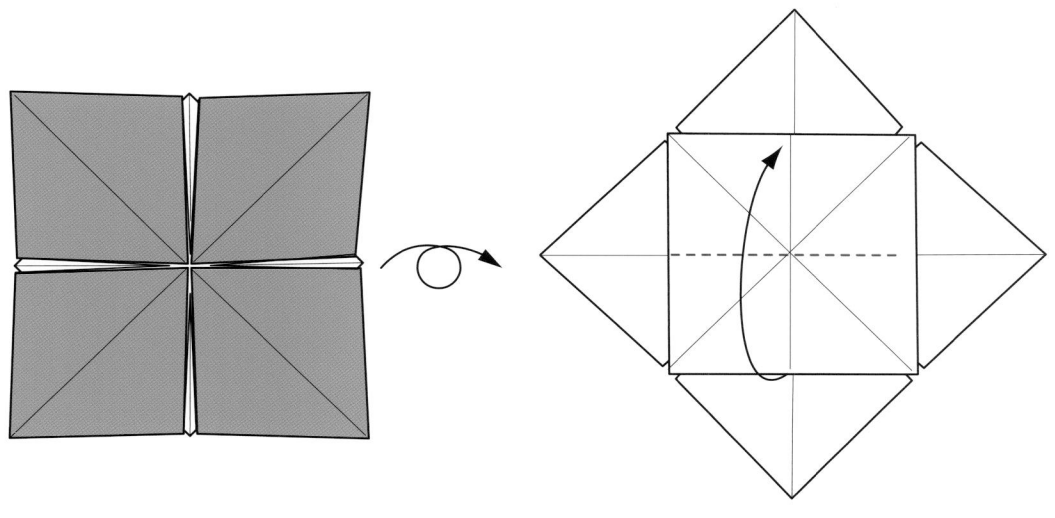

9   It will look like this. Turn over.

10   Fold the edge up.

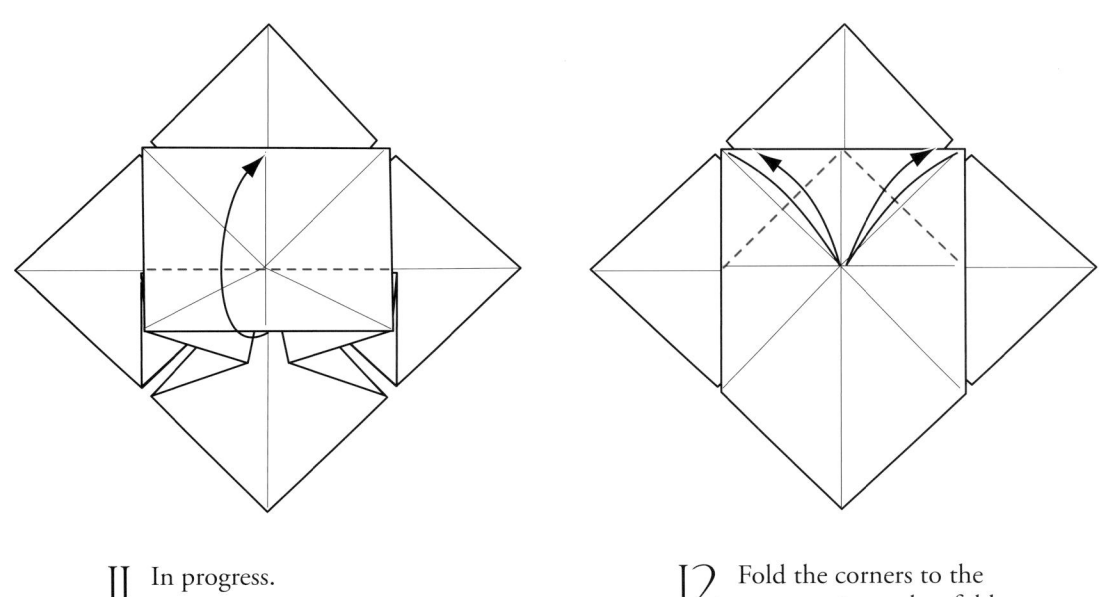

11   In progress.

12   Fold the corners to the center point and unfold.

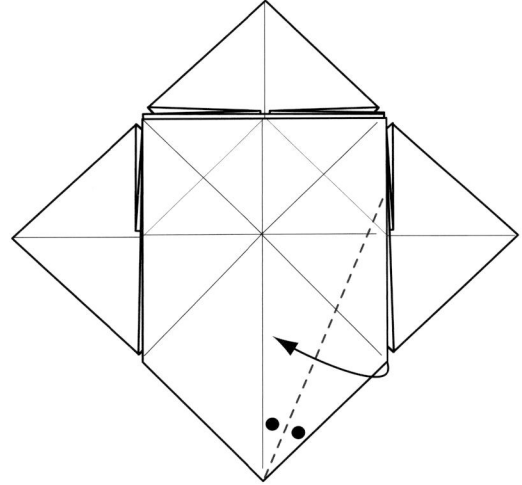

I3 Fold the angle bisector.

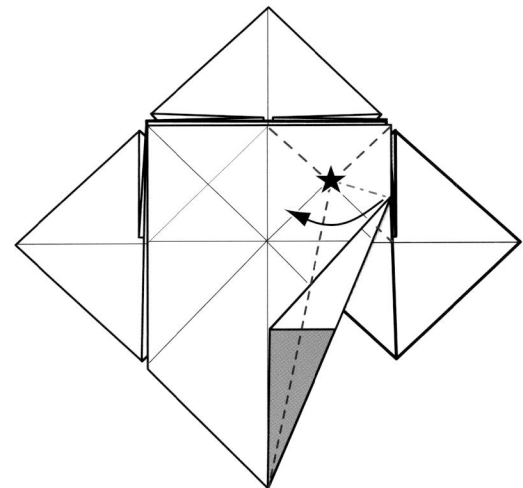

I4 Fold the edge to the center while standing the corner up.

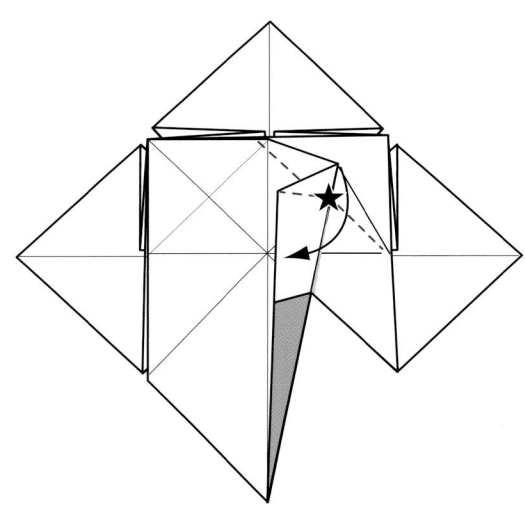

I5 Fold the corner down.

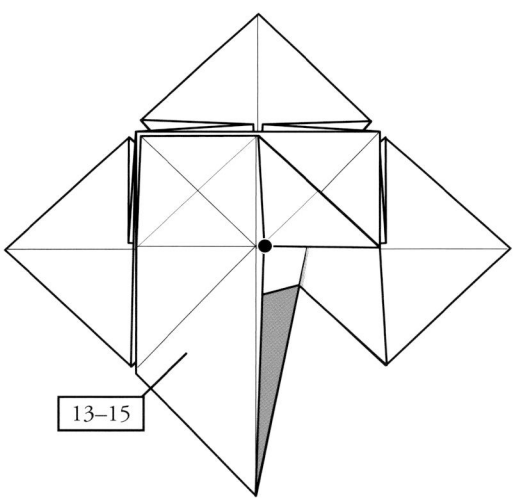

I6 Repeat steps 13 to 15 on the other side.

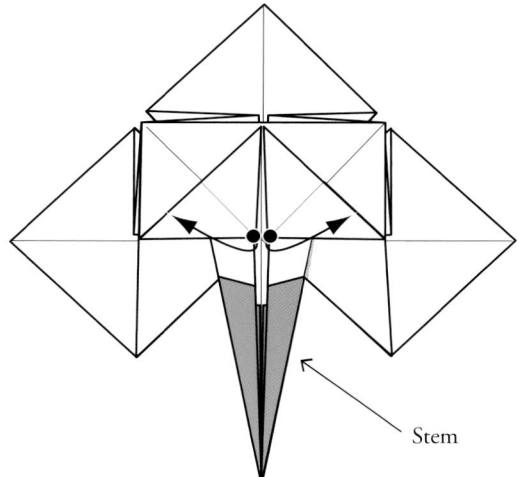

17 Open the corners slightly.

Stem

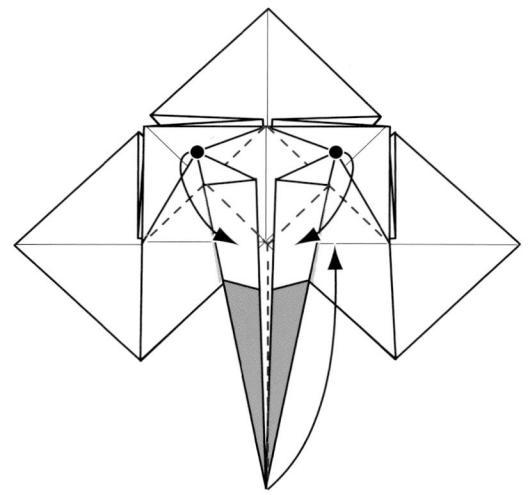

18 Fold the stem in half. Then fold the corners down and lift the stem so it stands up.

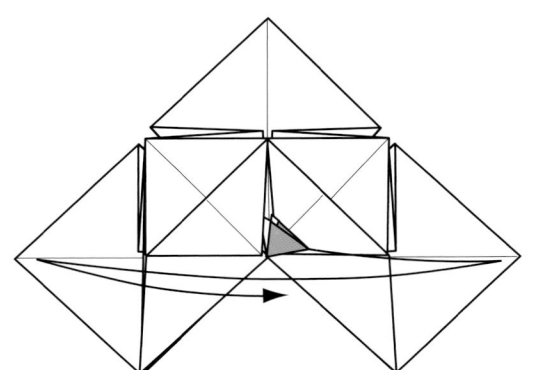

19 Crease the stem well by folding to the left and the right.

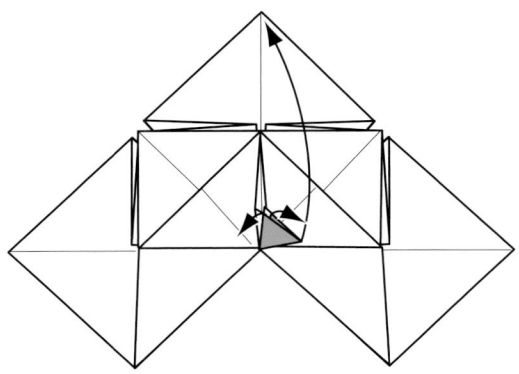

20 Open the stem and squash.

ABOUT THE ROSE

Roses (woody perennials from the genus *Rosa*) have been cultivated for millennia. The earliest cultivation is thought to date back 5,000 years in China. Many species were bred for their ornamental flowers; others were bred for their scent and became important ingredients in perfume making. There are different meanings associated with the different colors. Most people know that red roses symbolize love, but not everyone knows that pink is an expression of appreciation, orange indicates desire or enthusiasm, and white represents purity.

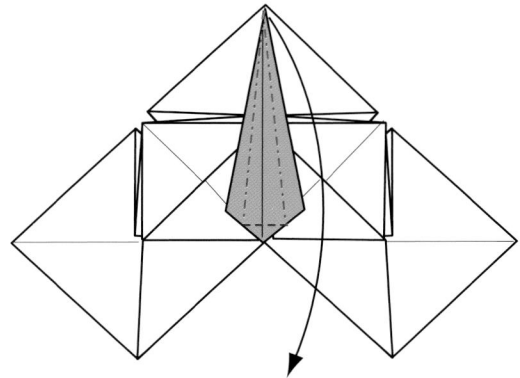

21 Petal fold the stem to narrow it.

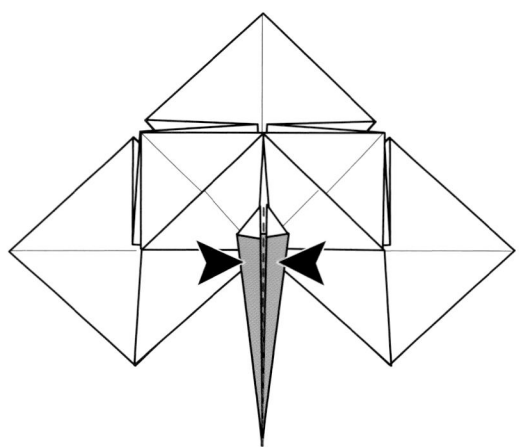

22 Fold the stem in half.

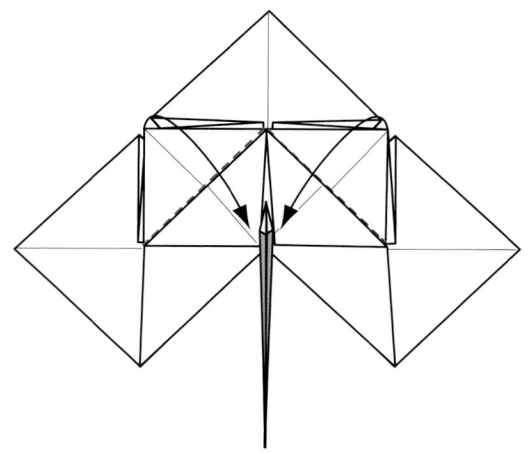

23 Fold the corners down.

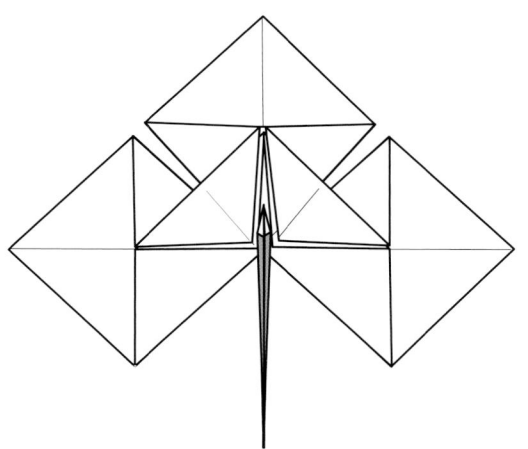

24 It will look like this.

25 Start shaping the leaves:
fold the corners as shown.

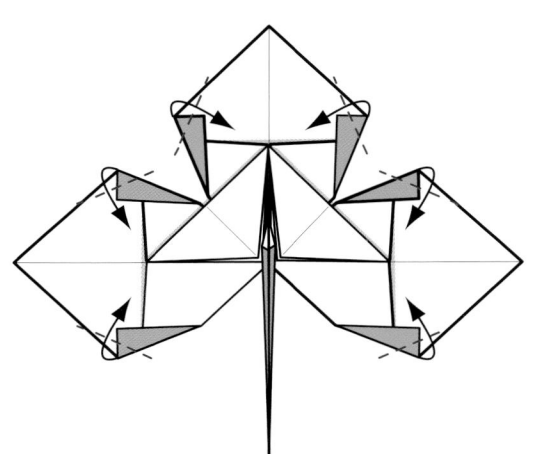

26 Fold the corners, aligning
the edges.

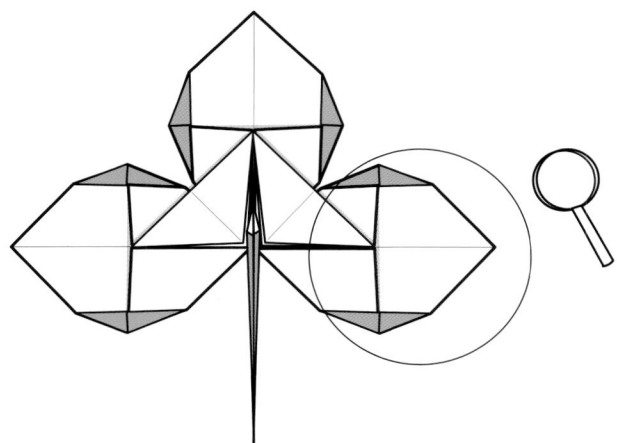

27 Magnified view next.

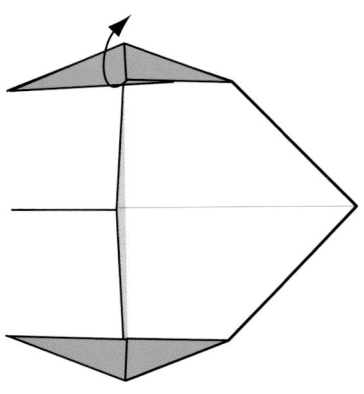

28 Open.

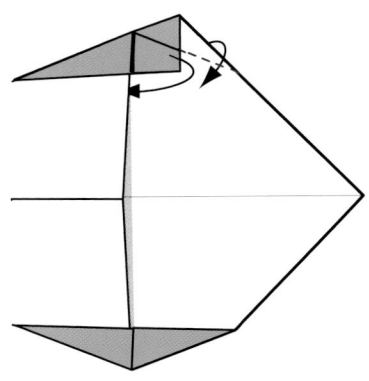

29 Fold the flap inside the pocket, locking it in place.

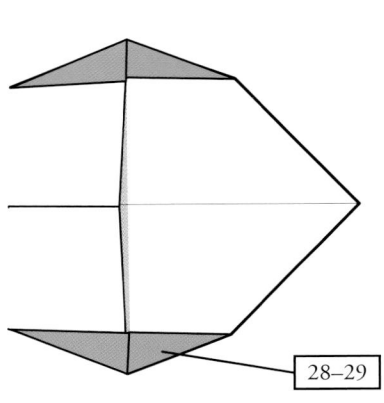

28–29

30 Repeat steps 28 to 29 on all the corners.

31 Turn over.

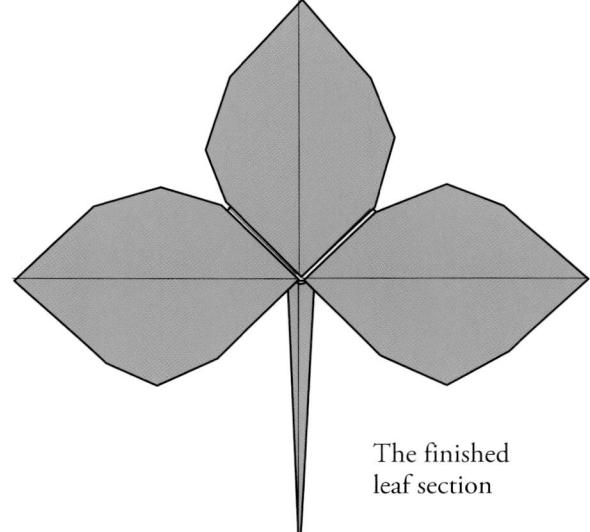

The finished leaf section

ASSEMBLY

Position the flower over the leaves as desired and glue in place.

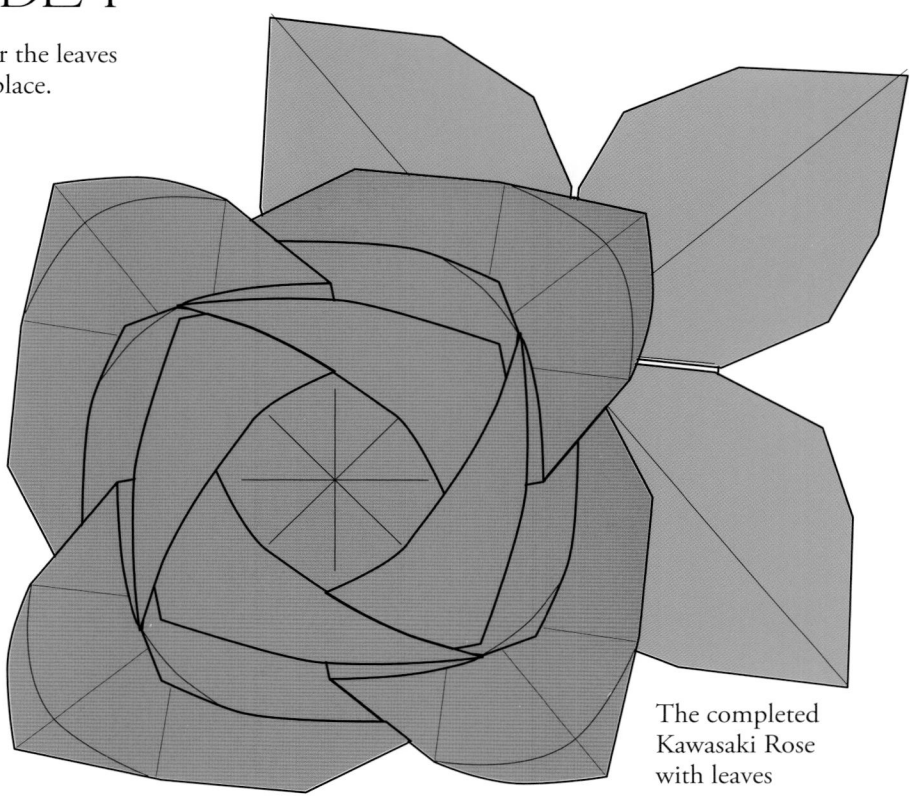

The completed
Kawasaki Rose
with leaves

ORCHID
Designed and diagrammed by Alexander Oliveros Avila

Alexander Oliveros Avila is a Colombian origami artist who lives in Bogota, where he sometimes works as a tourist guide and environmental educator. He has been folding origami since 1995 and designing models of his own since 2002. The models of his own design include simple and intermediate level models of objects, animals and plants that are inspired by his love of music and nature. He specializes in models that use paper with different colors on each side.

"I developed this orchid in 2003. I was inspired by some of the early models by my friend, Aldo Marcell (see page 140), although the process is a bit different. The final details were designed to create a model of the hybrid orchid created by orchid producer Cesar Wenzel. The one shown here was folded with two different sheets of recycled paper, glued together.

—Alexander Oliveras Avila

You will need three pieces of paper for this model: one for the flower, one that you will cut in half make two leaves, and one that you will cut into pieces for the stem. Use one piece of 20-cm (7.8-inch) square paper to fold the flower. The paper used for the flower shown has a different color on each side.

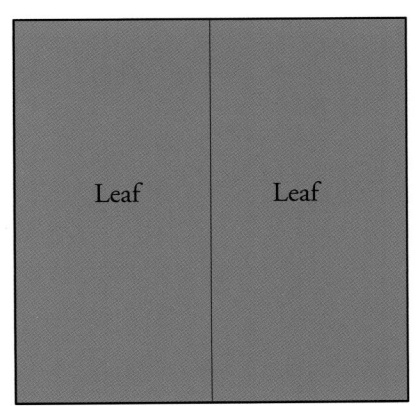

Orchid Flower

20-cm square

Leaf   Leaf

25-cm (9.8-inch) square

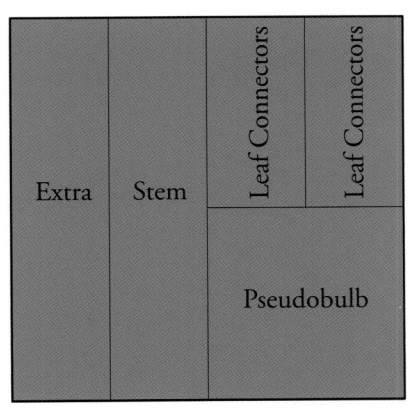

Extra   Stem   Leaf Connectors   Leaf Connectors

Pseudobulb

25-cm square

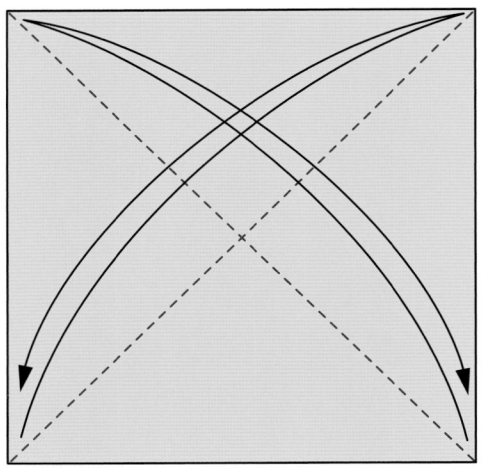

1 With the color for the lip (lower portion of the orchid) up, fold in half along both diagonals. Unfold.

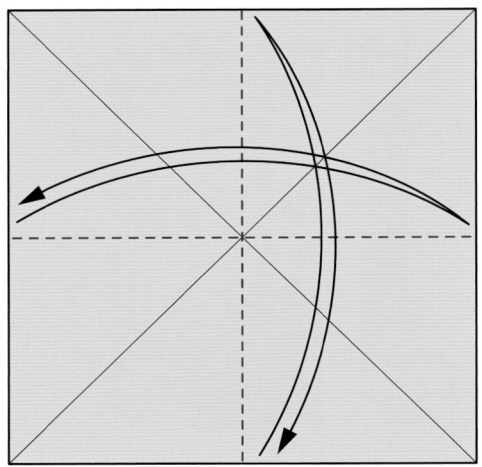

2 Fold in half horizontally and vertically. Unfold.

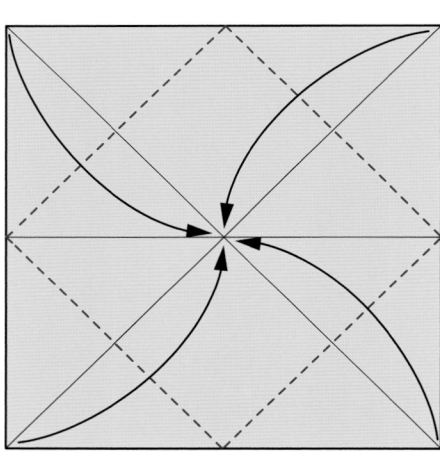

3 Blintz fold: bring the corners to the center point.

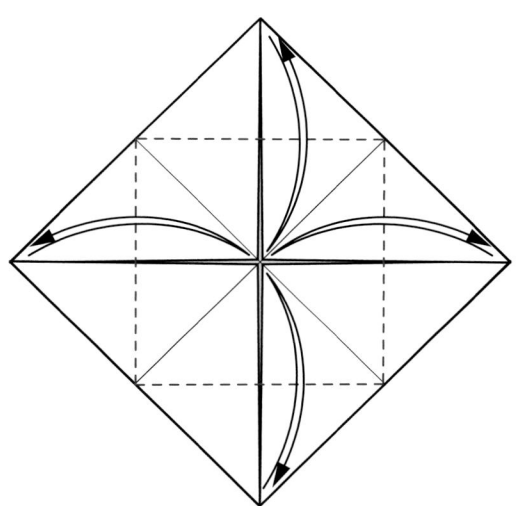

4 Blintz fold again. Unfold.

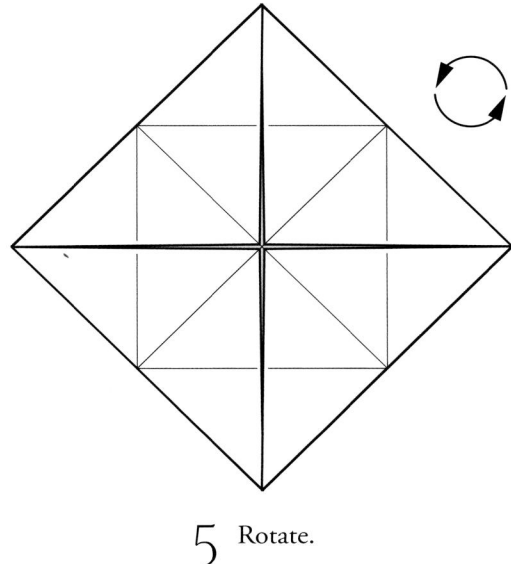

5 Rotate.

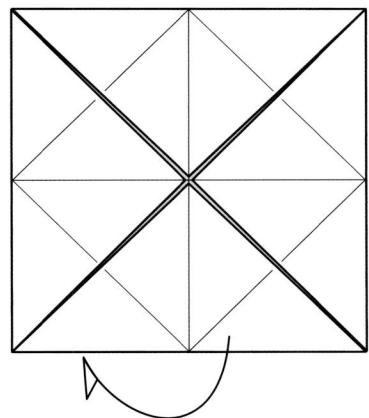

6 Fold the flap behind.

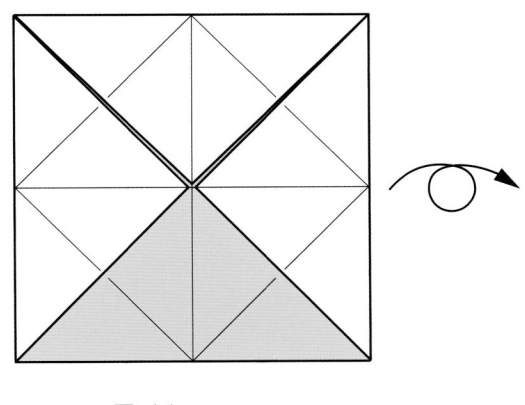

7 Turn over.

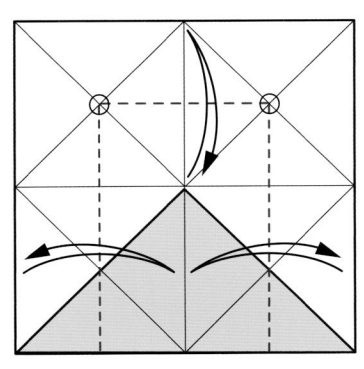

8 Crease as indicated.

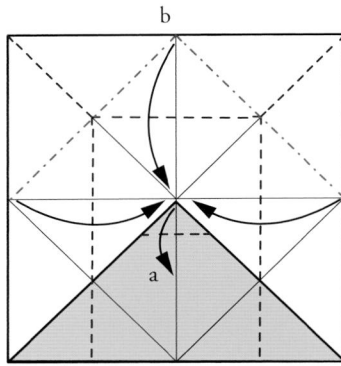

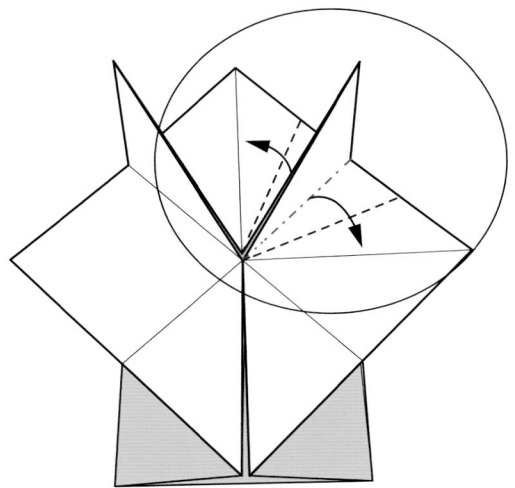

9 Valley fold the tip (a), then collapse as indicated (b).

10 Open out the sides of the flap, creating new creases to start making it flat.

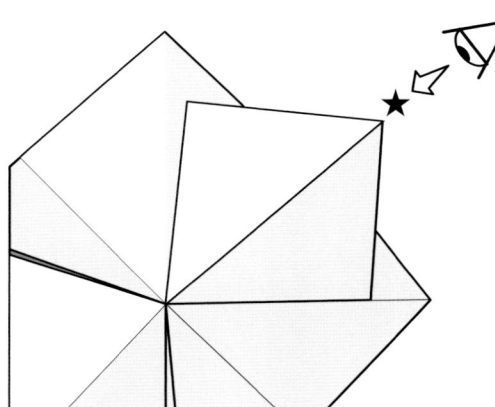

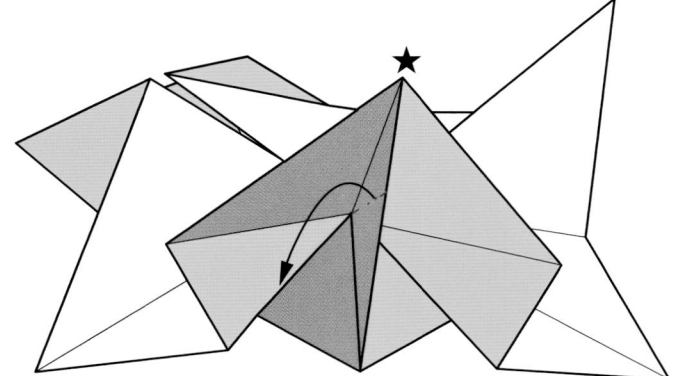

11 View from inside the flap is next (indicated with a star).

12 Fold the edge inside the flap, making the model completely flat.

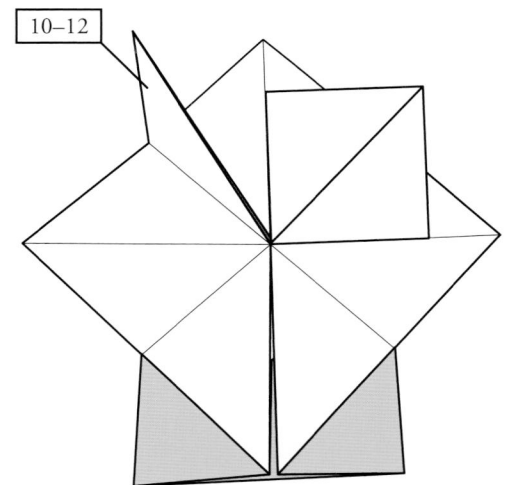

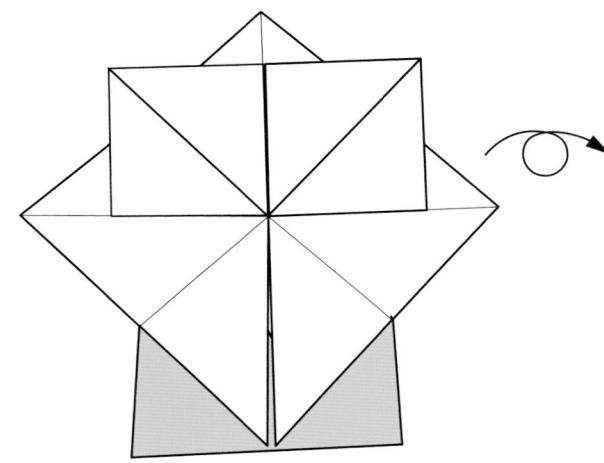

13 Repeat steps 10 to 12 on the other side.

14 Turn over.

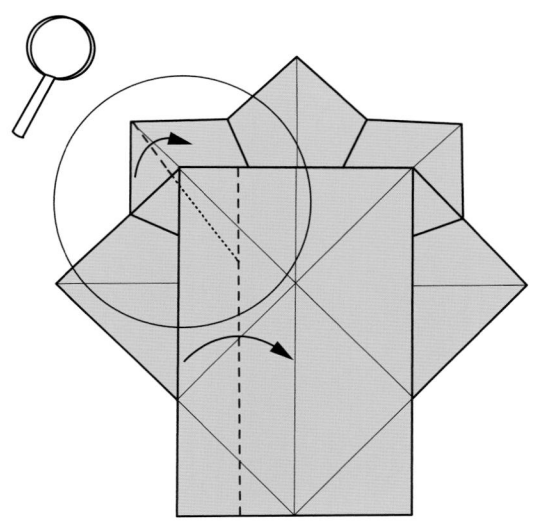

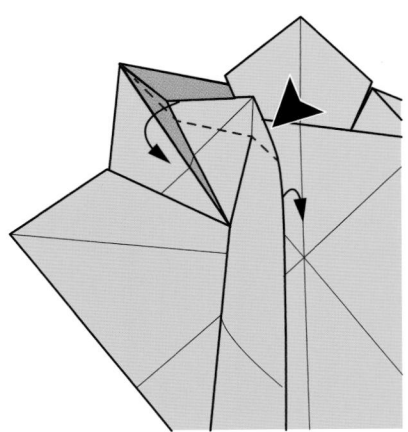

15 Fold the edge to the center, beginning a swivel (it won't lie flat). Detailed view next.

16 Swivel and squash so the model lies completely flat.

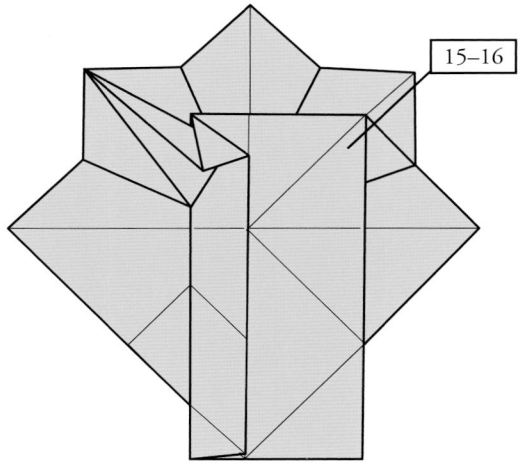

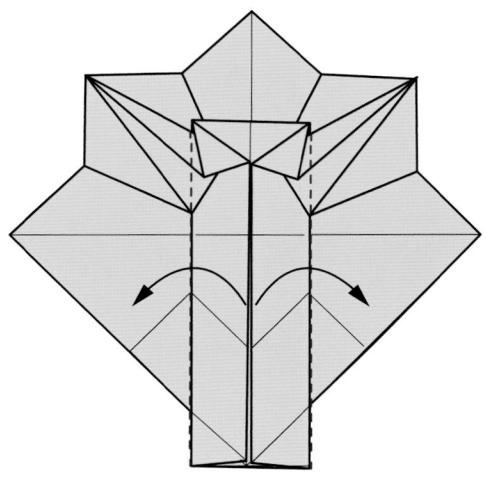

17 Repeat steps 15 and 16 on the other side.

18 Open the flaps to the sides.

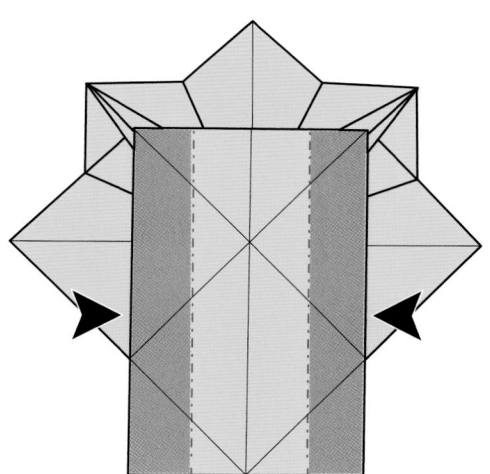

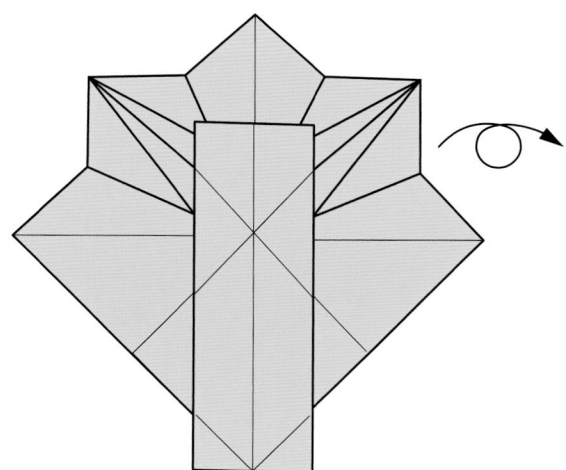

19 Sink the gray areas indicated. Note that the sinks will be closed by the corners that were squashed.

20 Turn over.

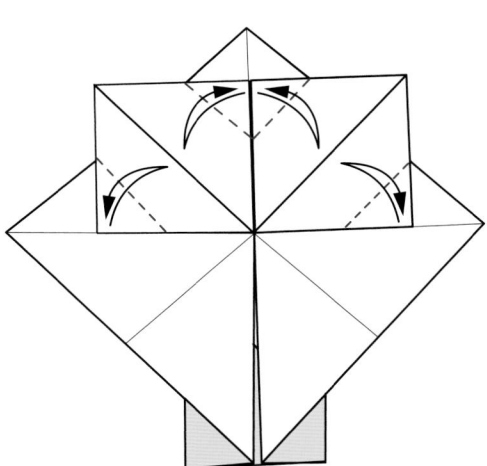

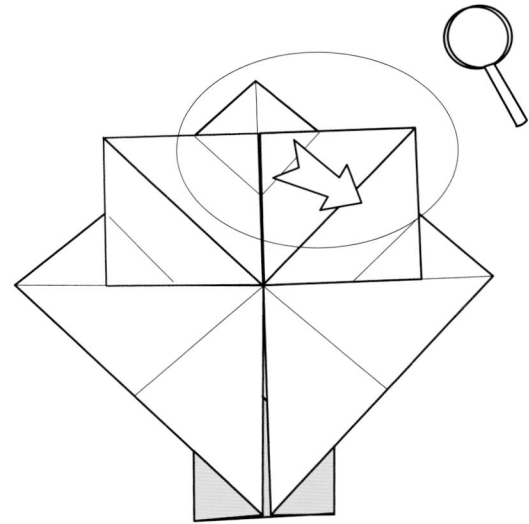

21 Crease the corners indicated.

22 Open the corner completely. Detailed view is next.

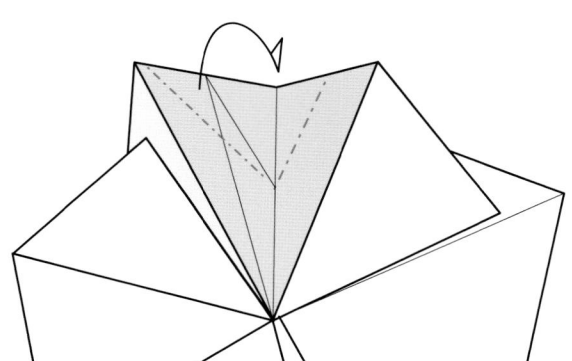

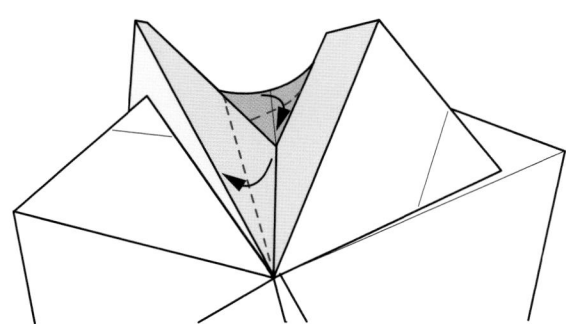

23 Use part of the crease formed in step 21 and add another almost to the corner to start an inside reverse that will not lie flat.

24 Fold the edge over to the center while squashing the excess paper from the back, making it lie flat.

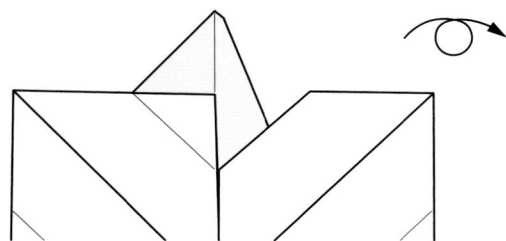

25 Turn over.

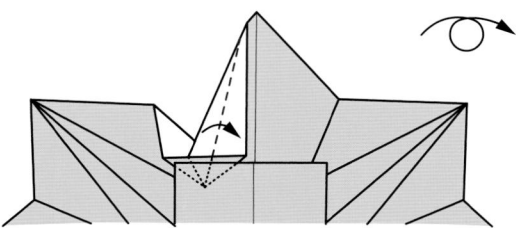

26 Fold the edge toward the center, narrowing the flap. Turn over.

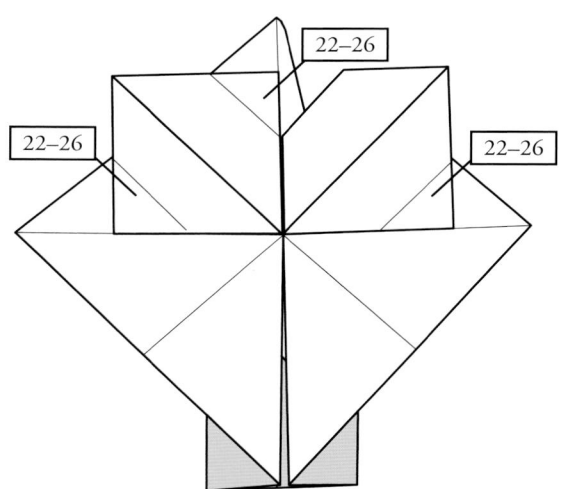

27 Repeat steps 22 to 26 on the other corners formed in step 21.

28 Detailed view is next.

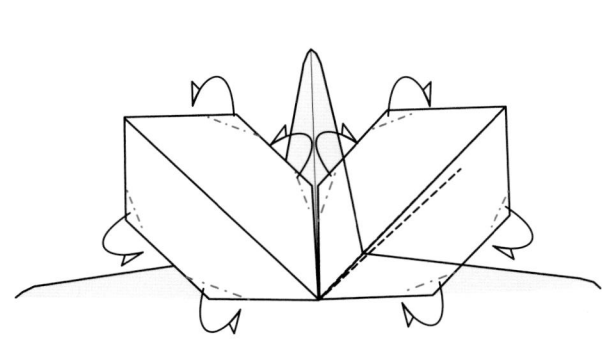

29 Mountain fold to round the corners, shaping the petals.

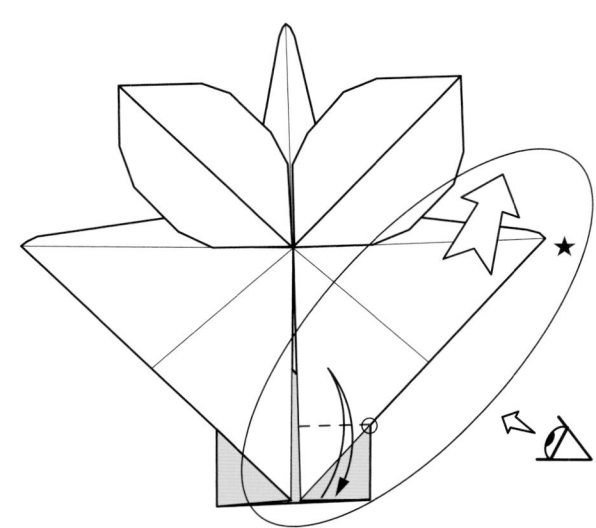

30 Crease the corner shown and open the flap to view the area beneath (indicated with a star).

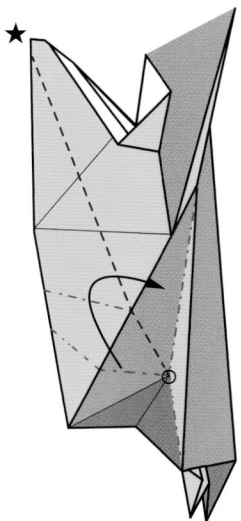

31 Make a new valley fold from the reference point indicated to the edge of the flap near the corner. Collapse as indicated to expose the lip color on the front.

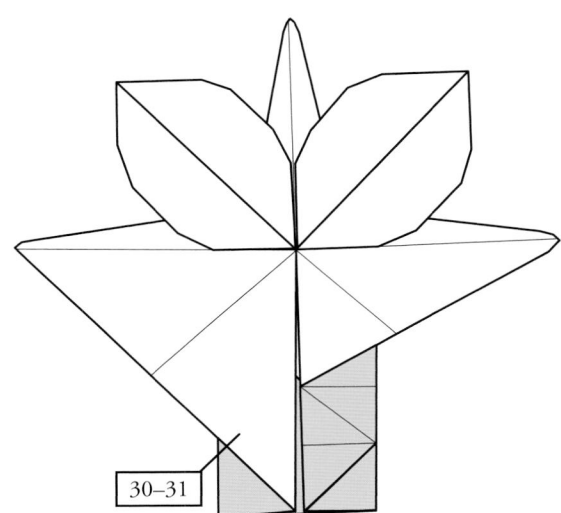

30–31

32 Repeat steps 30 and 31 on the other side.

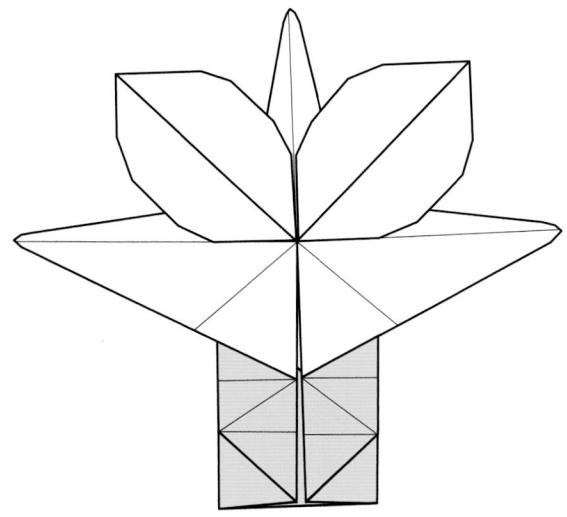

33   It will look like this.

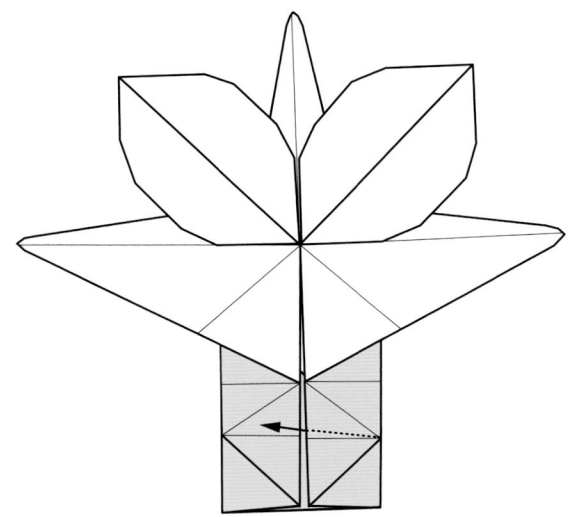

34   Untrap the triangular flap.

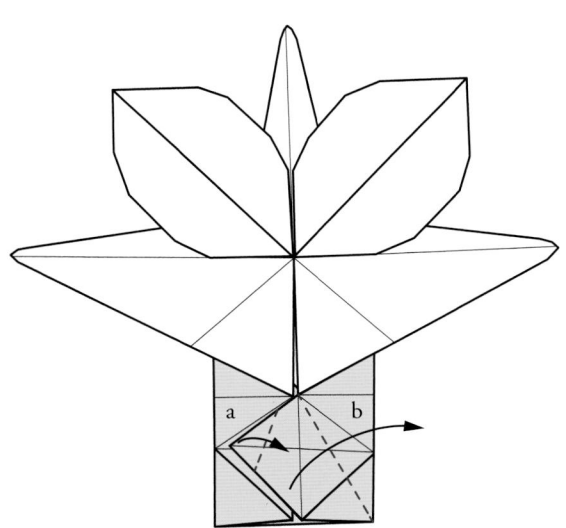

35   Valley fold the corner inward (a), then valley fold the flap (b).

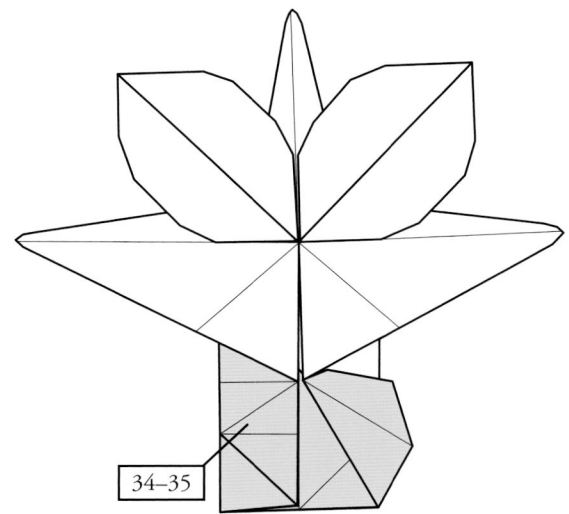

36   Repeat steps 34 to 35 on the other side.

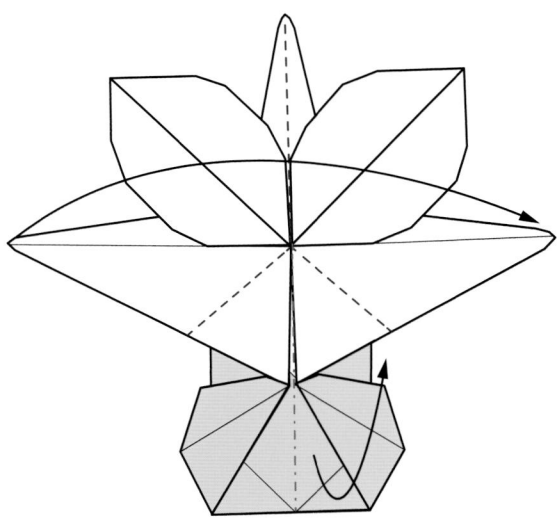

37 Fold in half, crimping the lip of the orchid.

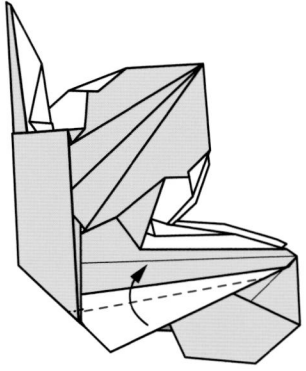

38 Valley fold the lateral sepal to narrow it. Repeat on the other side. View from under the lip next.

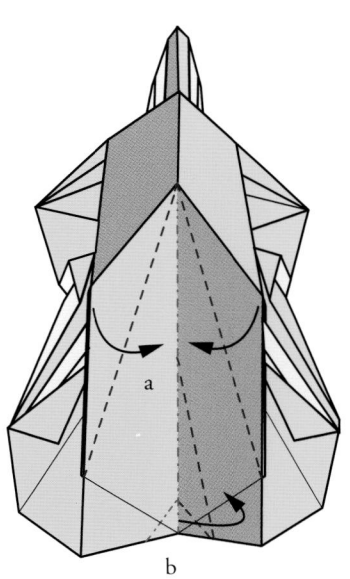

39 Reverse fold as indicated first (a) then fold the corner over (b) to lock the flap in position.

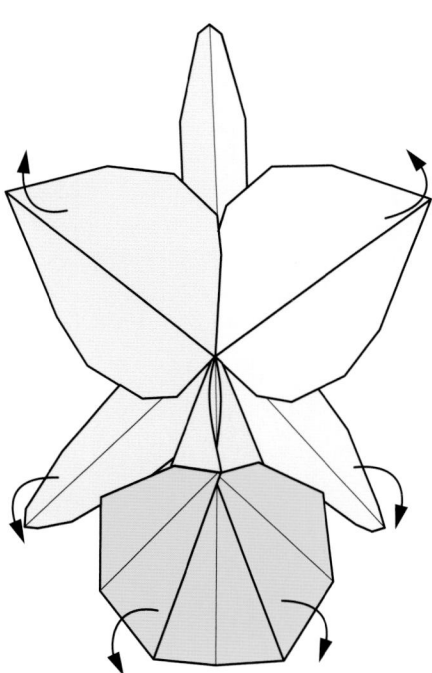

40 Curl the petals, sepals and lip to shape them.

Orchid 123

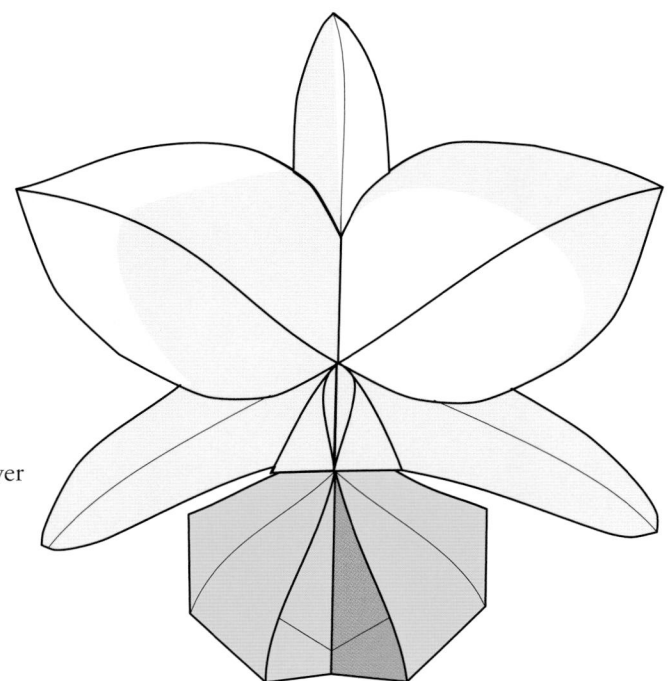

The finished Orchid flower

LEAVES

Use a piece of 25-cm square green paper to make the leaves. Cut the paper in half to make two leaves.

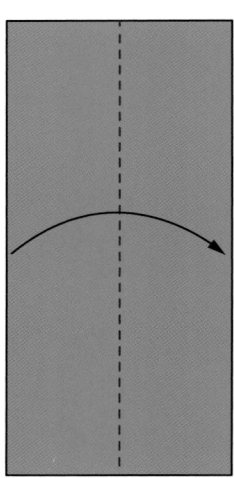

I Fold in half vertically.

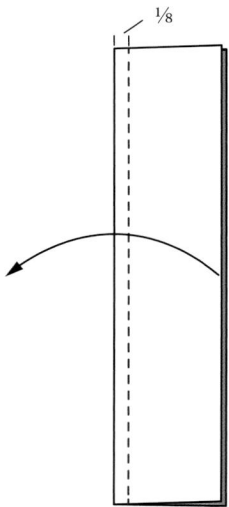

2 Create a pleat about ⅛ the width of the folded paper.

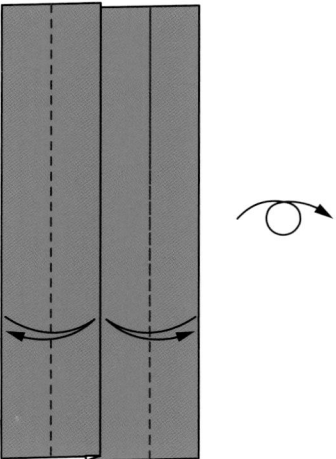

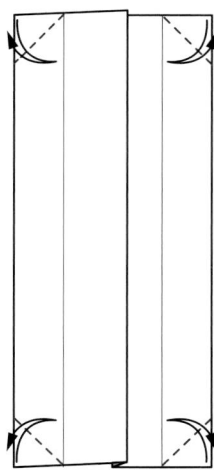

3 Fold the outer edges to the inner edge. Unfold. Turn over.

4 Fold the corners as shown and unfold.

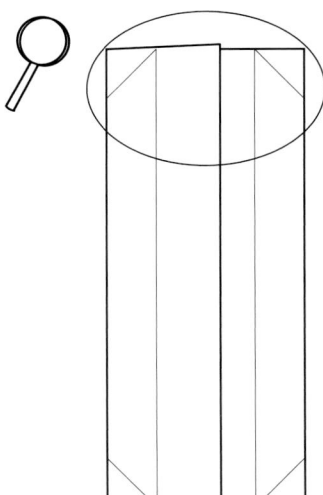

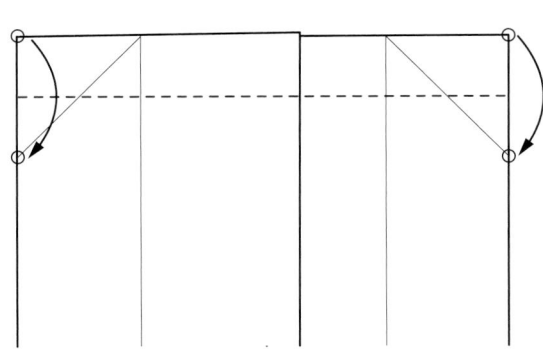

5 Detailed view is next.

6 Fold the edge over to the intersection points of the creases and side edges.

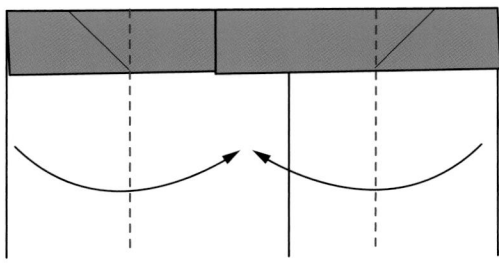

7 Fold the edges to the center.

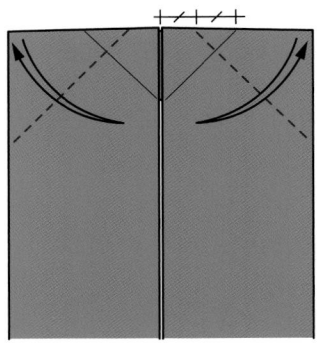

8 Fold the corners as indicated. Unfold.

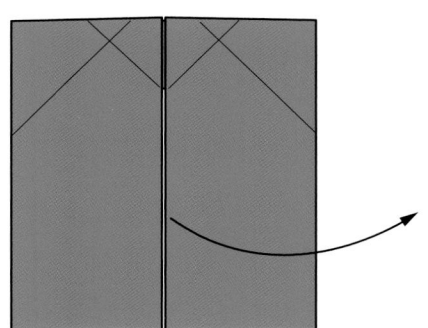

9 Open one side.

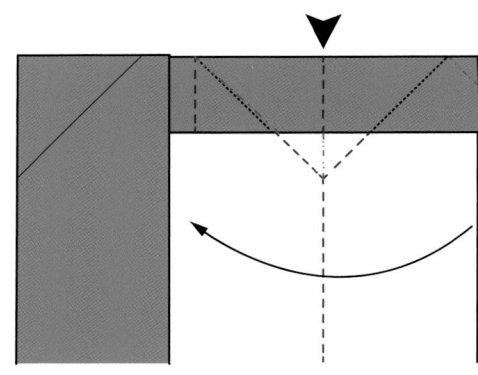

10 Collapse as indicated on existing creases.

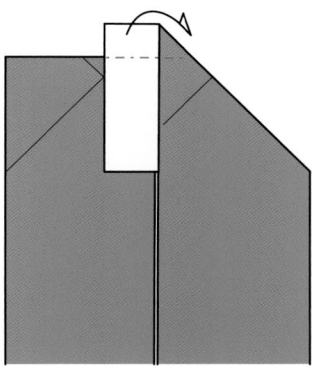

11 Mountain fold the flap inside.

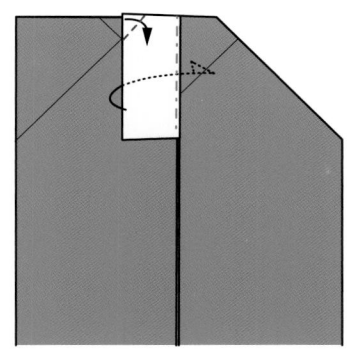

12 Fold the flap inside.

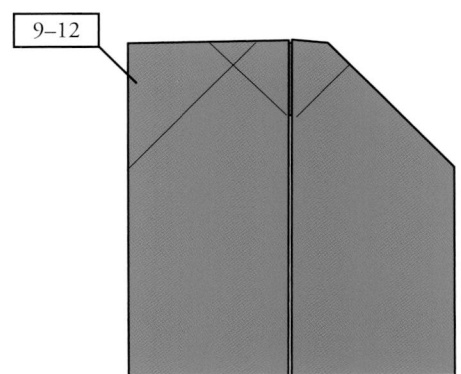

9–12

13 Repeat steps 9 to 12 on the other side.

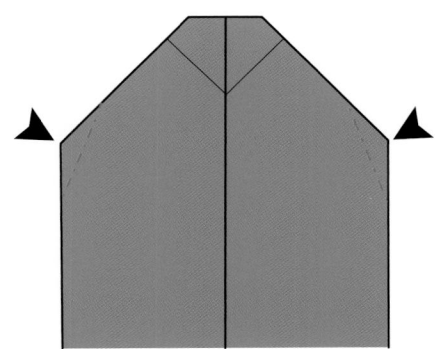

14 Make closed sinks at the corners.

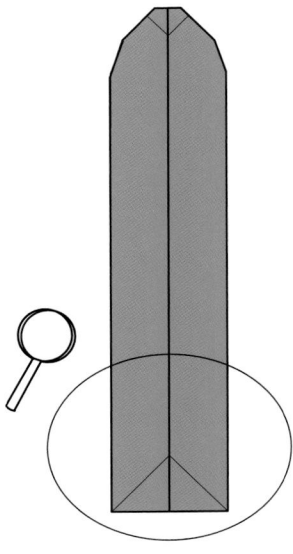

15 Detailed view of the bottom next.

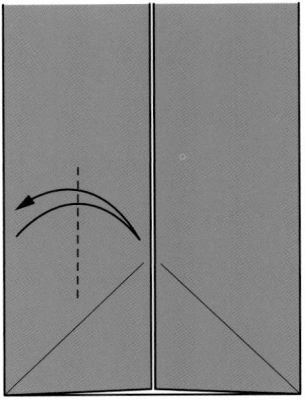

16 Fold the edge to the corner and pinch as indicated.

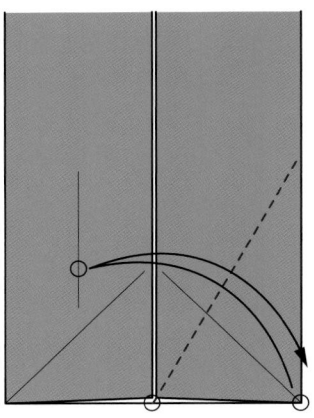

17 Bring the corner to the crease and unfold.

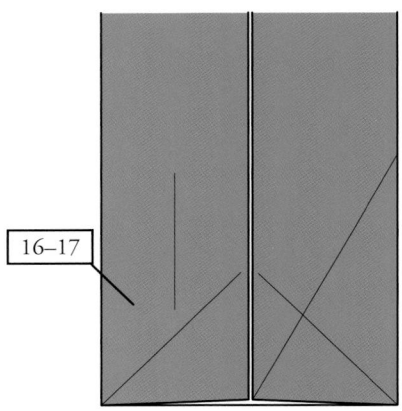

18 Repeat steps 16 and 17 on the other side.

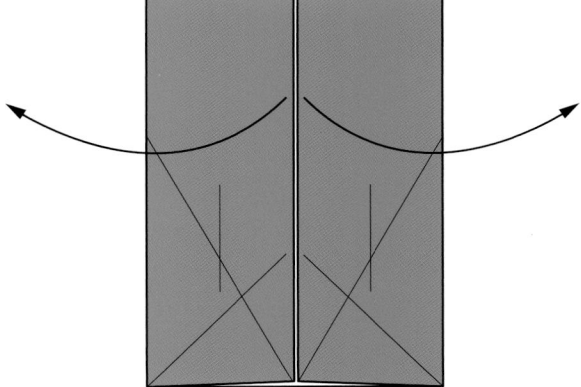

19 Open the flaps.

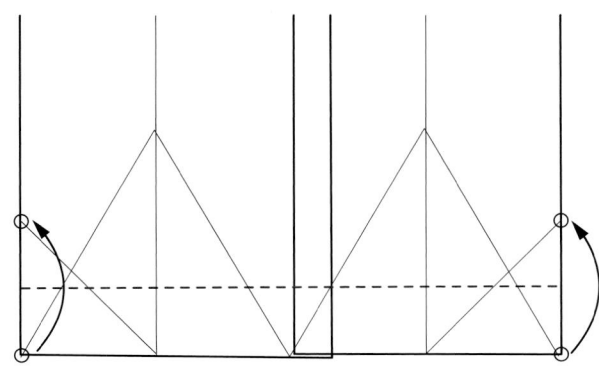

20 Fold the edge up to the reference points shown.

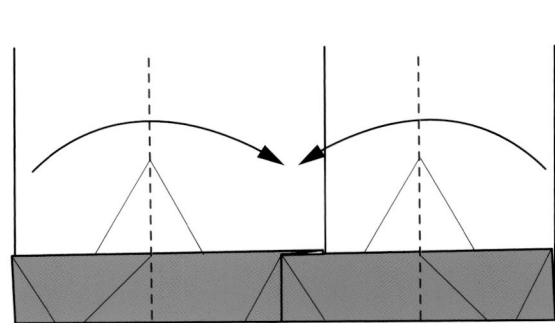

21 Fold the edges back to the center.

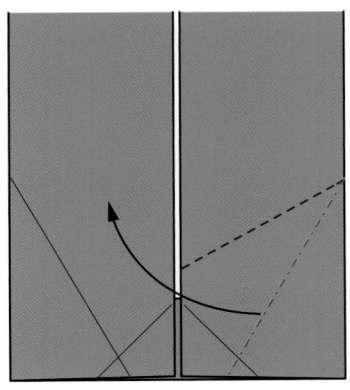

22 Swivel on existing creases.

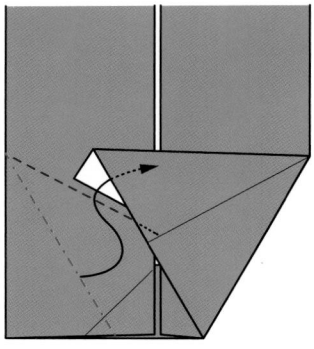

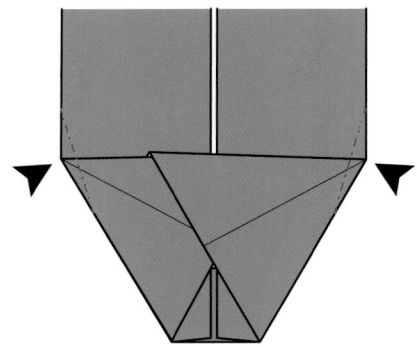

23 Swivel the other side, tucking the excess paper inside the flap created in step 22.

24 Make closed sinks at the corners to round the model out.

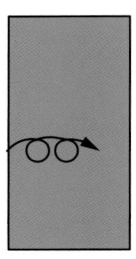

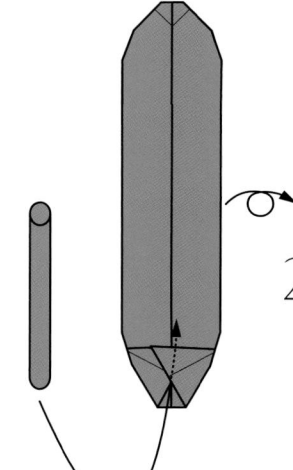

25 Make a connector using one of the small squares, cut in half vertically. Roll up one half into a long, thin tube.

26 Insert the connector into the opening at the bottom of the leaf.

27 Repeat steps 1 through 26 to make a second leaf.

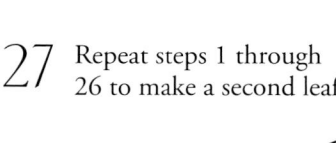

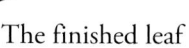

The finished leaf

STEM

Use one long rectangular piece to make the stem:

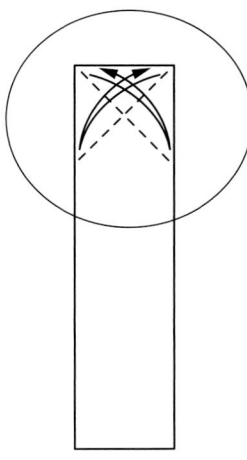

1 Fold the corners diagonally as shown and unfold.

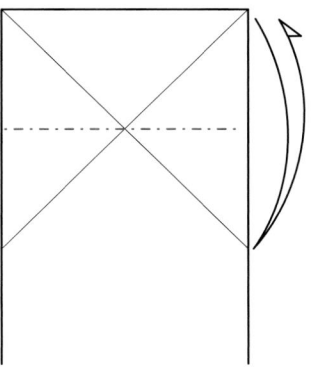

2 Mountain crease across the intersection.

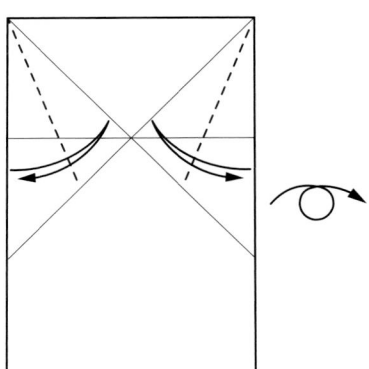

3 Fold the angle bisectors and unfold. Turn over.

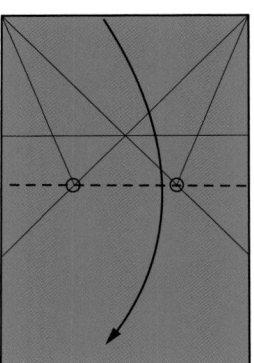

4 Fold the edge down through the reference points shown.

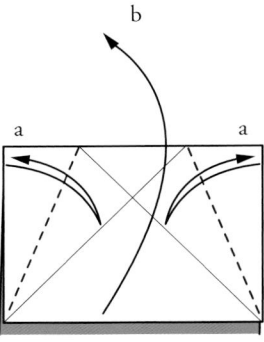

5 Crease the angle bisectors (a) then unfold back to step 4 (b).

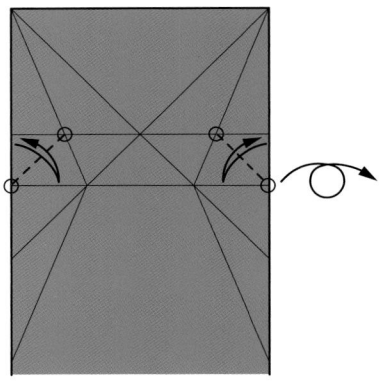

6 Fold diagonally between the reference points and unfold. Turn over.

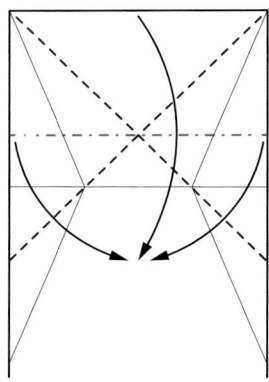

7 Collapse a waterbomb base.

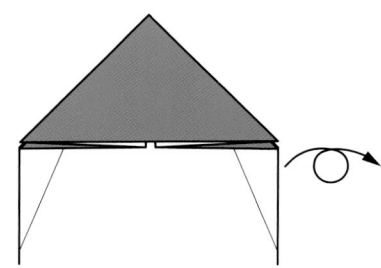

8 Turn over.

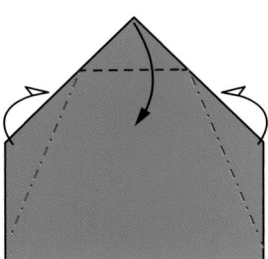

9 Using the existing creases, fold the corners behind and fold the tip down, allowing the back to flip out. The result will not lie flat.

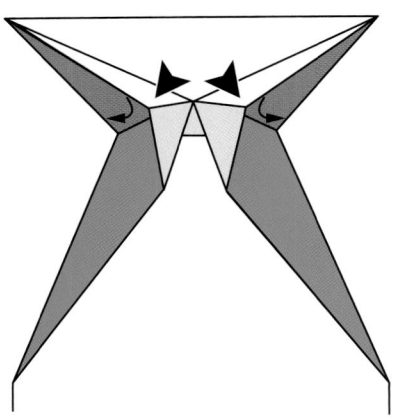

10 Squash to make the model flat.

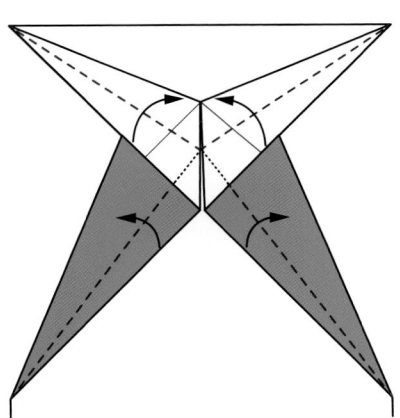

11 Fold as indicated, with a swivel.

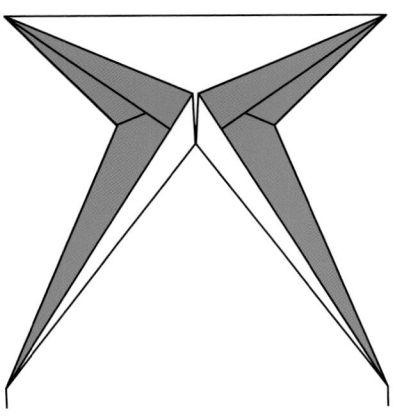

12 It will look like this.

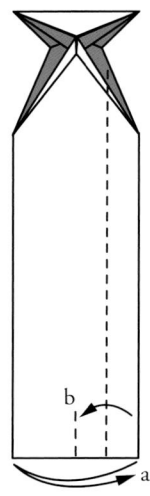

13 Fold the bottom in half and pinch by the edge (a), then fold the edge to the pinch (b).

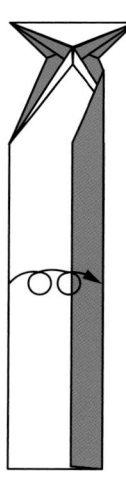

14 Roll the other edge over and over to narrow the stem.

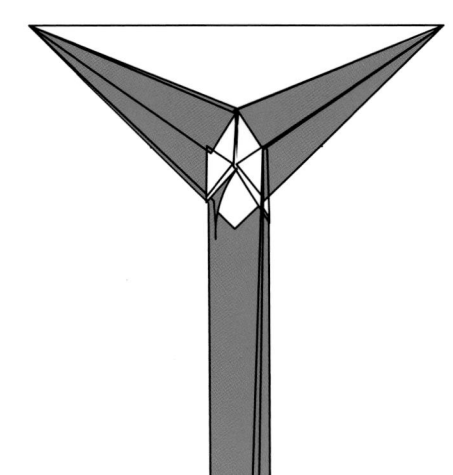

The finished stem

PSEUDOBULB

Use the other small square to make the pseudobulb:

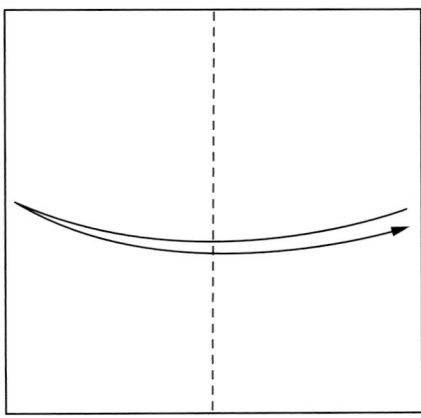

1 With the white side up, fold in half vertically and unfold.

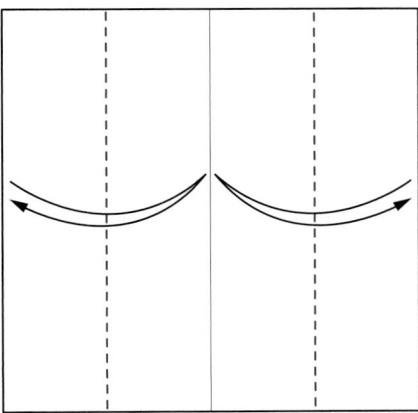

2 Fold the edges to the center and unfold.

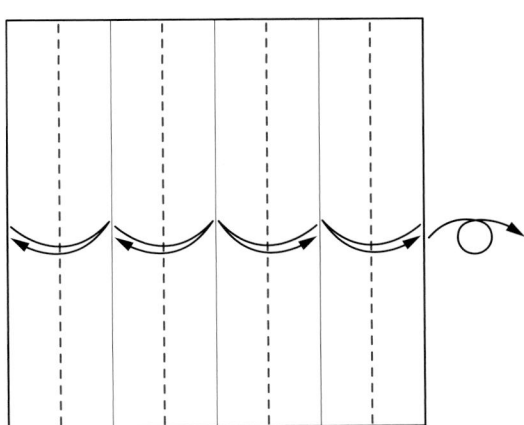

3 Fold the eighths and unfold. Turn over.

4 Fold the corners in and unfold.

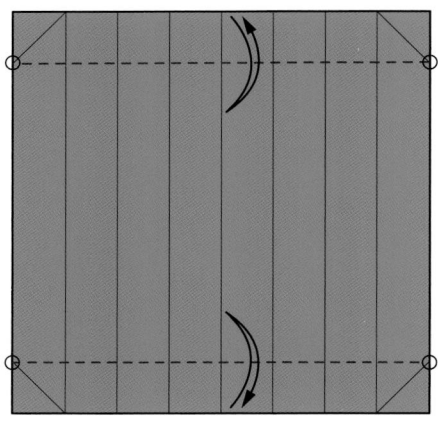

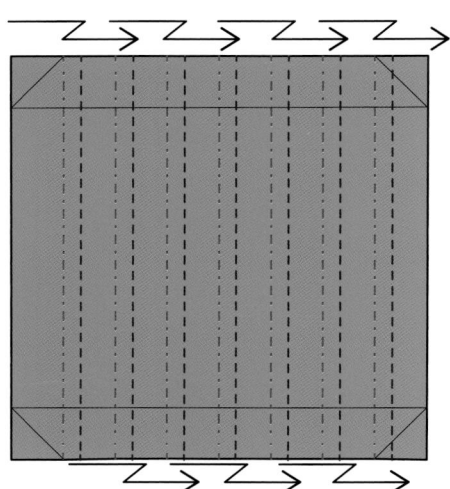

5 Crease through the reference points shown and unfold.

6 Reinforce the existing mountain creases, then make valley creases as shown to pleat.

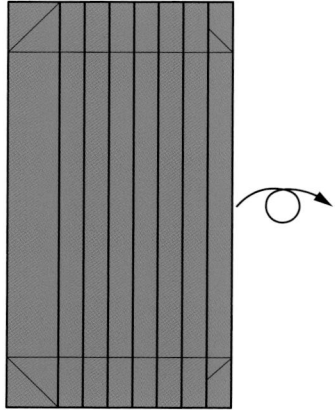

7 Turn over.

8 Fold the corners in on existing creases.

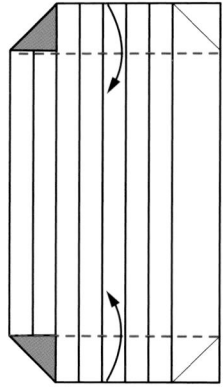

9 Fold the edges in on existing creases.

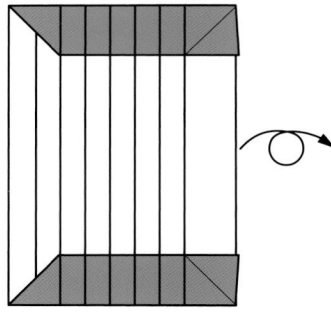

10 Turn over.

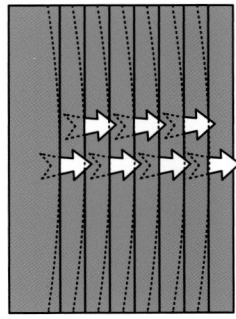

11 Pull out some paper at the center of the pleats to make a convex shape.

ABOUT THE ORCHID

Species belonging to the orchid family (*Orchidadeae*) number in the thousands. Even though we generally think of orchids as delicate tropical flowers, they are hardy flowers that can be found on all continents (except Antarctica) and in all climates (including the Arctic north). Many are cultivated for showy blooms and fragrance, but at least one variety is prized for its flavor: vanilla beans come from orchids. The flower is named for a figure from Greek mythology. Orchis was the son of a nymph and a satyr who attacked a priestess of Dionysus while drunk. Although he was killed for the insult, he was later transformed by the gods into a flower.

There are a number of symbolic meanings that are associated with different types of orchids, but all orchids are associated with delicate beauty and elegance.

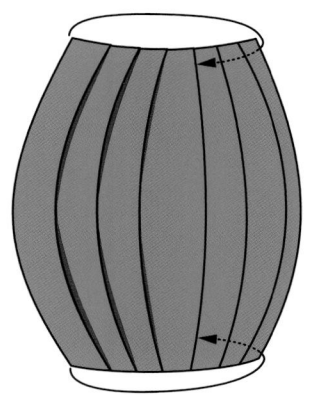

ASSEMBLY

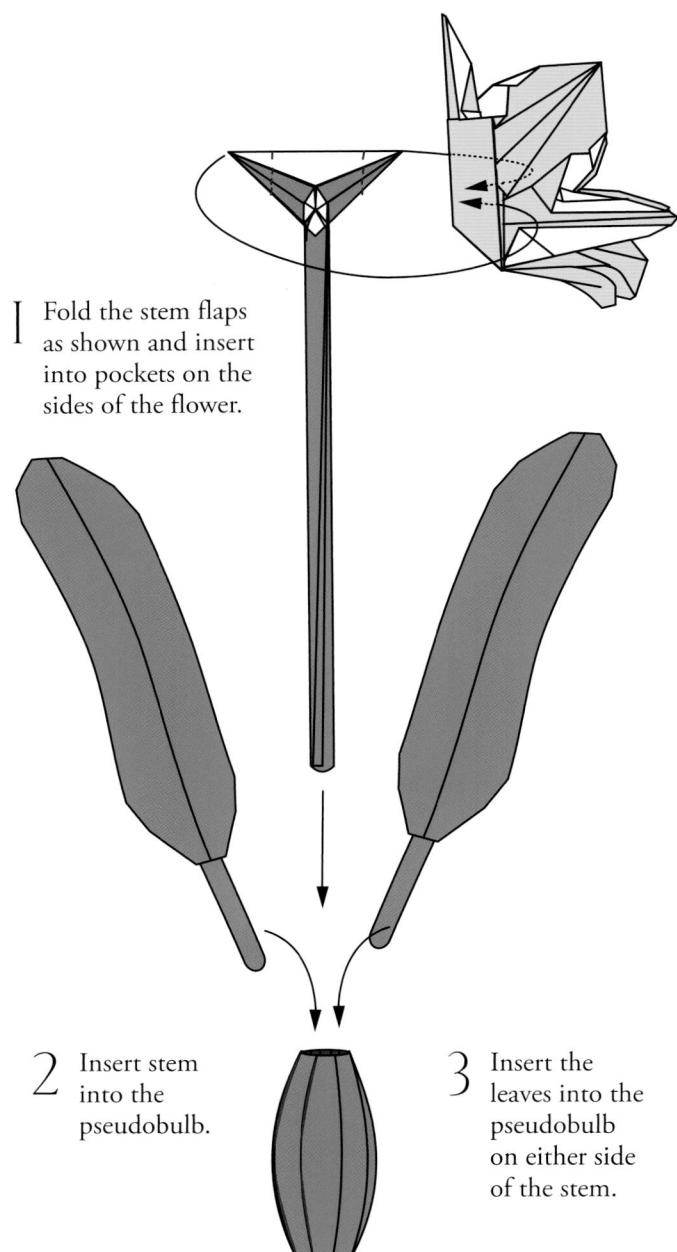

I2 Form into a cylinder, fitting the tab of one end into the pocket of the other.

I Fold the stem flaps as shown and insert into pockets on the sides of the flower.

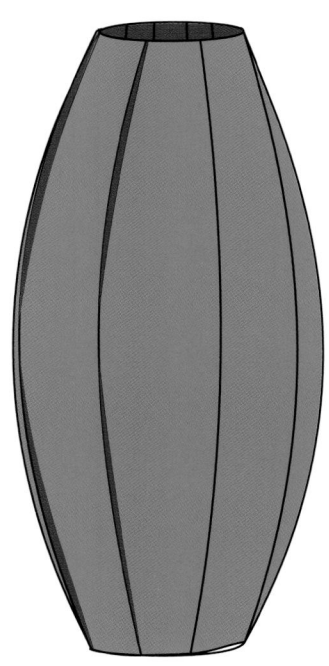

The finished pseudobulb

2 Insert stem into the pseudobulb.

3 Insert the leaves into the pseudobulb on either side of the stem.

The completed
Orchid with
leaves, stem, and
pseudobulb

ZINNIA

Designed by Aldo Marcell;
diagrammed and folded by Marcio Noguchi

"I started exploring the idea of developing a flower with lots of petals using only one sheet of paper in 2005, after folding flowers with multiple pieces of paper. This was the result.

I've tried a number of different materials, and so far I've had the best results using a foil gift wrap that has tissue paper layered over it with white glue. But I am still trying new material out, any thin but resistant paper. Right now, I am making something with triple tissue paper."

—Aldo Marcell

Aldo Marcell is a plant biologist, tour guide, and environmental educator from northern Nicaragua. He learned about origami as a child, but it became a passion for him as he got older and was able to combine his interest in folding with his love of nature and plants. Naturally, plants and flowers are what he enjoys folding most, but he also likes exploring geometric and modular shapes. He loves to teach origami to others and hopes to publish an origami book of his own one day.

Use a 35-cm (13.75-inch) square to make this flower.

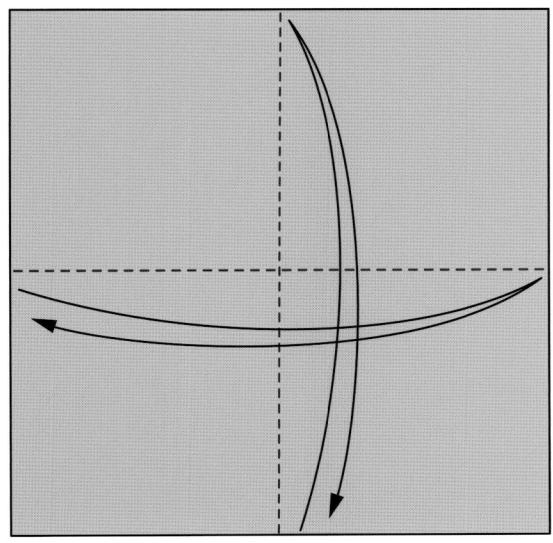

I Fold in half horizontally and vertically. Unfold.

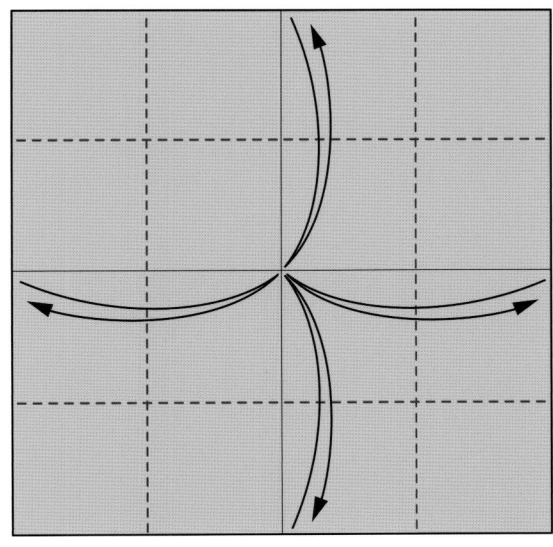

2 Fold in quarters horizontally and vertically. Unfold.

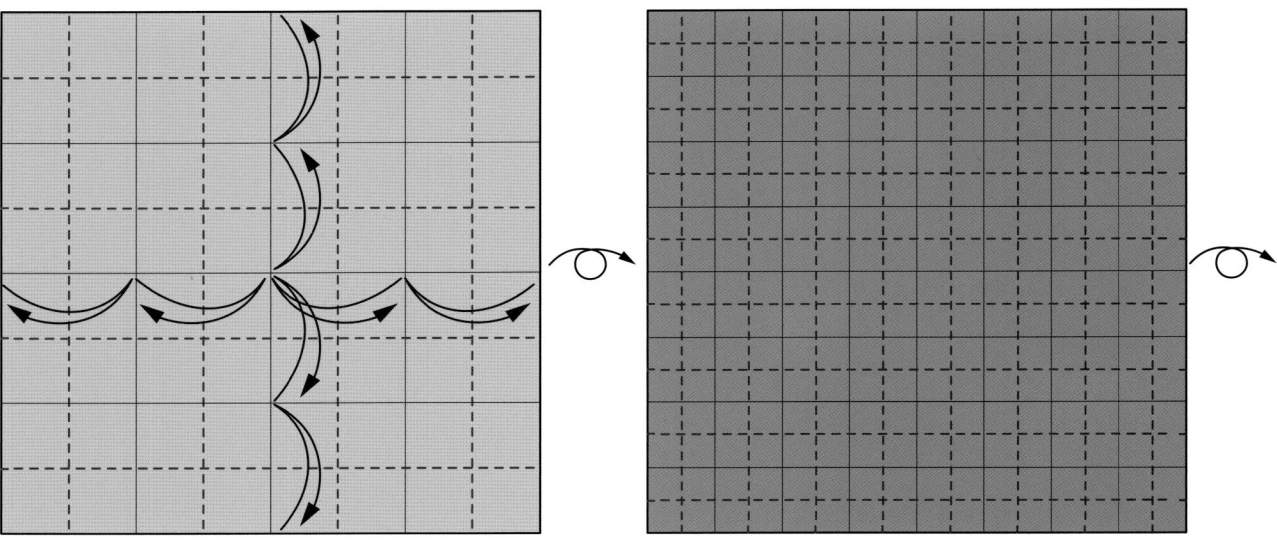

3 Fold in eighths horizontally and vertically. Unfold. Turn over.

4 Fold in sixteenths horizontally and vertically. Unfold. Turn over.

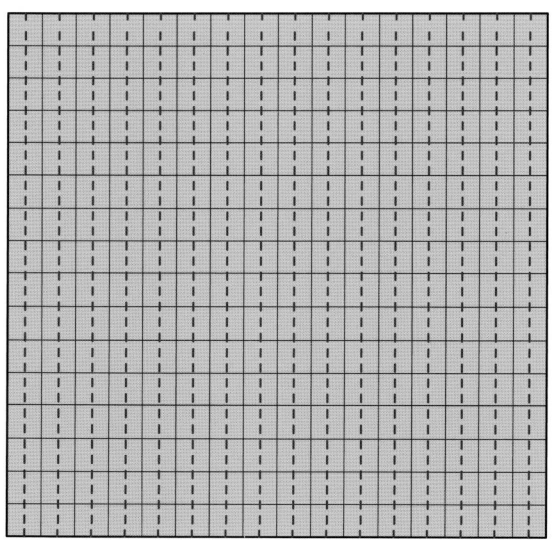

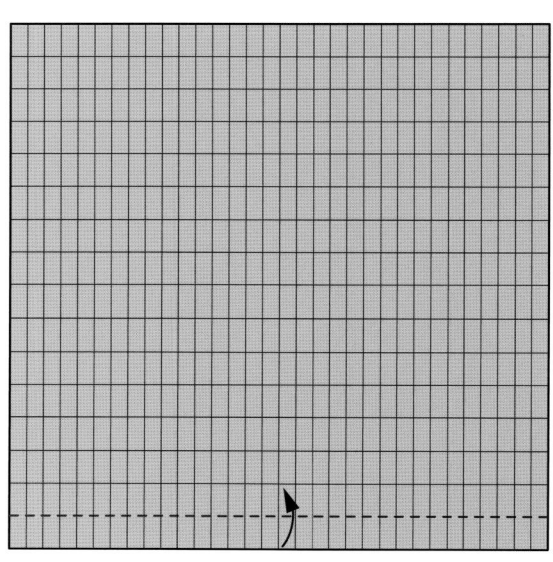

5 Fold vertically in thirty-seconds. Unfold.

6 Valley fold up on the first crease.

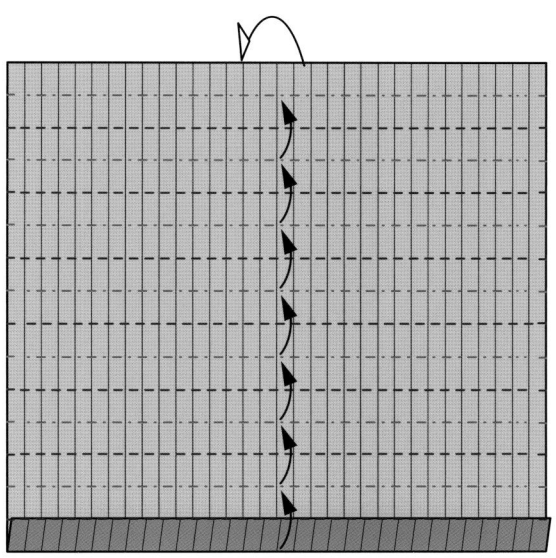

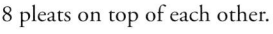
8 pleats on top of each other.

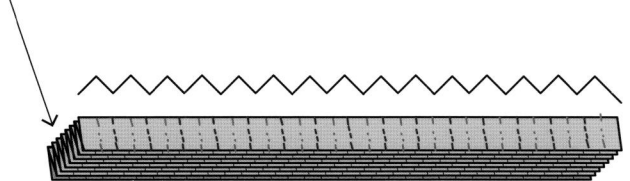

7 Valley fold up on the first crease, then pleat up (alternating mountain and valley folds) for the rest of the length.

8 The result is a long row of eight pleats on top of each other. Make a new sequence of horizontal pleats.

16 pleats

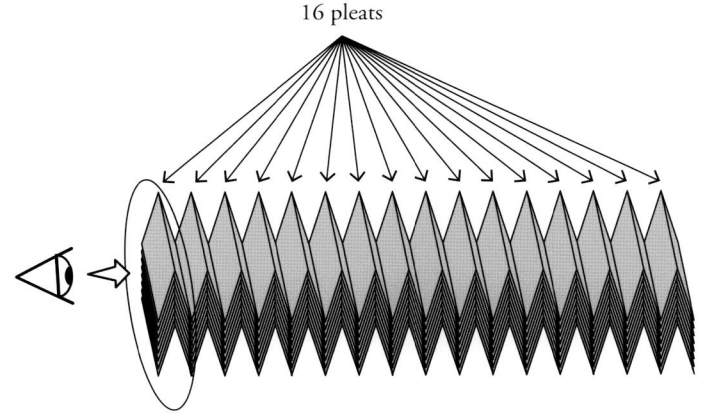

9 View the pleats from the side, focusing on the first pleat in the next step.

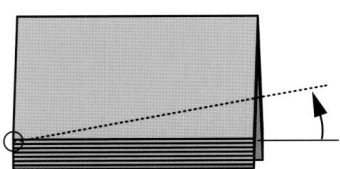

10 Pull the top pleat up at a slight angle. Repeat on the 15 pleats below.

ABOUT THE ZINNIA

Zinnias are part of the family *Asteraceae*. They are native to the southwestern United States, Mexico and Central America, and are named for the German botanist, Johann Gottfried Zinn, who brought them to Europe after finding them in the New World. They are known for their long stalks with solitary flowers in a range of bright colors. Zinnias are attractive to pollinators like butterflies and hummingbirds, so gardeners often plant them for this reason. There are different meanings associated with the different colored zinnias: scarlet means constancy, white means goodness, and yellow is for remembrance, to name a few.

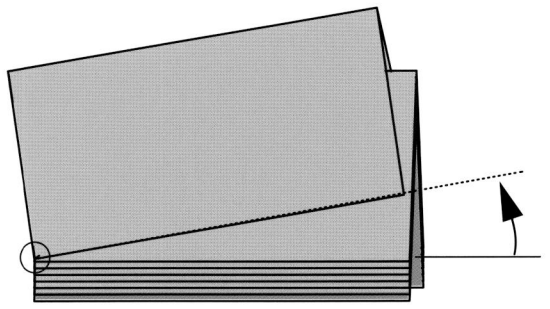

11 Pull the next row of pleats up at a slight angle.

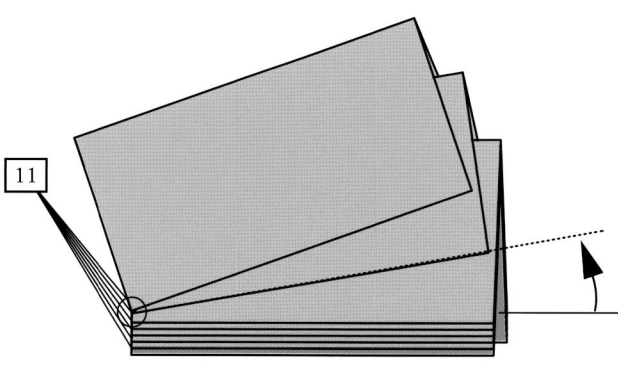

12 Continue fanning out the pleats on all layers, resulting in an almost 90° angle between the top row and the bottom row of pleats. See next step for expected results.

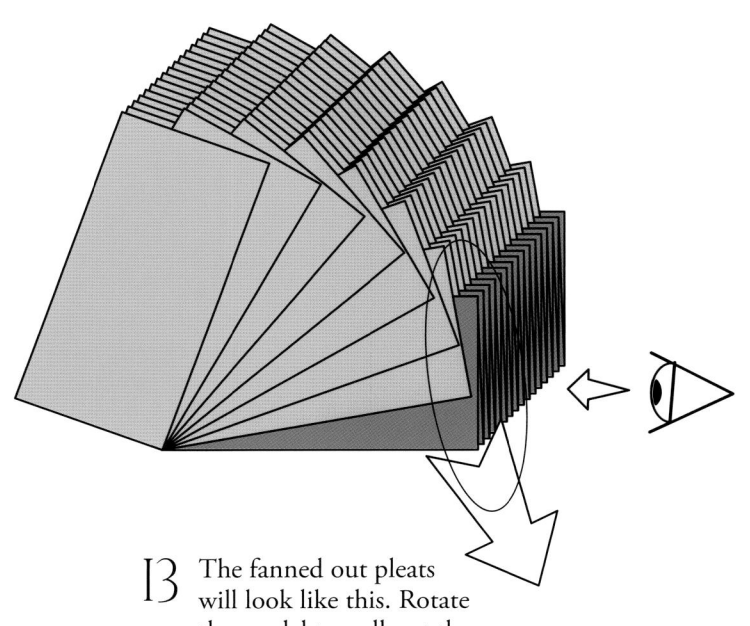
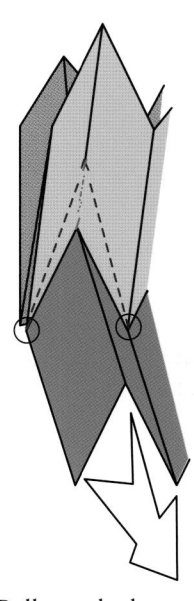

13   The fanned out pleats will look like this. Rotate the model to pull out the bottom row. See next step.

14   Pull out the bottom row as indicated, so that this row of pleats will be perpendicular to the others. Flatten the pleats.

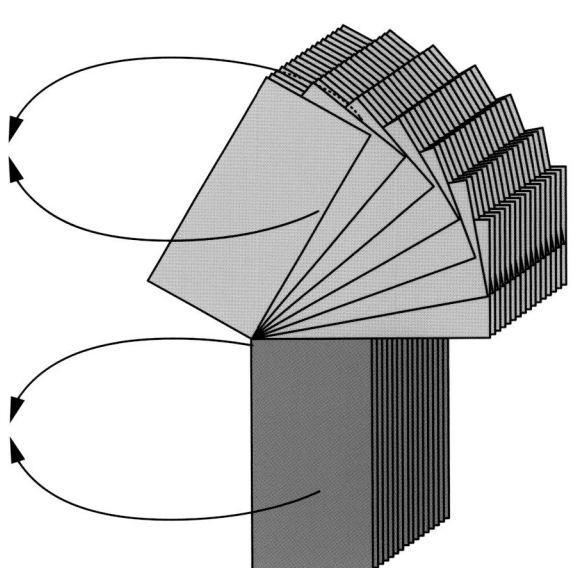
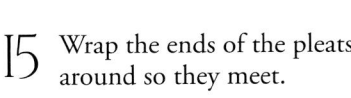
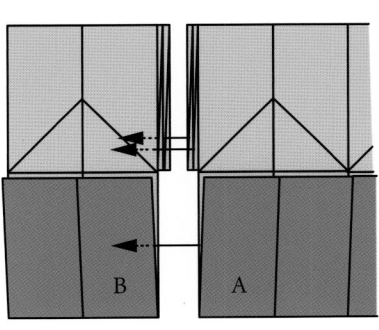
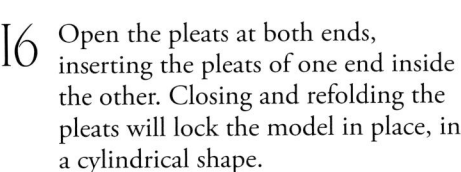

15   Wrap the ends of the pleats around so they meet.

16   Open the pleats at both ends, inserting the pleats of one end inside the other. Closing and refolding the pleats will lock the model in place, in a cylindrical shape.

17   View from the bottom next.

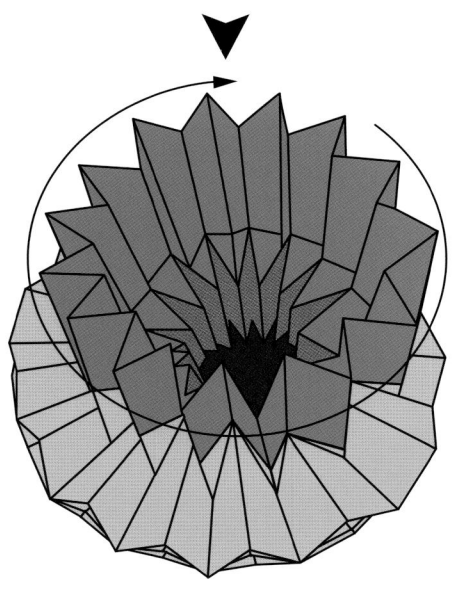

18   Twist the pleats while pushing them down toward the center one at a time. See next step for the result.

19   Turn over.

20   Repeat the twisting on the innermost ring of pleats on this side, while pushing them down toward the center one at a time.

The completed Zinnia

The leaves shown with the Zinnia in this photo
were made using the model found on page 179.

BLEEDING HEART

Designed by Daniel Robinson; diagrammed by Andrew Hudson

Daniel Robinson, an industrial designer from Pennington, New Jersey, has been doing origami for more than 25 years. His work has been published and displayed in museums all over the world. The inspiration for his designs comes from nature. He focuses on capturing not only the features of a subject but also its essence, and on creating models that are enjoyable for other origami enthusiasts to fold. Daniel Robinson believes that the product of origami is secondary to the process; it is the transformation of a simple sheet of paper into something evocative and stimulating that conveys the real magic of origami.

"This model of a bleeding heart is folded from a 16-inch square of handmade origami paper. The paper is 100% abaca fiber. The design goals for this model were to create a process that allows the folder to simulate both the fibrous texture of the stem as well as the delicacy of the blooms, all through simple shaping. I also wanted to showcase the flower's opening process (hence, a branch with multiple blooms). The final model should look natural, lazily drooping under its own weight.

—Daniel Robinson

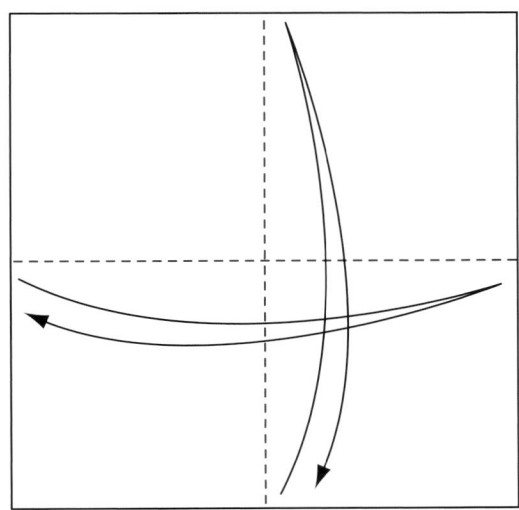

1   With the white side up, fold in half horizontally and vertically.

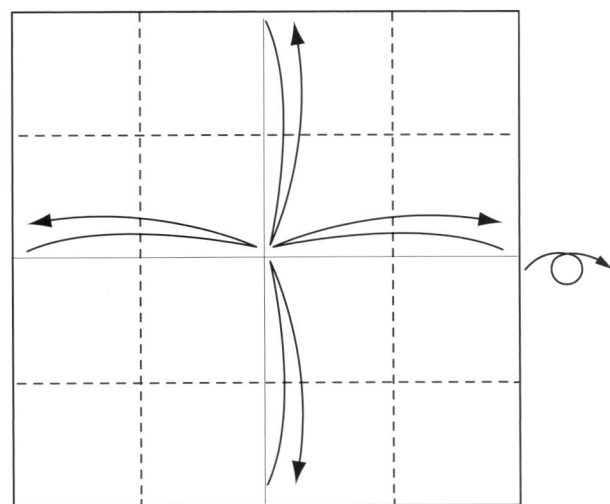

2   Fold in quarters and unfold. Turn over.

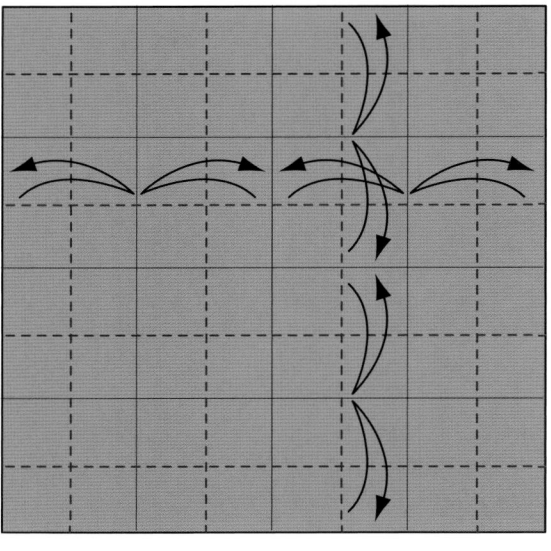

3   Fold in eighths. Unfold.

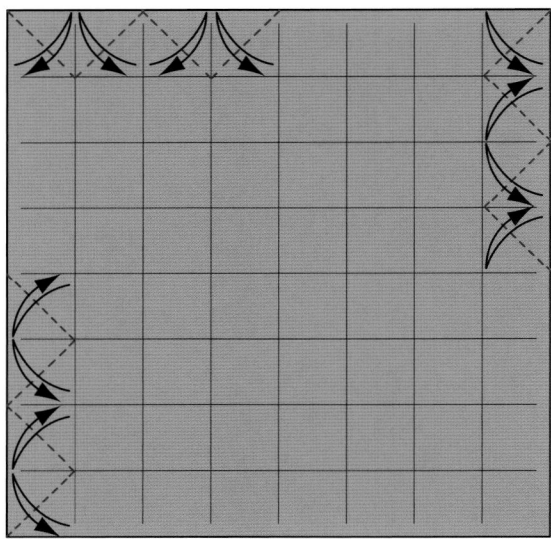

4   Crease the diagonals.

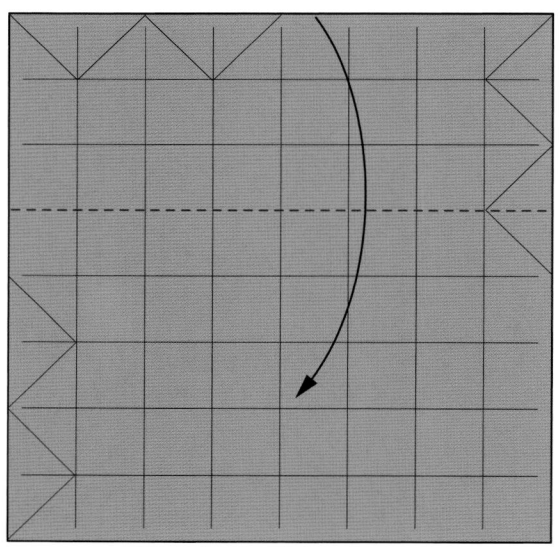

5   Fold the top edge down as indicated.

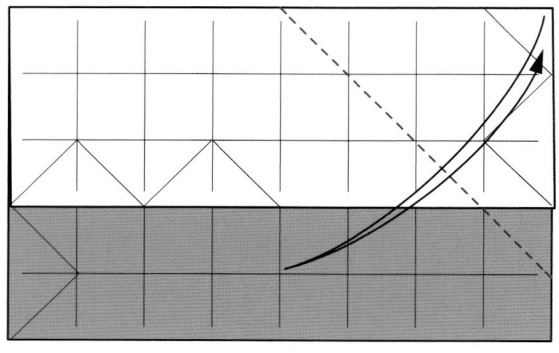

6   Fold the diagonal shown and unfold.

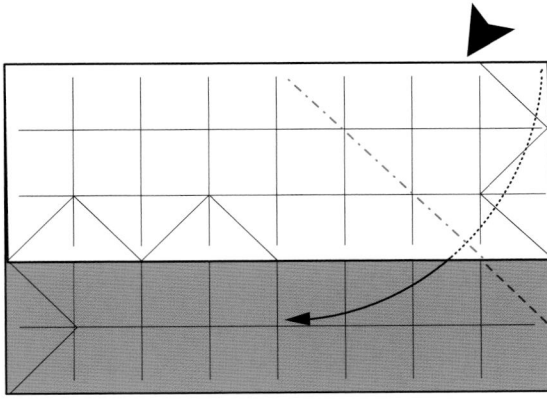

7   Reverse fold.

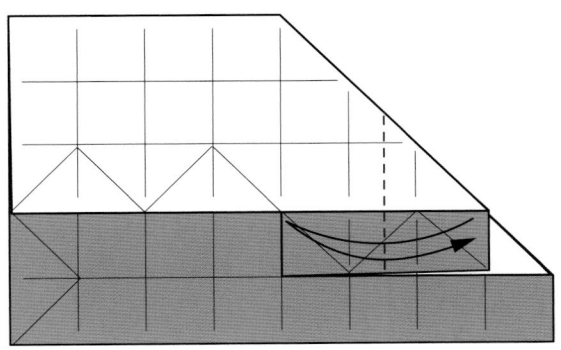

8   Fold the flap to the edge as indicated and unfold.

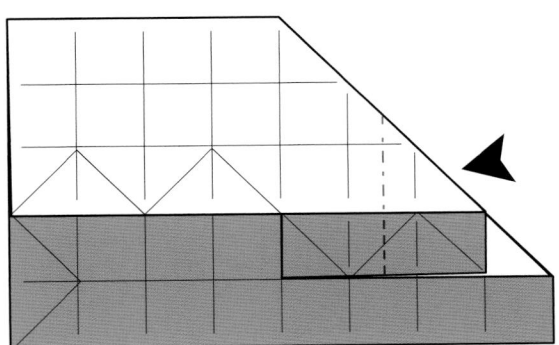

9   Reverse fold.

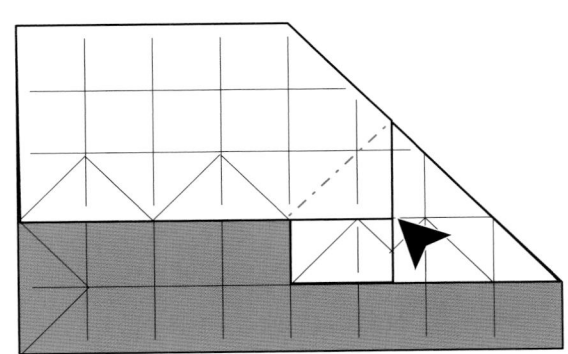

10   Reverse fold.

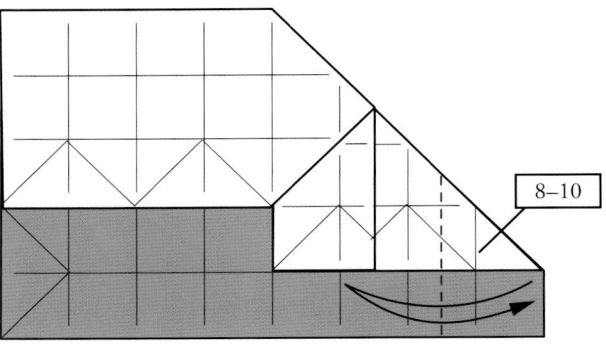

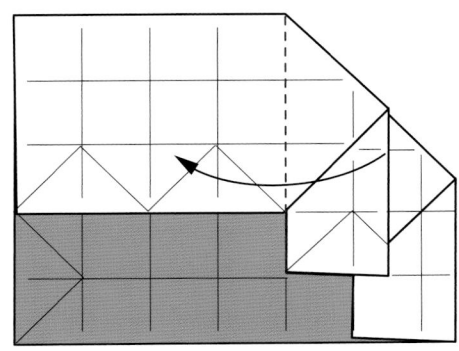

11 Repeat steps 8 to 10 on the lower flap.

12 Valley fold over.

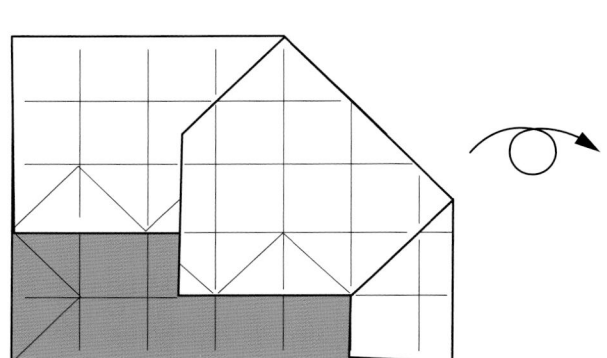

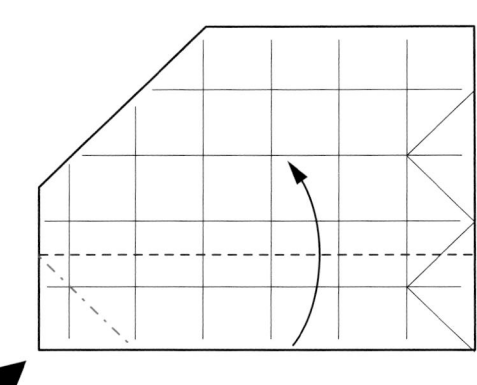

13 Turn over from side to side.

14 Valley fold the bottom edge up to the crease shown, squashing the corner.

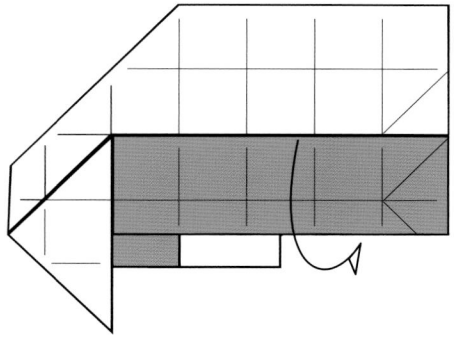

I5   Wrap the layer behind.

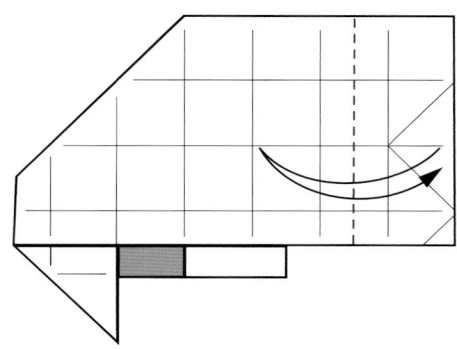

I6   Fold and unfold.

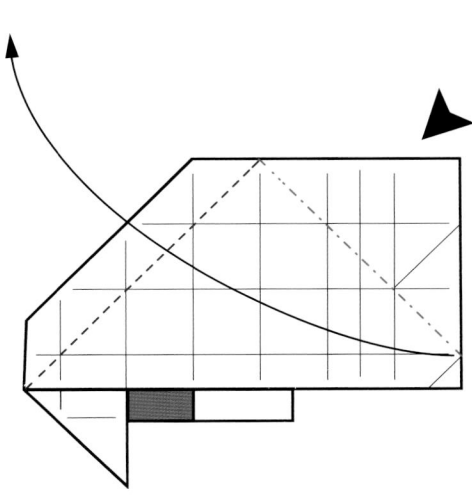

I7   Swivel fold.

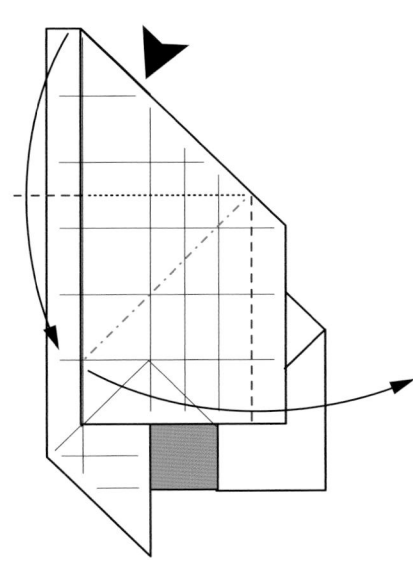

I8   Swivel fold.

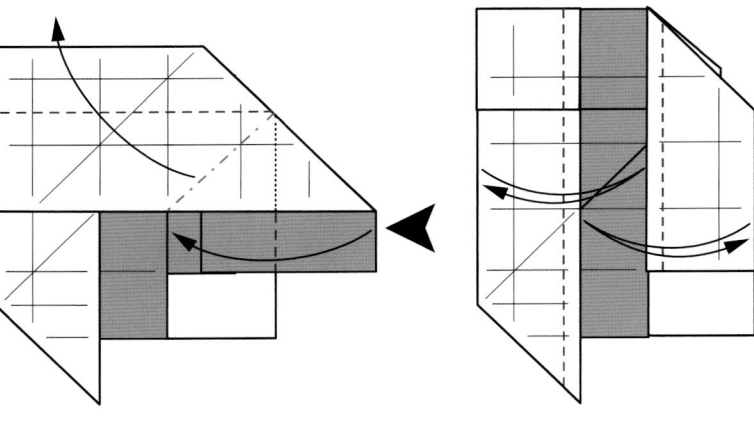
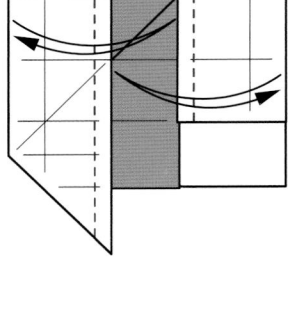
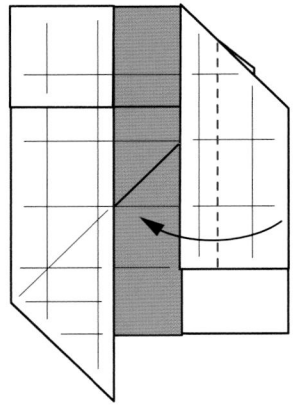

19 Swivel fold.

20 Fold the outer edges to the inner edges shown as indicated.

21 Fold the flap over to the other side.

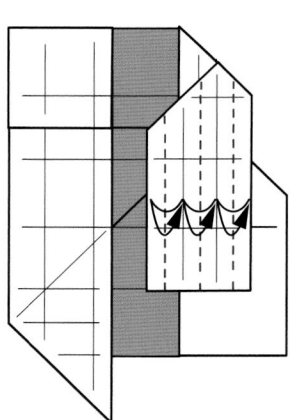
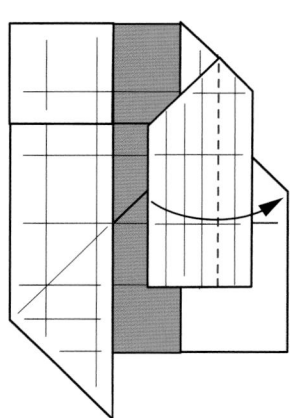
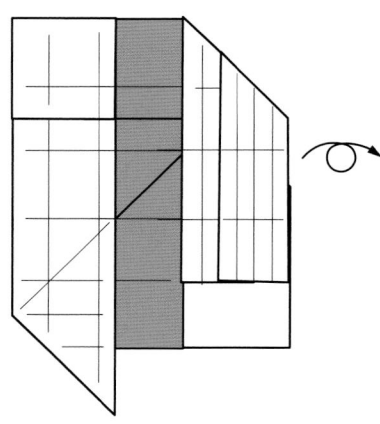

22 Fold the sections in half vertically and unfold.

23 Fold the flap back to step 21.

24 Turn over from side to side.

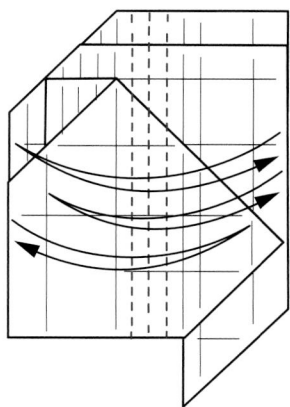

25 Pre-crease through all layers.

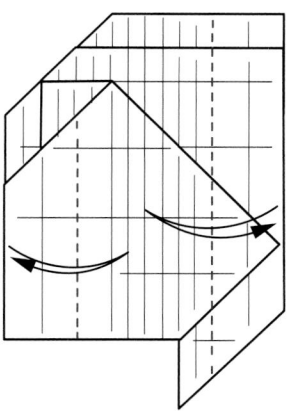

26 Pre-crease through all layers.

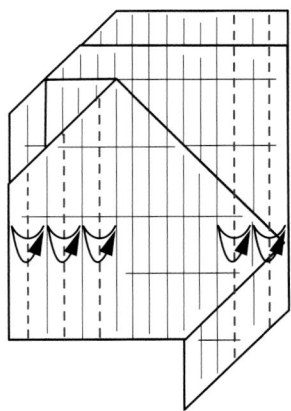

27 Pre-crease as indicated.

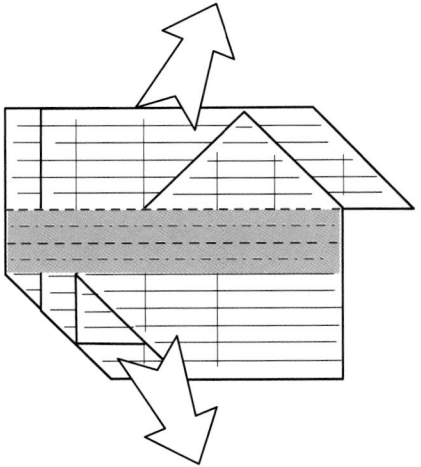

28 Open the model completely and pleat the shaded area. See next step for details.

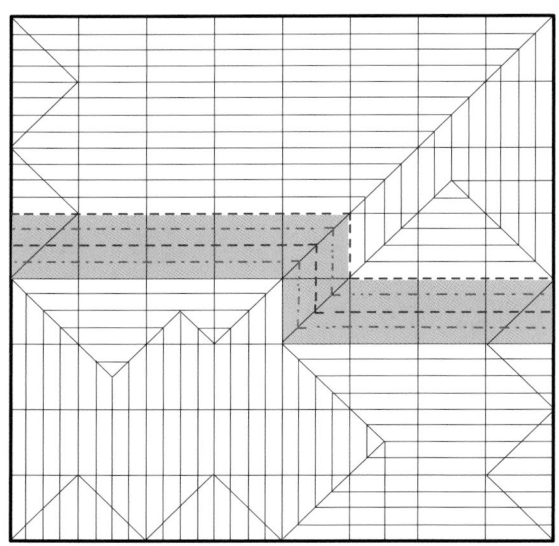

29 Pleat as indicated.

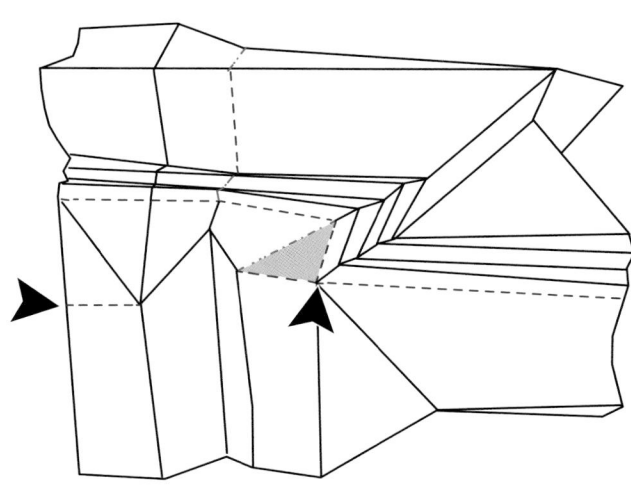

30 Push down on the corner of the shaded triangle, flipping it around its hypotenuse, and pulling up the lower half of the model. Only new or changed creases are shown.

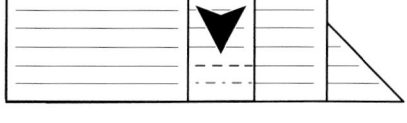

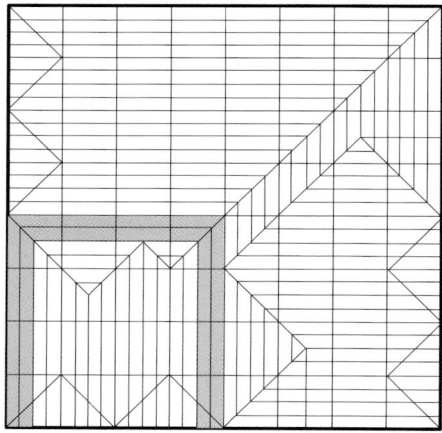

31 Open sink. The shaded areas of the crease patterns in the next steps indicate the areas to be worked.

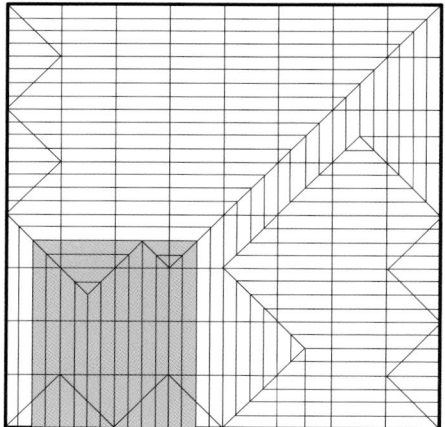

32 Open sink the two middle flaps. The shaded area indicates the area to be worked on in the crease pattern.

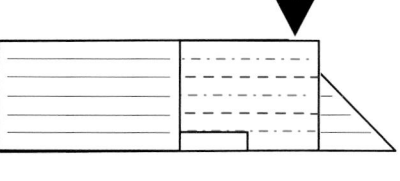

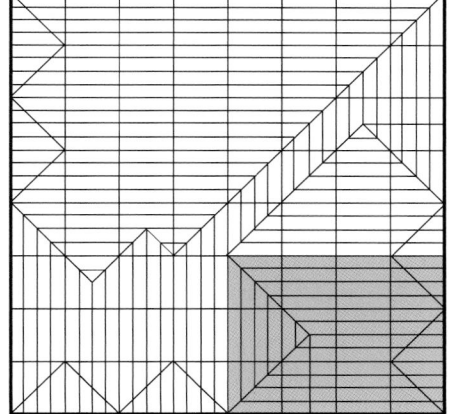

33 Open sink the inside layer. The shaded area indicates the area to be worked on in the crease pattern.

1 Unit

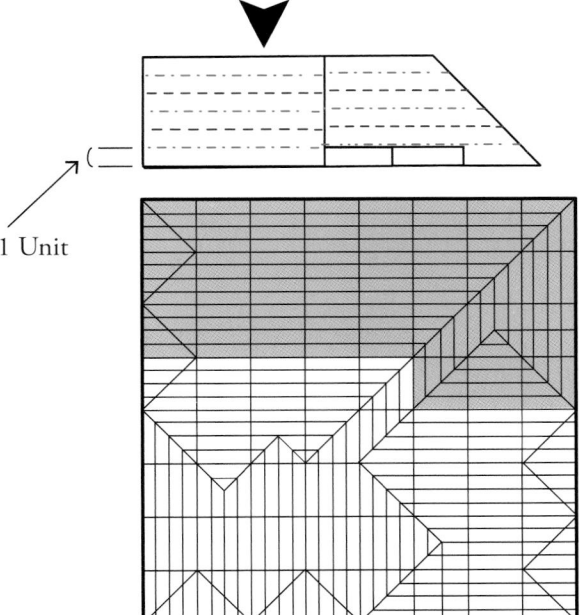

34 Open sink the outer layers. If you've done the previous steps correctly, you will have three six-unit flaps in the middle, with a thick four-unit flap on the right (see next step for result). The color will be on the inside, visible along the bottom of the model.

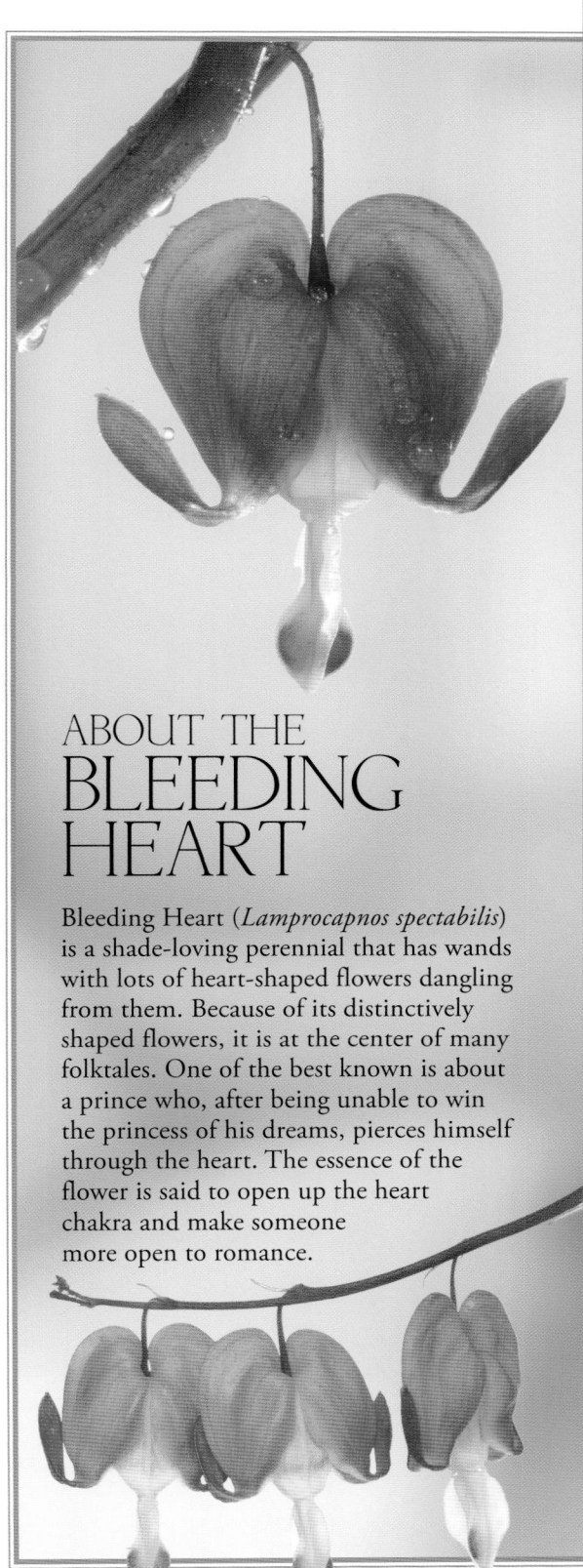

ABOUT THE BLEEDING HEART

Bleeding Heart (*Lamprocapnos spectabilis*) is a shade-loving perennial that has wands with lots of heart-shaped flowers dangling from them. Because of its distinctively shaped flowers, it is at the center of many folktales. One of the best known is about a prince who, after being unable to win the princess of his dreams, pierces himself through the heart. The essence of the flower is said to open up the heart chakra and make someone more open to romance.

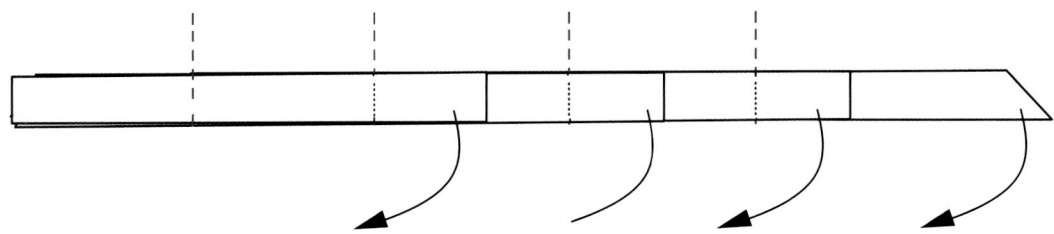

35 Fold each flap out to establish the hinge creases. The end flap should be folded four units out as well so that the flaps are spaced equally, and all six units long.

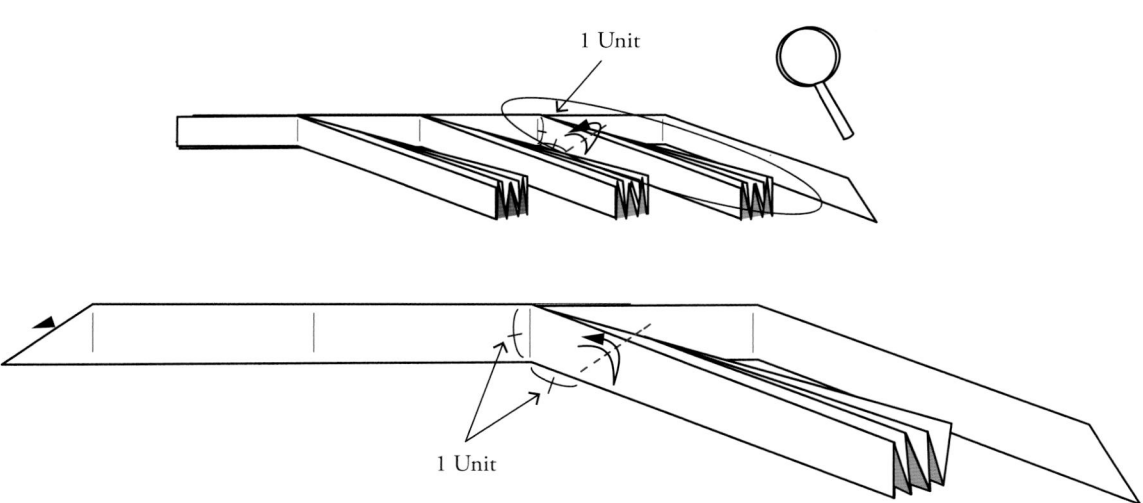

1 Unit

1 Unit

36 Pre-crease the entire flap 45°, starting one unit from the axis of the model. Open the flap.

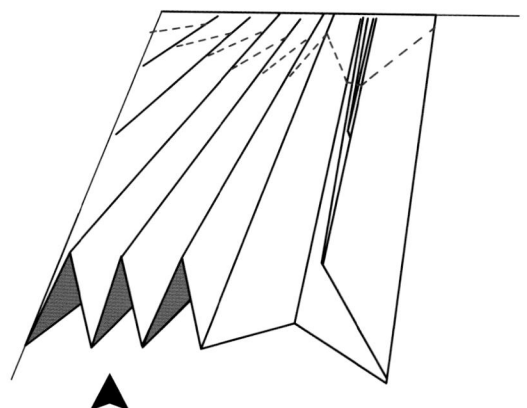

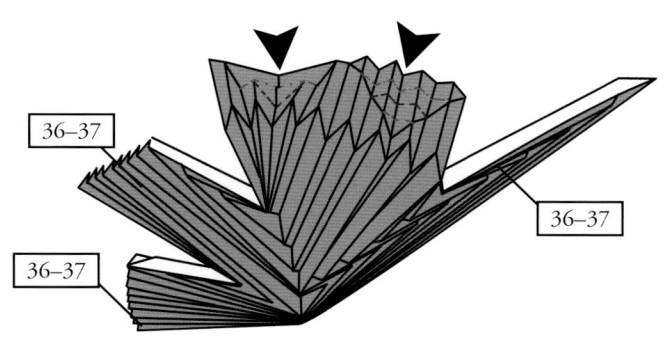

37 Open sink upward. Include the ridge flap with the first pleated layer. See step 38 for more details.

38 View from below. Perform two Elias stretches using the diagonal creases shown, made in step 4. Repeat on the other three flaps.

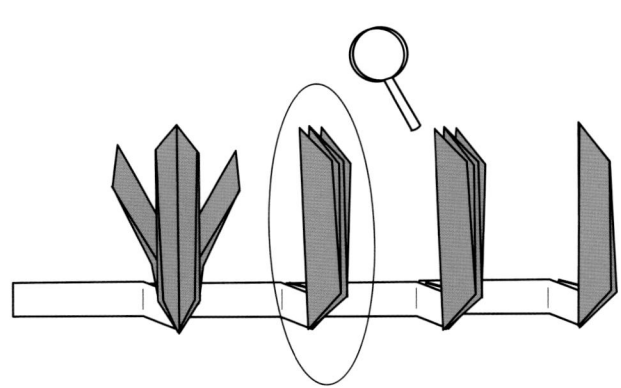

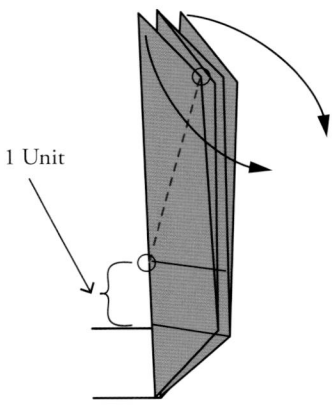

1 Unit

39 It will look like this; the points on the far left flap are spread to show the structure. Steps 40 to 44 will focus on the three-point flaps.

40 Fold a line connecting the points indicated. Repeat behind.

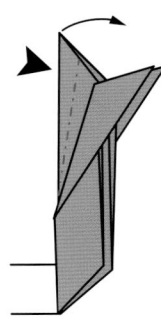

41 Reverse fold, bisecting the angle.

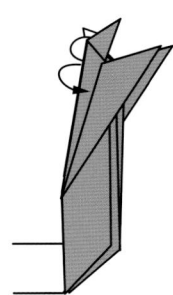

42 Wrap the raw edges around to the front, changing the color. This will be easier if you unfold the flap a little bit.

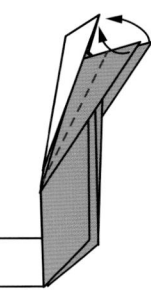

43 Bisect the angle. Repeat behind.

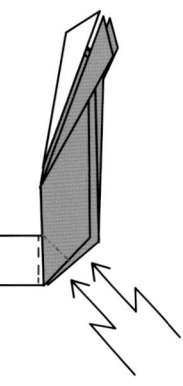

44 Crimp symmetrically. The mountain folds should be soft and rounded, not sharp.

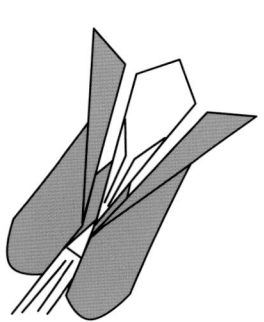

45 The result will look like this.

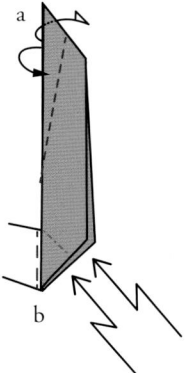

46 For the bud at the end, start with an outside reverse fold (a), then crimp as in step 44 (b).

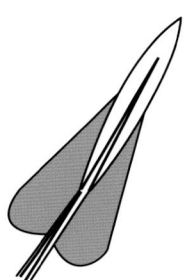

47 The bud will look like this.

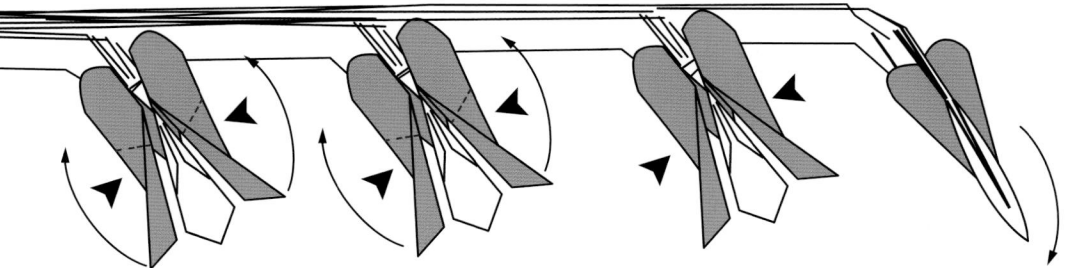

48 Notes on final shaping: fold the petals up on the left two flowers to show a progression between the bud and the fully formed bloom. Then pinch around the middle of each flower to make the heart shape clear from the front of the model. Bend the stem down so it has a gentle, drooping curve to it.

The completed Bleeding Heart wand

A MIURA-KEN BEAUTY ROSE, OPUS 482

Designed and diagrammed by Robert J. Lang

Born and raised in Atlanta, Georgia, Robert J. Lang worked as a physicist and engineer before becoming an origami artist full time. Dr. Lang is one of the pioneers of the cross-disciplinary marriage of origami with mathematics. He is consulted on applications of origami to issues in engineering while being noted for origami designs of great detail and realism. His work has been shown worldwide, from the Museum of Modern Art in New York to the Nippon Museum of Origami in Japan.

Dr. Lang lectures widely on origami and its connection to the world of science and teaches workshops on both artistic techniques and applications of folding in industrial design. A Fellow of the Optical Society of America, a member of the IEEE Photonics Society, and a past Editor-in-Chief of the IEEE Journal of Quantum Electronics, he was recently selected as one of the inaugural Fellows of the American Mathematical Society. He is the author or coauthor of 14 books and numerous articles on origami. He currently resides in Alamo, California.

"I used a 48-cm (18.9-inch) square to make this bloom. For the calyx, I used a 13-cm (5.1-inch) square of dark green hanji. You can use double-hanji and fold the corners to make the pentagon; if you use watercolor paper, it is better to just cut out the pentagon and then fold that. For the leaves, I suggest using 5.5-cm (2.2-inch) squares of either double-thick hanji or watercolor paper."

—Robert J. Lang

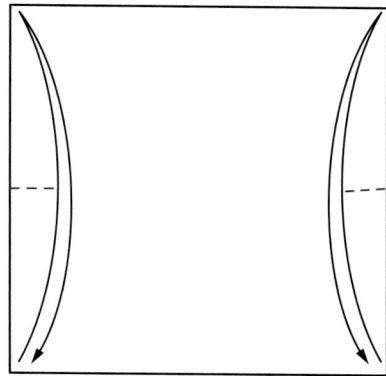

1 With the white side up, fold in half and pinch at the edges. Unfold.

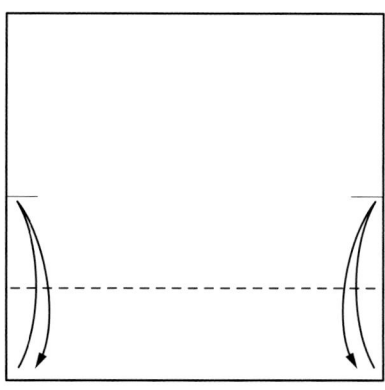

2 Fold to the pinches and unfold.

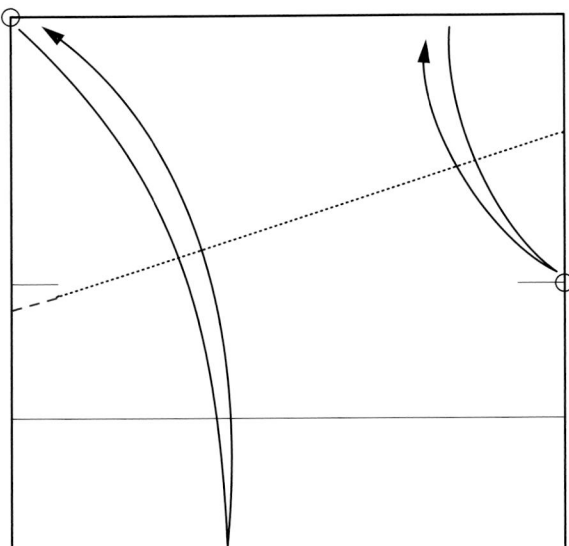

3 Bring the top left corner to the bottom edge while bringing the top edge to the crease intersection along the right. Pinch at the left edge and unfold.

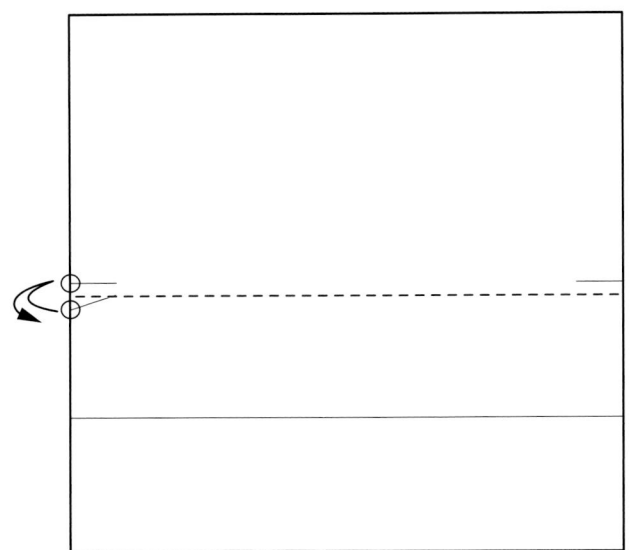

4 Bring the two crease intersections together and fold a horizontal crease all the way across the paper. Unfold.

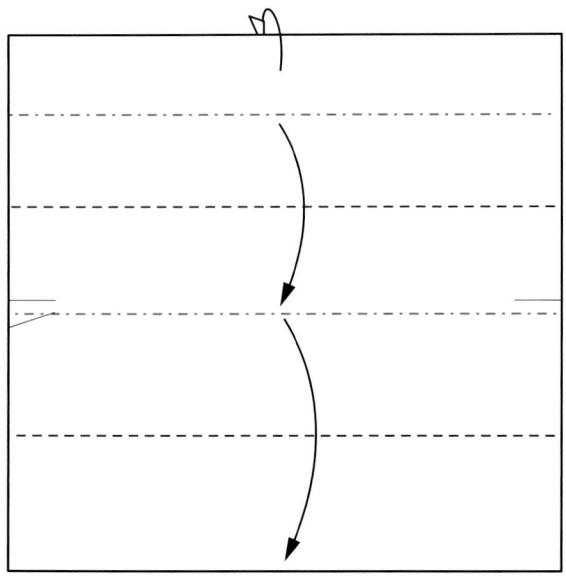

5 Using the first two creases as a guide, pleat the paper so that the distances between folded edges along the top and bottom are equal.

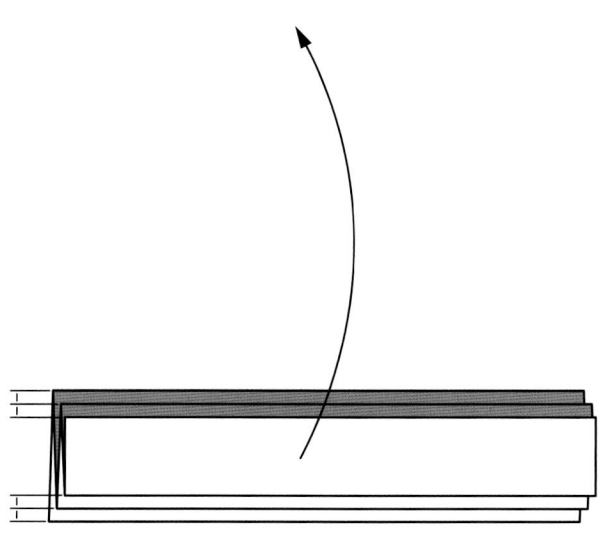

6 Unfold.

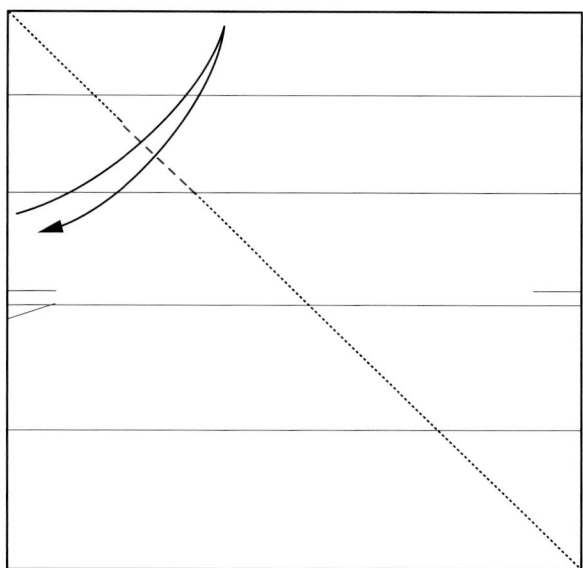

7 Make a pinch along the diagonal.

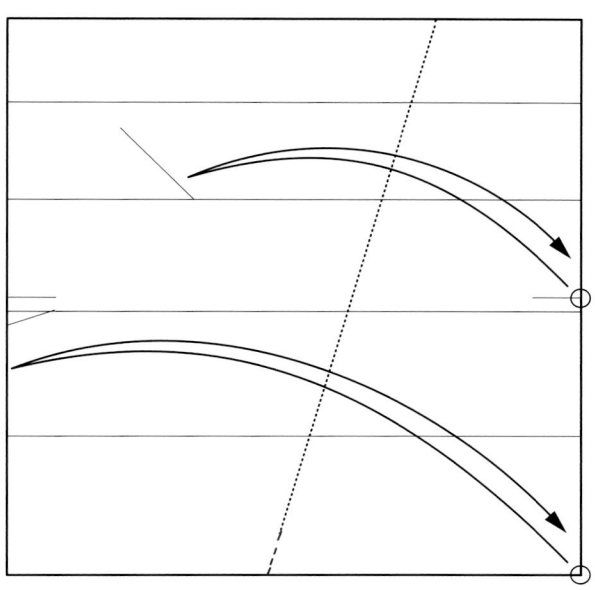

8 Bring two points along the right edge to the left and the diagonal pinch, making a new pinch along the bottom edge.

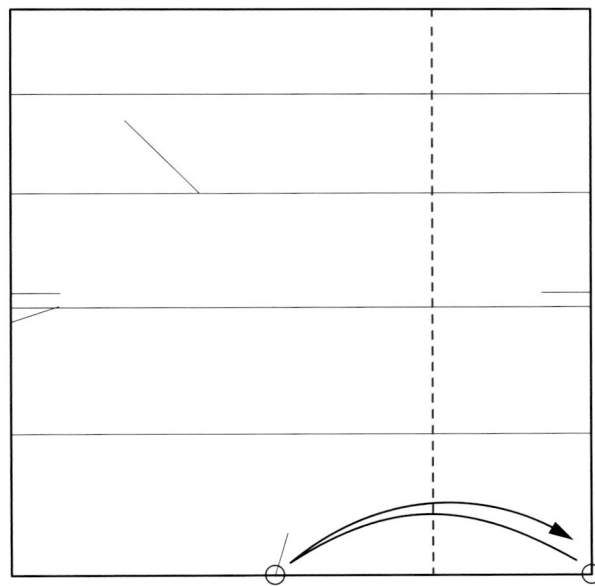

9 Bring the two points together, forming a vertical crease from bottom to top. Unfold.

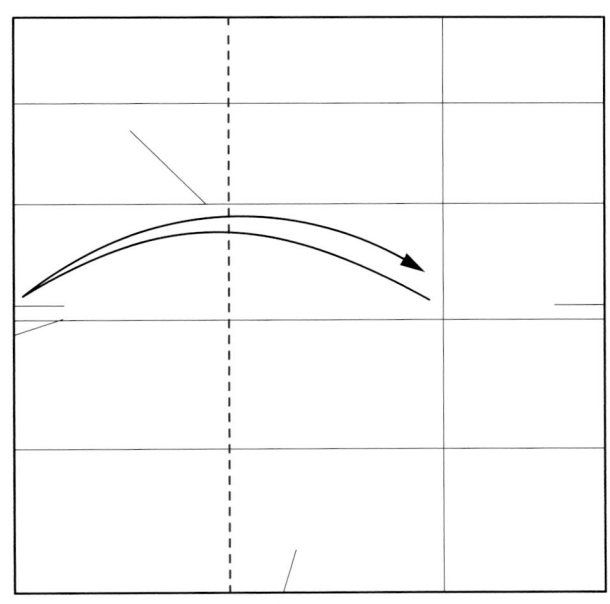

10 Fold and unfold.

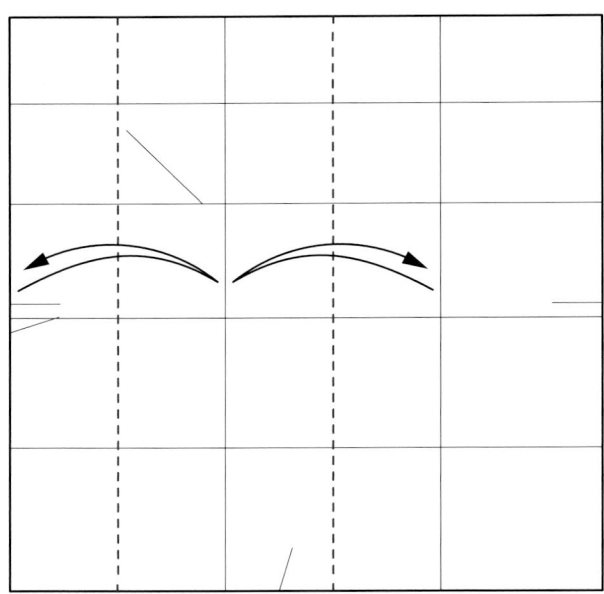

11 Fold and unfold.

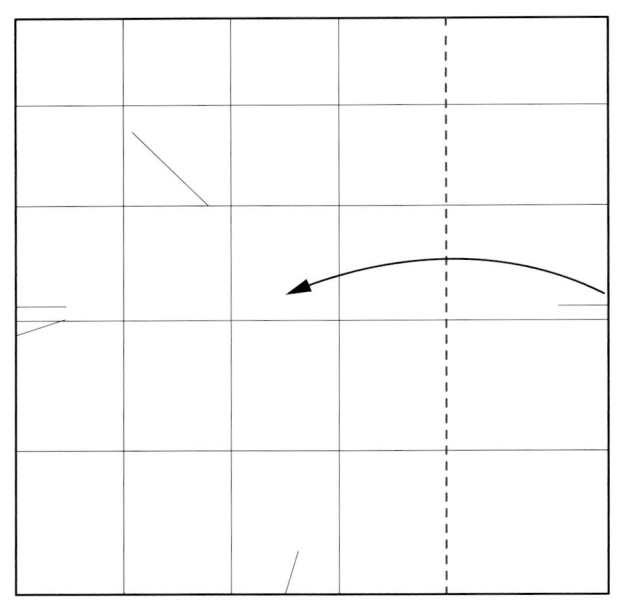

12 Fold the right edge in on the existing crease.

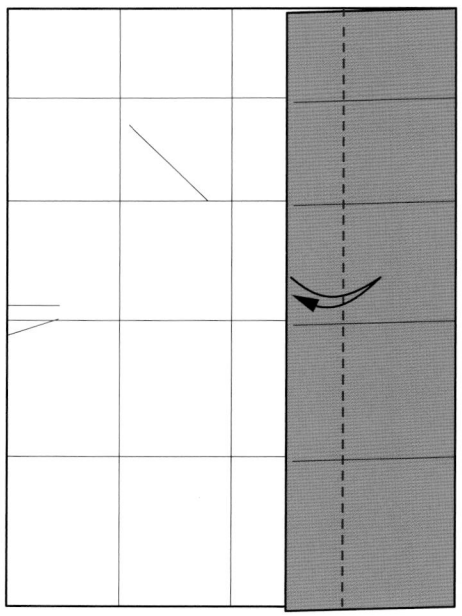

13 Fold and unfold, forming a crease aligned with the crease on the lower layer of paper.

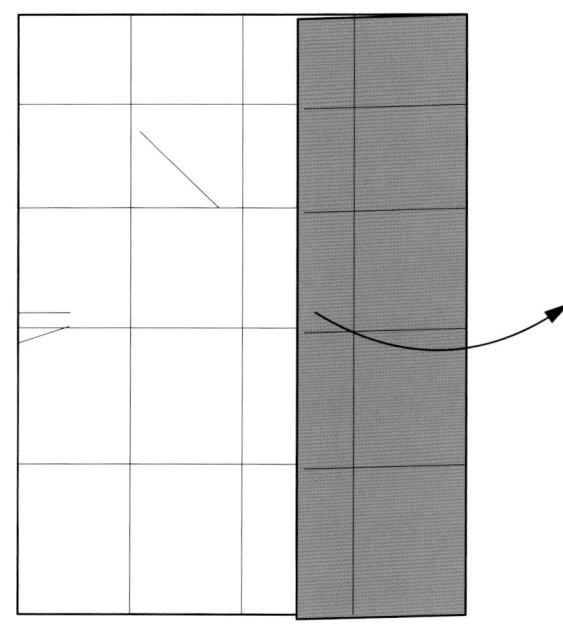

14 Unfold.

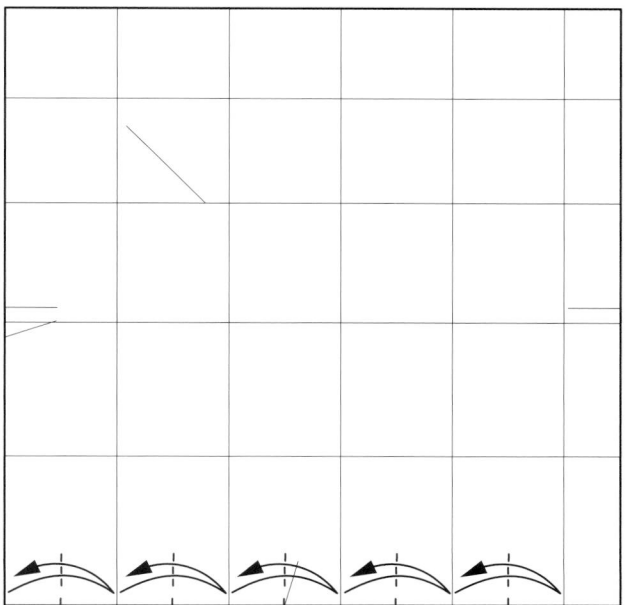

15 Divide each panel in half and pinch along the bottom edge.

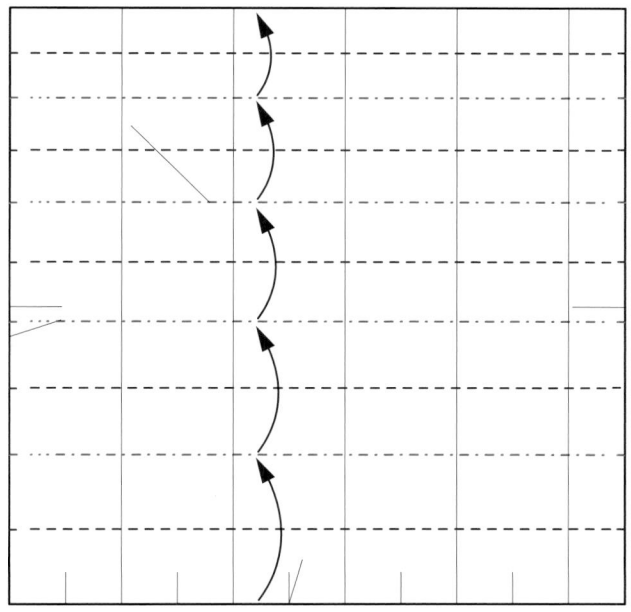

16 Pleat, making the mountain folds on existing creases and the valley folds so that all folds are aligned along the top edge.

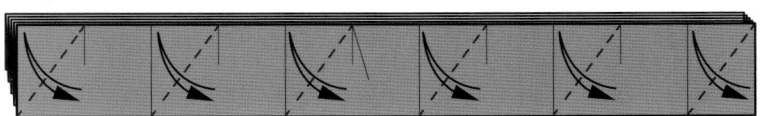

17 Crease through all layers.

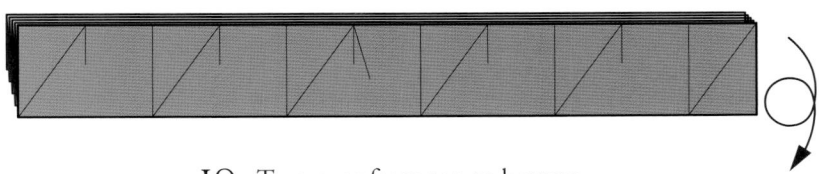

18 Turn over from top to bottom.

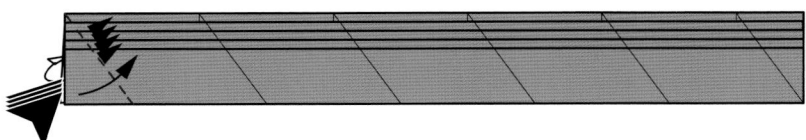

19 Reverse fold all layers (the reverse folds are all linked).

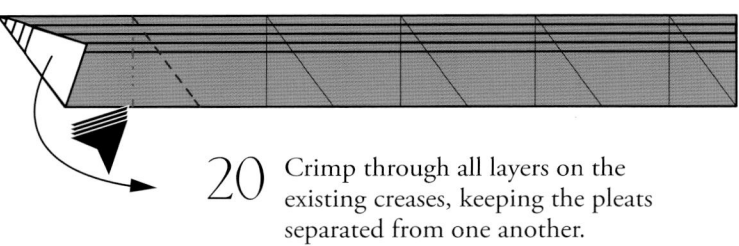

20 Crimp through all layers on the existing creases, keeping the pleats separated from one another.

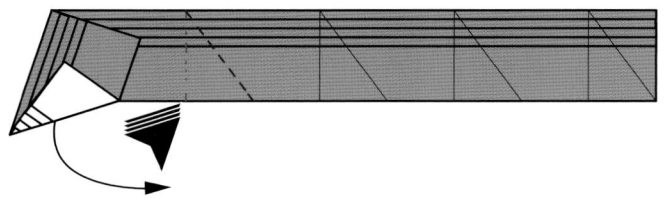

21 Crimp again through all layers on the existing creases.

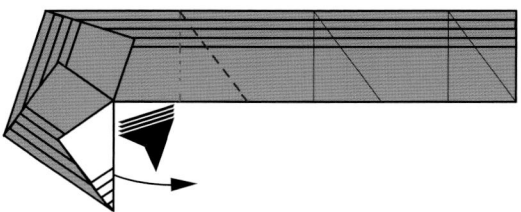

22 Crimp again through all layers on the existing creases.

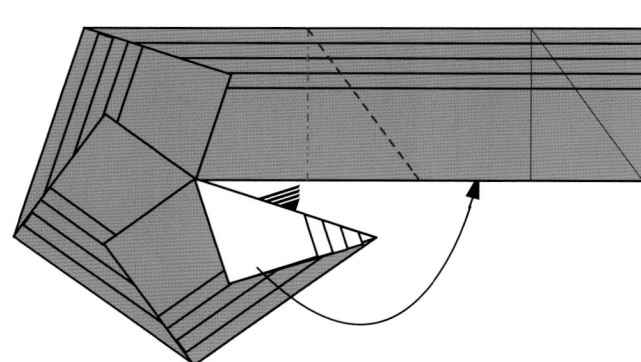

23 Crimp again, tucking each corner into a corresponding pocket. Note that raw edges on the left side should line up exactly with vertical creases on the right.

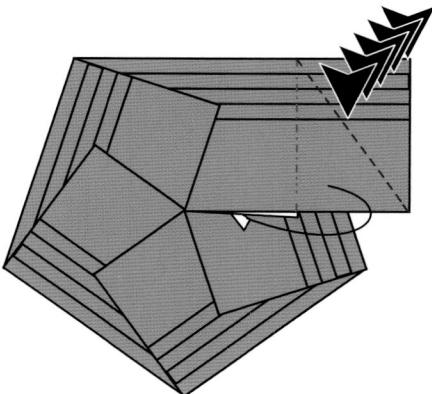

24 Reverse fold five edges, wrapping the paper over the coiled-up left side. Make sure the raw edges and creases are aligned and flatten completely.

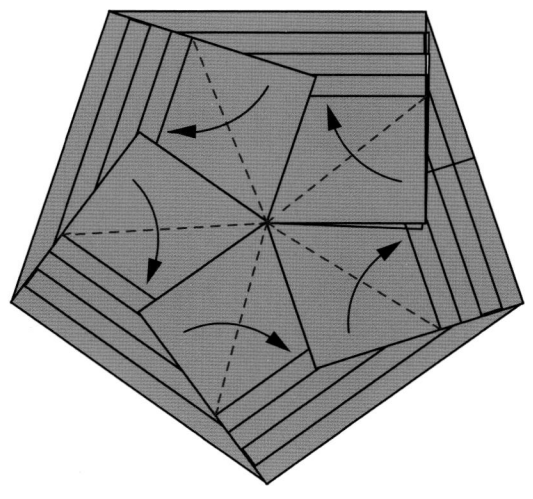

25 Fold the flaps counterclockwise.

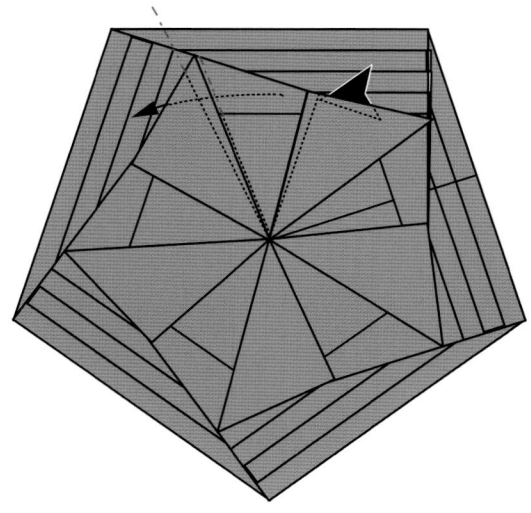

26 Reverse fold the topmost pleat.

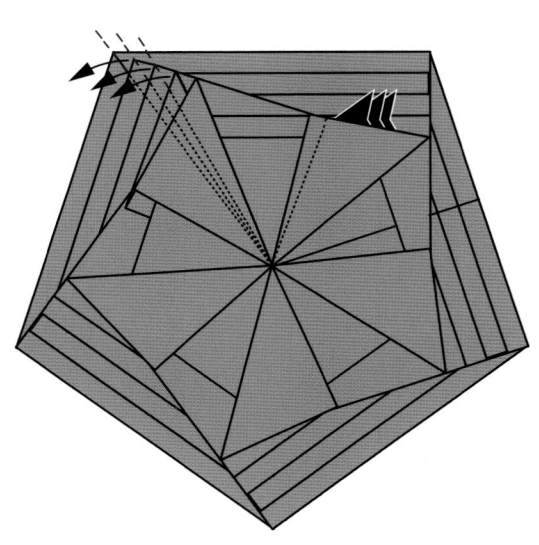

27 Reverse fold three more pleats.

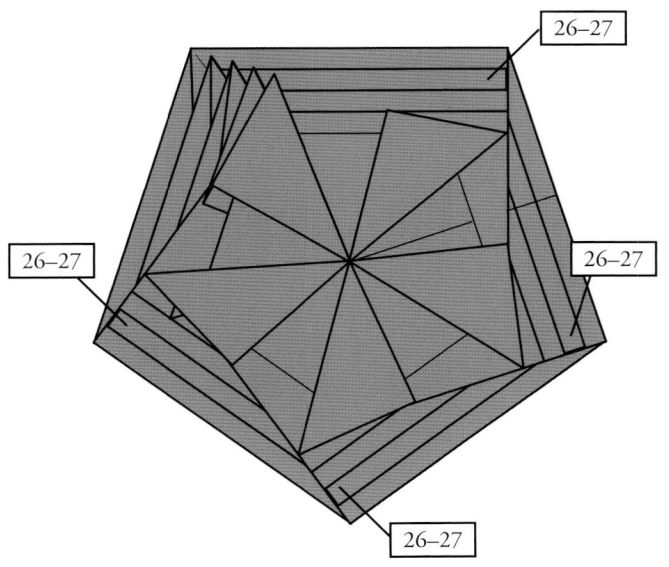

28 Repeat steps 26 and 27 on the remaining corners.

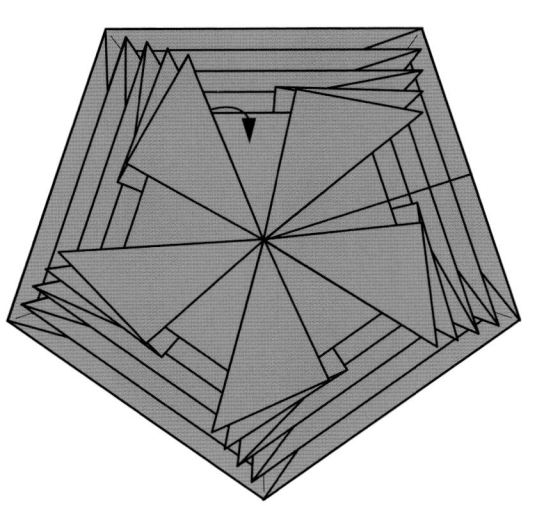

29 Pull excess paper out of the pocket as far as possible. The result will not lie flat.

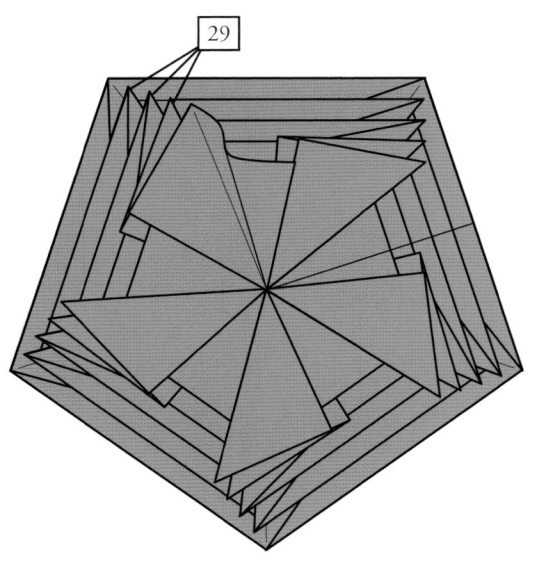

30 Repeat on the three corners below.

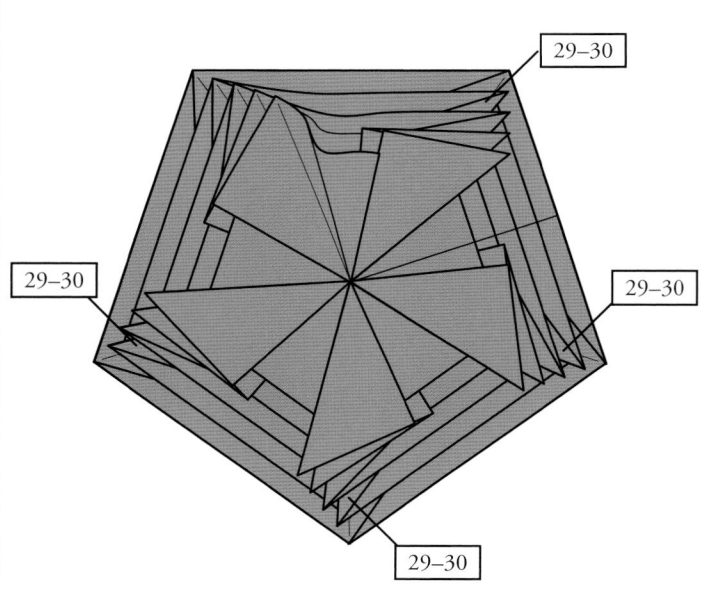

31 Repeat steps 29 and 30 on the remaining corners.

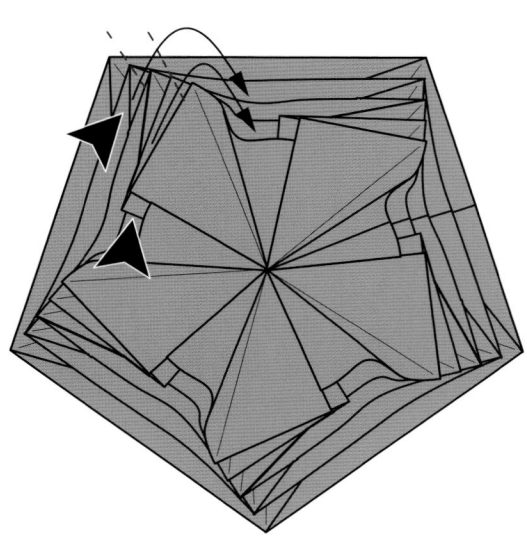

32 Reverse fold two of the edges.

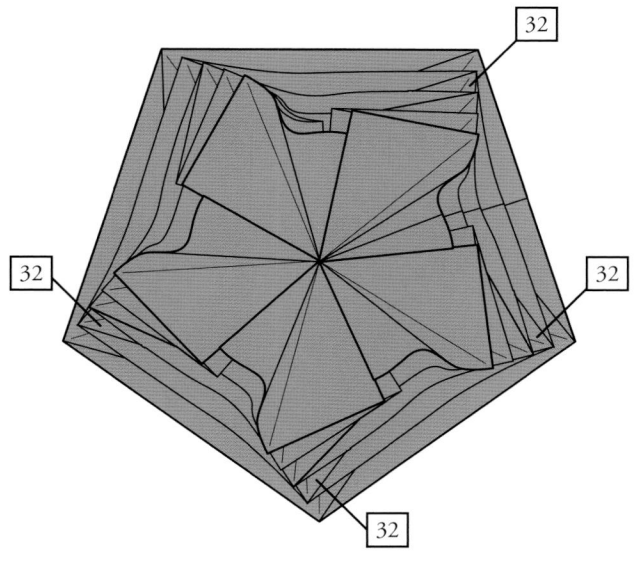

33 Repeat step 32 on the remaining corners.

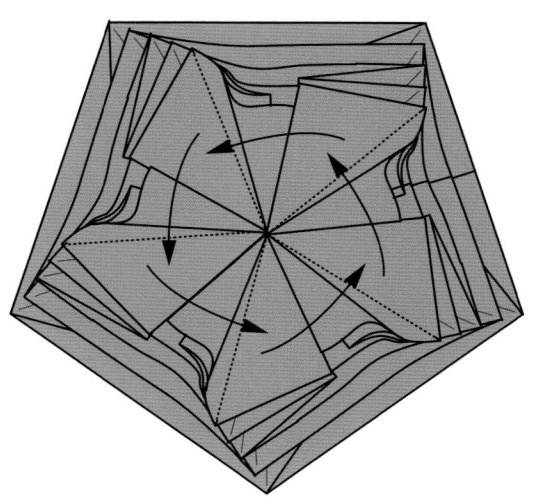

34 Lift and curl the innermost flaps around each other, forming a tight, upright cone. Each corner in the cone should have all of its layers lying smoothly in contact with one another, with three layers pointing clockwise and one layer counterclockwise. See next step for details.

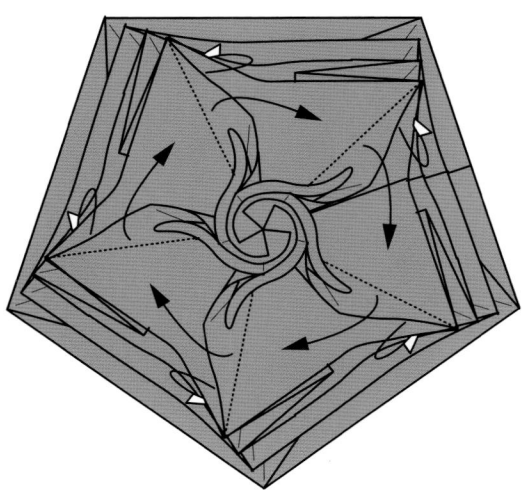

35 Lift and curl the next ring of corners into a looser cone; in this ring, each corner should have three layers pointing counterclockwise and one layer pointing clockwise. The petals should be positioned in the gaps between the petals of the innermost ring.

36 Lift and curl the next ring of corners into a looser cone; in this ring, each corner should have three layers pointing counterclockwise and one layer pointing clockwise and again, the petals should be positioned in the gaps between the petals of the innermost ring.

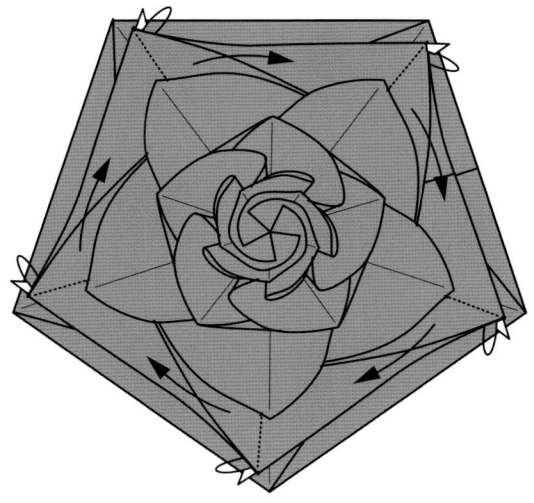

37 Lift and curl the next ring of corners into a very shallow cone as before.

38 Turn the model over.

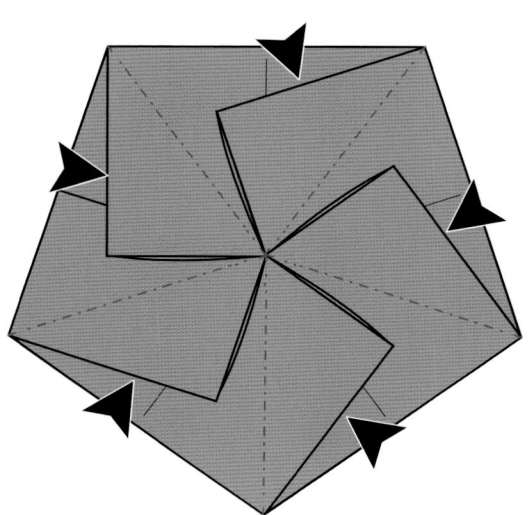

39 Reverse fold the corners into the interior of the model.

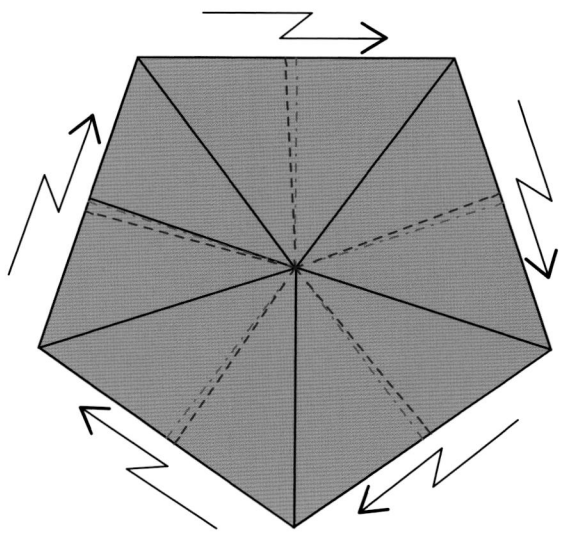

40 Form five narrow pleats. The paper will become slightly conical, with the edges pointing away from you.

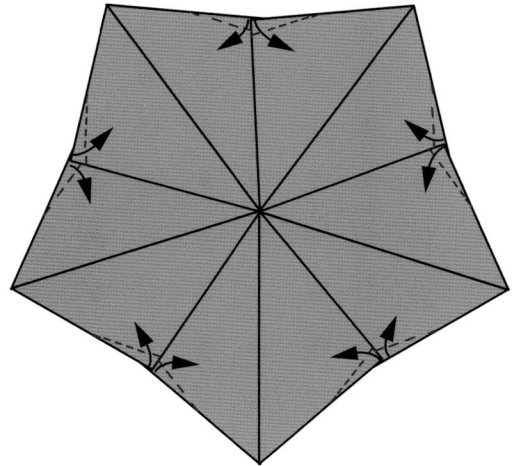

41 Valley fold the top of each pleat, squash-folding at the end of the pleat. This locks the pleat in place.

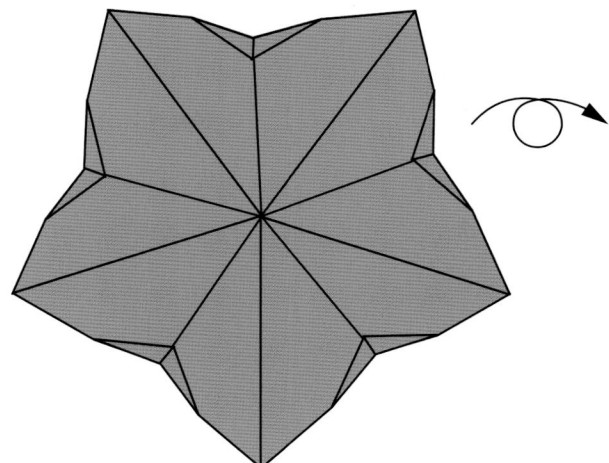

42 Turn the model over. Rotate the flower while adjusting the petal positions so that each ring of petals lies in the gaps between the petals of adjacent rings.

43 Adjust the petals and give each a slight curl.

The finished Rose

A Miura-Ken Beauty Rose, Opus 482   173

CALYX

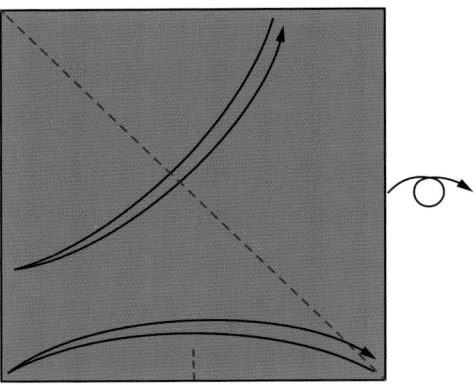

1 With the color side up, fold in half and pinch at the edge. Unfold, then crease on the diagonal and unfold. Turn over.

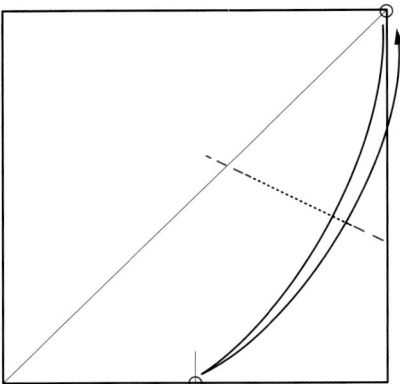

2 Bring the top right corner to the crease mark at the bottom. Pinch at the intersection and at the right edge. Unfold.

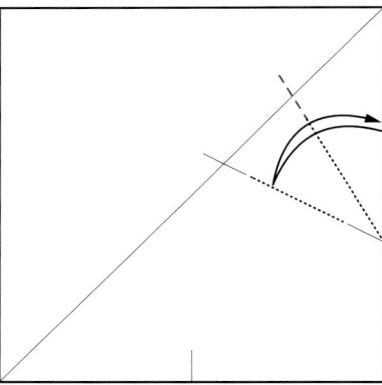

3 Fold the angle bisector. Pinch at the intersection and unfold.

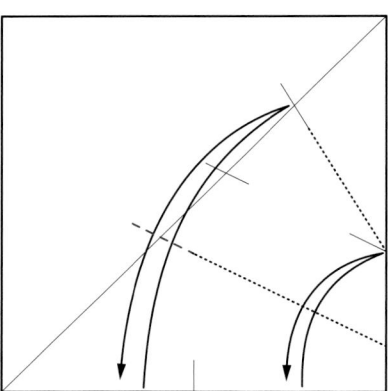

4 Fold the bottom edge to the crease mark to form the angle bisector. Pinch at the intersection and unfold.

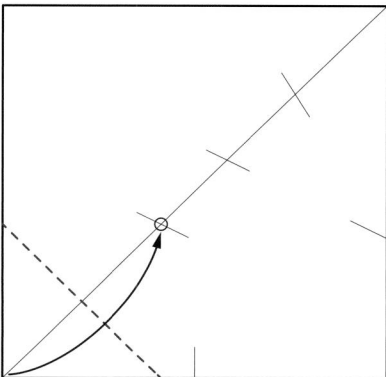

5 Fold the corner to the intersection point.

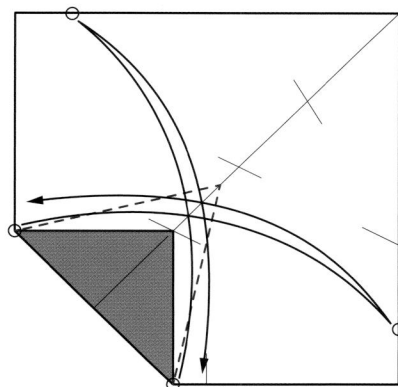

6 Fold the corners to the edges opposite and unfold.

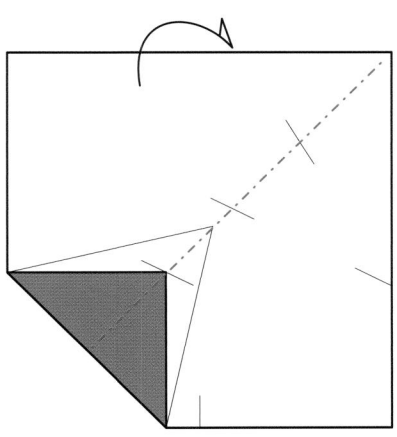

7 Mountain fold in half.

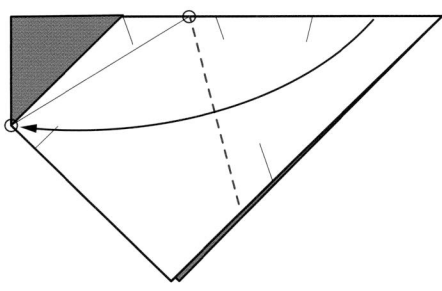

8 Fold the edge to the corner.

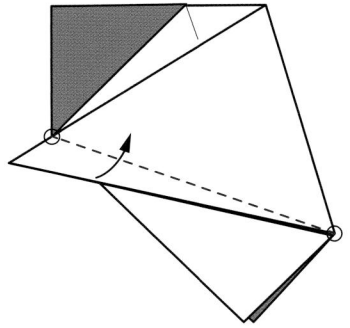

9 Fold between the points indicated.

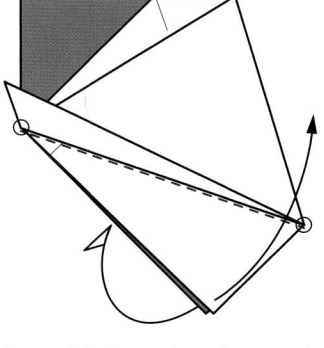

10 Fold along the edge, in the front and back.

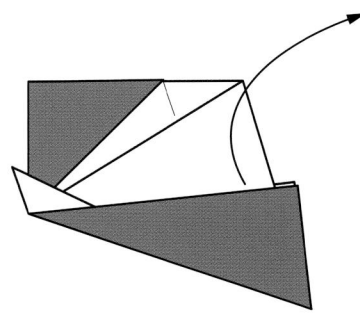

11 Unfold back to step 6, with the color side up.

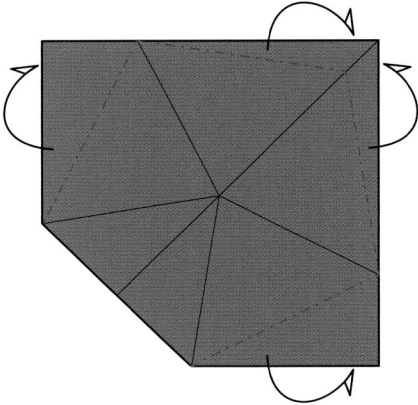

12 Mountain fold on existing creases to make a regular pentagon.

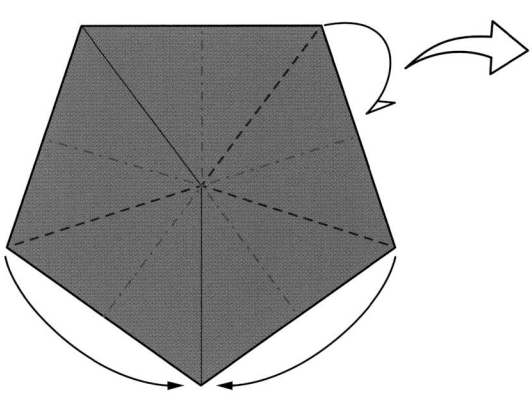

13 Collapse into a pentagonal preliminary fold.

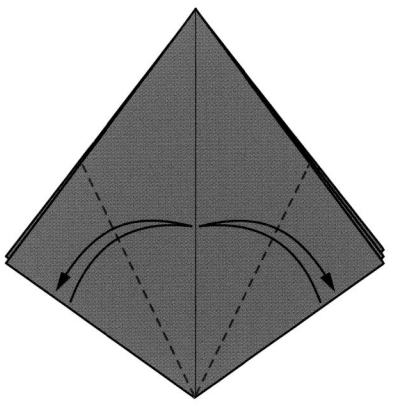

14 Fold the angle bisectors and unfold.

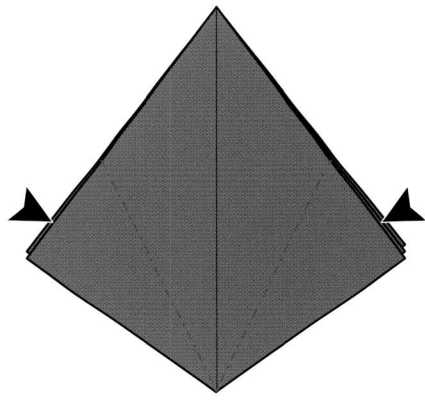

15 Reverse fold.

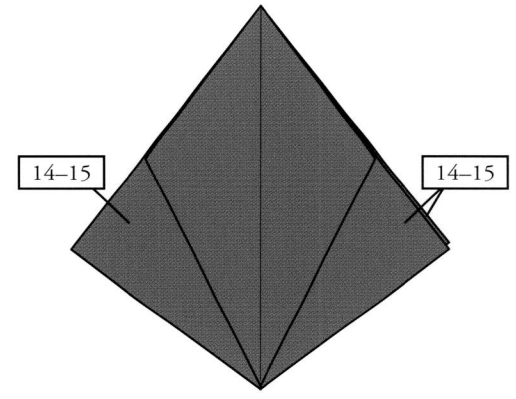

14–15   14–15

16 Repeat steps 14 and 15 on the remaining corners.

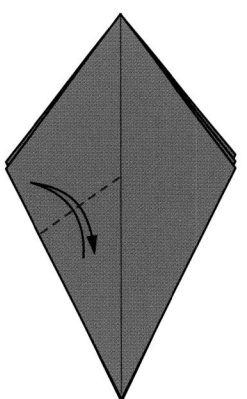

17 Lightly crease as shown on the top layer. This crease will be adjusted as needed.

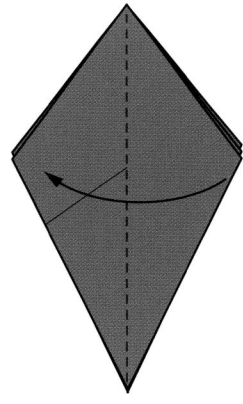

18 Fold one flap over to the other side.

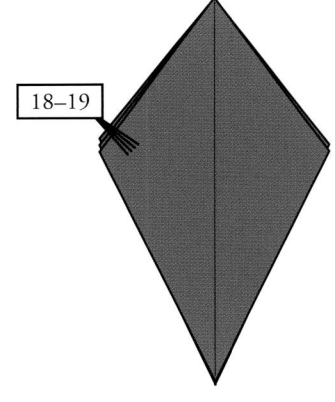

18–19

19 Repeat steps 17 and 18 to make the crease on all flaps.

ABOUT THE ROSE

According to Ayurveda, the traditional medical system of India, roses can balance disorders of the heart—both physical and emotional. Roses are known to be soothing, cooling, and moisturizing. Rose oil can be used to alleviate allergies and asthma, calm anger and help with depression. Rose water can be used as a natural toner for your skin. And rose petals, in preserves, can be used for a variety of medical purposes including reducing nausea and boosting the immune system.

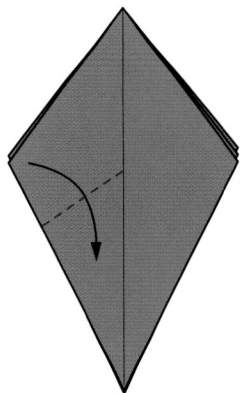

20   Fold the corner over on the crease. The result will not lie flat; we are starting the process of making the model 3D.

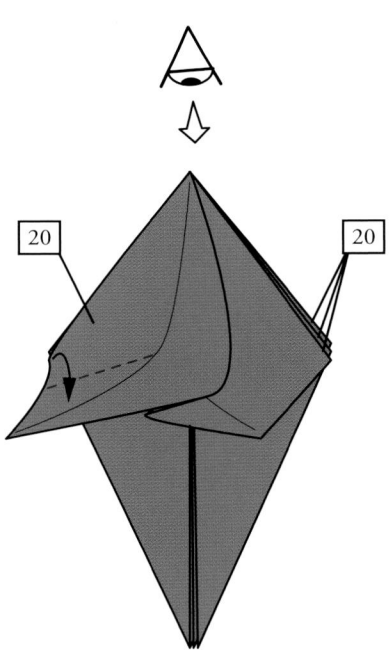

21   Repeat step 20 on the remaining flaps, making the model radially symmetrical. See next step for the result viewed from the top.

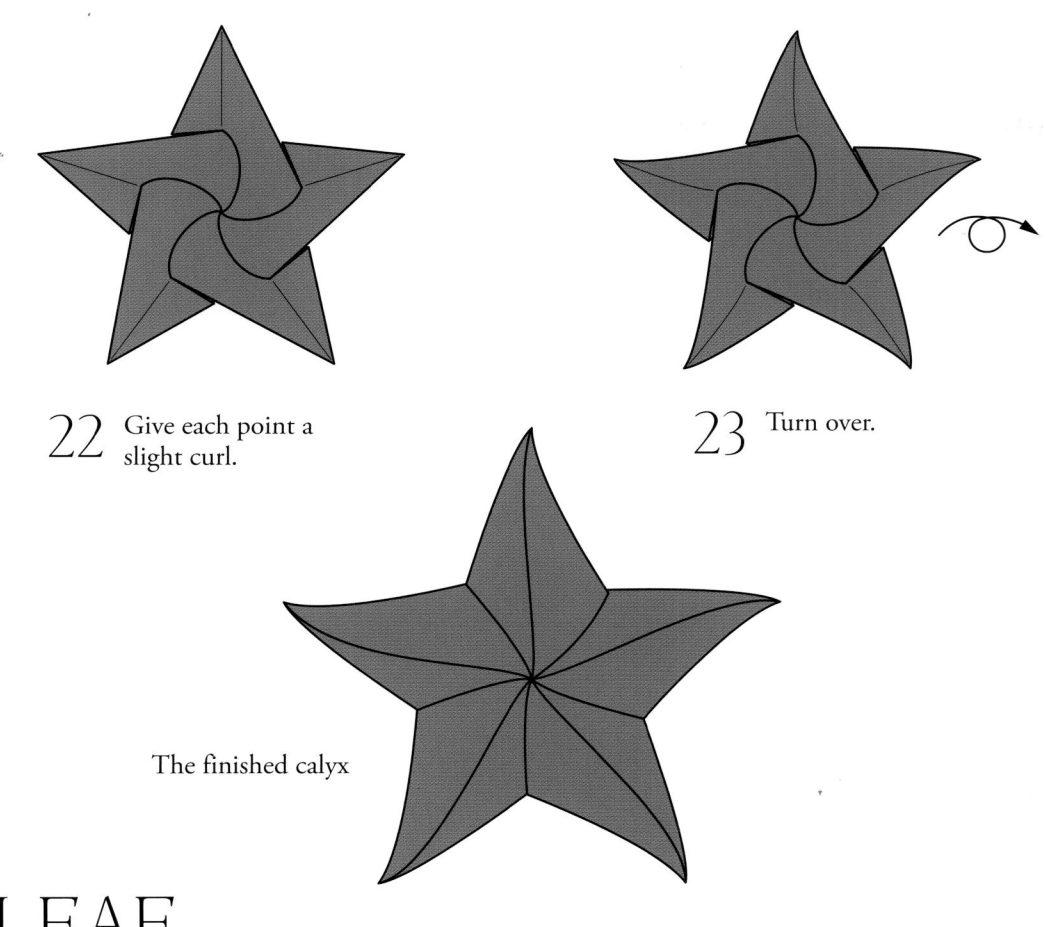

22 Give each point a slight curl.

23 Turn over.

The finished calyx

LEAF

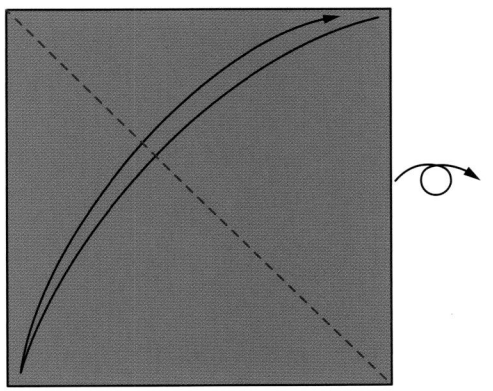

1 With the color side up, fold in half along the diagonal. Unfold. Turn over.

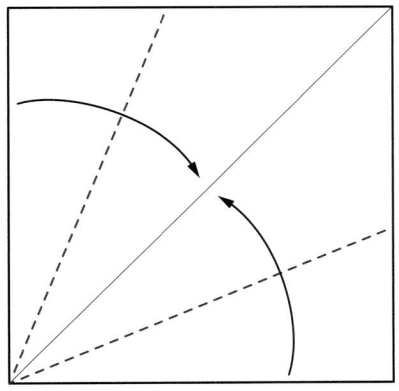

2 Fold the angle bisectors.

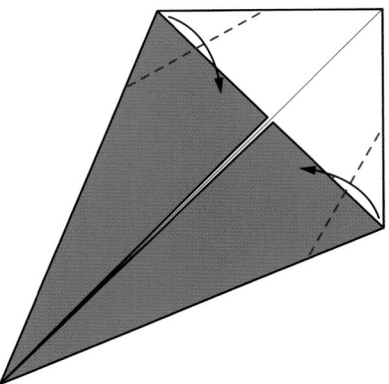
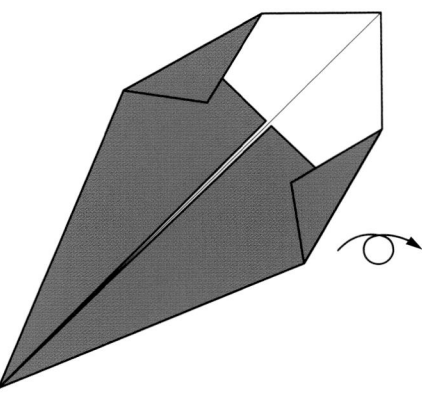

3 Fold the corners (there are no particular references for these).

4 Turn over.

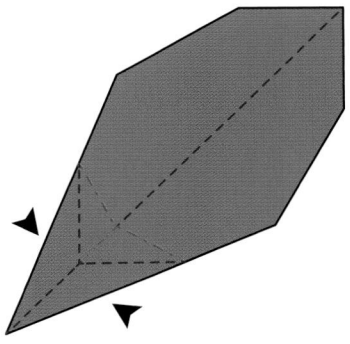
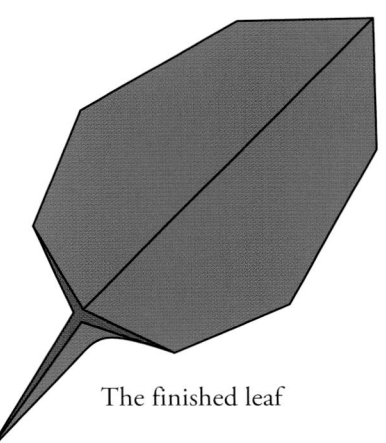

5 Rabbit-ear fold at the corner to form the stem, then valley fold the leaf slightly in half.

The finished leaf

Make six of these to form two groups of three leaves (see pages 26 and 27 about wiring elements and forming clusters).

The completed A Miura-ken
Beauty Rose, opus 482 with leaves

ORIGAMI WREATH
Designed by John Blackman

This wreath, designed and assembled by the creator of the Sweet Pea on pages 28–35, uses many of the flowers and leaves presented in this book (including Stemless Leaves, presented at the end of this project). It is an excellent example of how to create a large floral showpiece out of many different flower and leaf elements. You will be creating several elements—some loose and some bundled—and wiring them so the wires can be used like small picks, inserted into the foam wherever you want to place them.

ORIGAMI:

- 6 large Lilies (page 64), made from 9-inch squares, stem ends untwisted
- 9 medium Lilies (page 64), made from 6-inch squares, stem ends untwisted
- 5 Kawasaki Roses (page 90), made from 7-inch squares
- 9 Kawasaki Roses (page 90), made from 4-inch squares taped into clusters of 3.
- 40 Sweet Peas (page 28), made from 2-inch squares for the flower and 1-inch squares for the calyx and taped into 8 clusters of 5 flowers
- 70 small flowers made from 1-inch squares using the calyx model on page 32, taped into 7 clusters of 10 flowers. Note: when making flowers from these instructions, start with the white side up.
- 7 large calyxes (page 32) made from 1½-inch squares, 1 for each small-flower cluster
- 50 Stemless Leaves (page 188) made from 1 x 2-inch squares, taped into 10 clusters of 5 leaves
- 33 A-Miura-Ken Beauty Rose leaves (page 179) made from 2-inch squares and taped into 11 clusters of 3 units.
- 45 Bougainvillea leaves (page 46) made from 2-inch squares and wired (see page 26).

OTHER SUPPLIES:

- 12-inch foam wreath form
- Dark green tissue paper
- White glue (not a glue stick)
- Cloth-covered floral wire (18 to 24 gauge)
- Green floral tape
- Dry pastels for customizing the colors of the small flower and Sweet Pea clusters, if desired

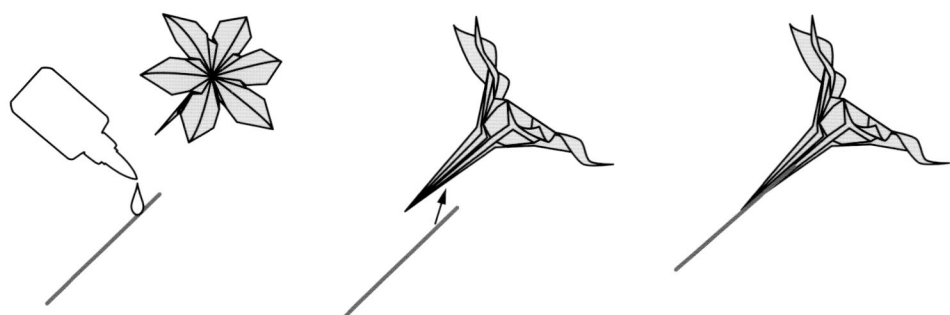

1 Wire the loose flowers: for all Lilies, glue a 2-inch length of wire into the folds of the stem. The wire should extend about an inch beyond the tip of the stem. Then wrap the stem and wire with floral tape; for the Kawasaki Roses, glue a length of wire under one of the overlapping folds in the base, then bend it so it points out from the flower. Tape the small Kawasaki roses together in clusters of three.

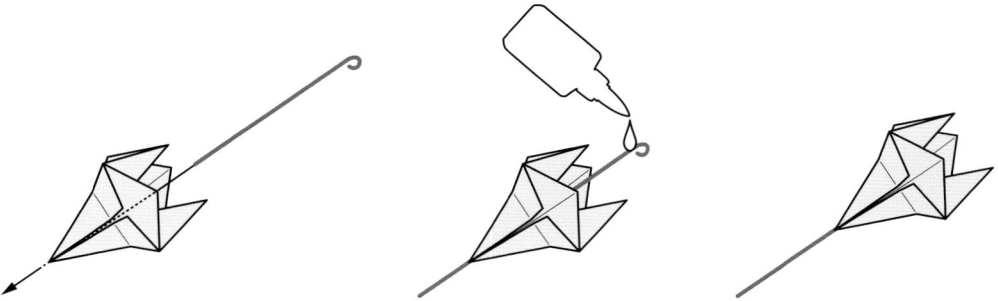

2 Cut ten 1½-inch lengths of cloth-covered wire for each cluster of small flowers made from the calyx. Form a small loop at one tip of each piece of wire to make eye pins. Push the tapestry needle into the cone of a flower from above to pierce a hole through the tip, out the back. Then thread the flowers with the eye pins. Place a small drop of glue on the loop just before pulling it into the flower. The loop should be hidden inside the flower and will keep the wire from sliding through.

3 Wire the seven large calyxes with bare floral wire using 1½-inch lengths made into eye pins. Add a drop of glue to the loop and insert the wire into a calyx. Then insert a bundle of small flowers (with a drop of glue on the tape at the base) into the opening of each calyx.

4 Prepare the wreath form: cut the green tissue paper into 1- to 2-inch strips. Wrap the strips around the wreath form to cover the foam and tack in place using the glue.

5 Add leaves to the outside and inside of the wreath by pushing the wire ends into the form. Don't use all the leaves; just use as many leaves as necessary to form the edges of the wreath shape. The front of the wreath should be left empty.

6   Add flowers to the front of the wreath in a similar fashion. Try to spread the various flowers around the wreath, but don't space them evenly.

7   Fill in the empty spots between the flowers and around the outside of the wreath with the remaining leaves.

STEMLESS LEAVES

Designed by John Blackman

The leaves shown below are a separate element; clusters of them can be used with many of the flowers shown in this book in larger arrangements. Cut a small square (2 inches/5 cm) in half to make two Stemless Leaves.

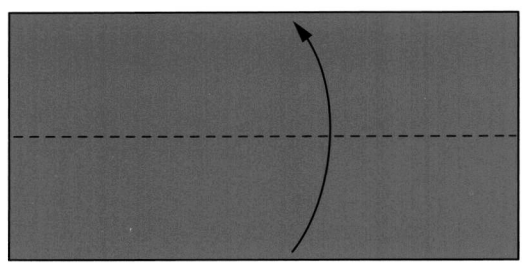

1 With the color side up, fold in half.

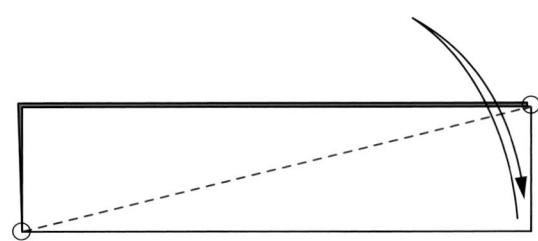

2 Fold the diagonal through both layers. Unfold.

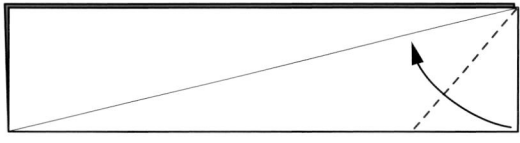

3 Fold the angle bisector.

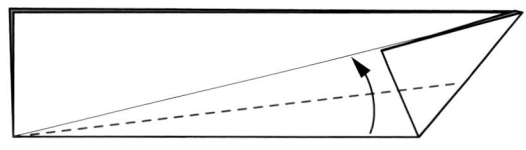

4 Fold the angle bisector.

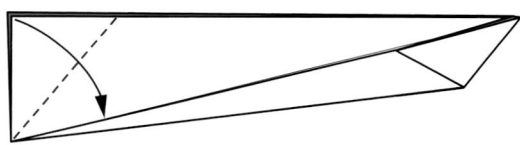

5 Fold the top layer down to form the angle bisector

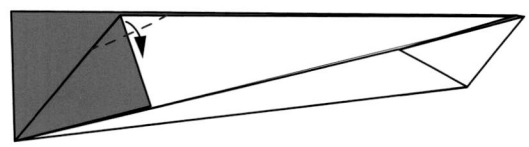

6 Valley fold the corner down a little.

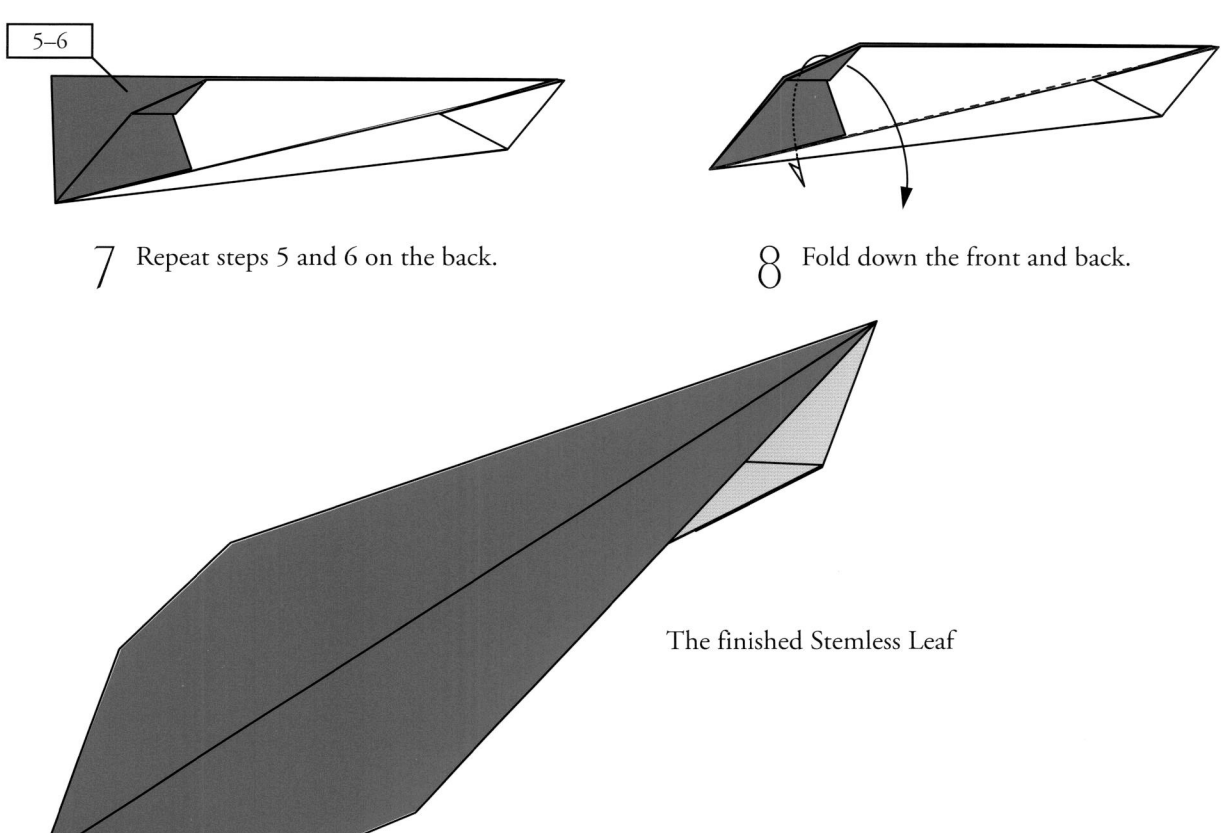

7 Repeat steps 5 and 6 on the back.

8 Fold down the front and back.

The finished Stemless Leaf

ASSEMBLY

1 Wire the leaves: insert a length of cloth-covered wire, leaving about an inch of wire extending past the base of the leaf, into the pocket on the underside of the model and glue in place. One of the leaves should have a longer wire than the others.

2 Use floral tape to wrap a cluster of leaves together.

ABOUT THE EDITOR

Sherry Gerstein is an editor and writer who has edited many origami books. She has been folding since she was 7 years old. She crafts and sells her own line of origami jewelry at etsy.com/shop/papergirlinct and aspires to create origami models of her own.

ABOUT THE ILLUSTRATOR AND DIAGRAMMER

The saying "every picture tells a story" is especially true of origami diagrams; they tell the story of the transformation of a piece of paper into a work of art.

It is the challenge of the origami diagrammer to employ the tools of the trade—symbols such as solid lines, dashed lines, arrows and more—to tell the story in a clear and sequential fashion. The clearest diagrams work in such a way that the casual observer isn't even aware of the work involved. For instance, a line of a certain weight translates into "edge"; a finer line translates into "existing crease," and a dotted line translates into "hidden edge." These are concepts—the language of technical illustration, as it were—that are very nearly self-explanatory. At least, they are quickly grasped by the reader.

While this book collects models created by several different people, all the models have one thing in common: their stories were all told by the same illustrator/diagrammer, Marcio Noguchi.

Born in Brazil to Japanese parents, illustrator Marcio Noguchi first learned about origami as a child. But he didn't become a serious enthusiast until the mid-2000s, after he moved to the US.

Since that time, Marcio Noguchi has illustrated and diagrammed a number of models for other creators. Some have appeared in books; others have been collected and distributed at the conventions of national origami societies in the US, the UK, and Japan. Says Noguchi, "Each diagram is a story. Each step indicates the before and the after, as well as the present action. It can tell about something as simple as a single fold or as complex as a big, one-step collapse. The best diagrams are so good that we feel are reading, even if we don't understand the language the actual text is written in."

He is a supporting member of the Japan Origami Academic Society and a member of the OrigamiUSA Executive Board of Directors. He lives in Westchester County, New York.

RESOURCES

PAPER:

While some of the projects in this collection can be made with standard 6-inch squares of paper, many call for much larger papers. You can find high quality papers of larger sizes at the following art supply stores:

Amazon.com

www.amazon.com
Amazon is a great place to start an online search. Not only will you find art papers in many colors and varieties to order, but you will also find links to many other online suppliers.

Dick Blick Art Materials

P.O. Box 1267
Galesburg, IL 61402-1267
800-8248-4548
www.dickblick.com
You can order online or use the store finder to find a retail location near you.

Etsy.com

www.etsy.com
You can find crafting supplies in addition to the crafts themselves on this online marketplace. Sellers carry fine papers in sheets; others carry floral crafting supplies.

Fineartstore.com

You can find an excellent supply of fine art papers on this web site, but if you are ever in Rochester, New York, you can visit their retail location:
150 West Main Street
Rochester, NY 14614
800-836-8940
585-546-6509
Fax: 585-546-5023
www.fineartstore.com

New York Central Art Supply

62 Third Avenue
New York, NY 10003
212-473-7705
Orders: 800-950-6111
Fax: 212-475-2513
www.nycentralart.com

Paper Source

www.paper-source.com
This art-and-craft store chain has many locations; check the store finder on their web site or place orders online.

The Paper Studio

www.paperstudio.com
This online-only site carries unryu and lokta papers in addition to many other varieties of decorative papers.

FLORAL SUPPLIES:

The florist's equipment you will need to create these projects can be found at the following craft suppliers:

A.C. Moore

www.acmoore.com/storelocator
This craft store chain has many brick-and-mortar stores on the east coast. Check their website to find a store near you. An online presence is in the works for this year.

Hobby Lobby

www.hobbylobby.com
Hobby Lobby arts and crafts stores are in many locations nationwide. If one isn't in your area, order online through their website.

Joann.com

www.joann.com
Joann is an arts and crafts store chain with many locations. If you don't have a Joann store in your area, check their web site for crafting and floral supplies of all kinds. While they carry some origami paper, they don't carry the large sheets needed for some of these projects.

Michaels.com

www.michaels.com
Like Joann above, Michaels is a mainstay of crafters with many stores, in addition to a significant online presence. Michaels also carries some origami paper, but not in large sheets.

Save-on-crafts.com

www.save-on-crafts.com
Online wedding, party, and home decorating supplies at a discount.